WHAT WE MUST KNOW ABOUT COMMUNISM

WHAT WE
MUST KNOW
ABOUT COMMUNISM

HARRY AND BONARO OVERSTREET

W · W · NORTON & COMPANY · INC ·
NEW YORK

Library of Congress Catalog Card No. 58-11110

PRINTED IN THE UNITED STATES OF AMERICA
W

Our censure should be reserved for those who would close all doors but one. The surest way to lose truth is to pretend that one already wholly possesses it.

GORDON W. ALLPORT

CONTENTS

FOREWORD

A STRANGE new force has entered our world, the strangest and most enigmatic in all history. Equipped with a formula and a strategy, and starting in one of the most backward countries of Europe, it has, in a brief forty years, taken control of one-third of the world's people and one-fourth of the world's territory.

How has this amazing development happened? What is the character of this new force which has seemed to come from nowhere and which has declared its intention of reaching everywhere?

The problems that harass our country today in relation to Communism can best be summed up as problems of our unreadiness. This unreadiness characterizes virtually all of us. It is a product of our having looked away from problems that have been clamoring for our attention, and of our having been satisfied with half truths where nothing less than whole truths could serve us. The unreadiness, in short, is a product of our widespread mental and emotional drift in a world where the adversary has not been drifting.

This adversary has, in the name of Marxism-Leninism, been moving ahead, step by calculated step, toward the building of a monolithic State, armed with the weapons of a nuclear age; and this State has learned the peculiar art of practicing totalitarianism at home and piecemeal conquest abroad while offering itself to the world as the vanguard of "peace," "liberation," and "anti-imperialism."

We have written this book because we had to. There comes a point where the world's peril turns into every individual's responsibility. So far as the problem of Communism is concerned, this point, we feel certain, has long been reached and passed. The time has come when each of us is obligated to study the character of this new force which claims the human future as its own, and to convert such knowledge into awareness of what is at stake and what needs to be done.

Communism is not a subject about which we can ever hope that our learning will be sufficient and final. It has, to be sure, aspects so basic that we can assume they will remain permanent as long as the ideology and the system remain in the world. These aspects we need to understand thoroughly and to pin down in our minds—definitively. On the other hand, we would say that we ourselves have never before tackled a subject where the "answers" so startlingly and so constantly explode into new questions, and where the known so tenaciously brings us up against the unknown, the permanent against the changing.

Because we think of this book as a project in initial and not in final exploration, we have included a bibliography of the works we have found most useful to us, a reference list of periodicals that have proved to be a continuing source of information, and a list of centers from which new materials of dependable scholarship are constantly being made available.

It would be impossible for us to make full acknowledgment to all who have given us help. Our thanks go to every person who, in book, or pamphlet, or newspaper, or interview has given us the information and insight we have needed. We owe a very special debt to certain friends who, having been absorbed with the problem of Communism far longer than we, have been able to put at our disposal their libraries of research materials, without which we could not have written this book. Our thanks go likewise to those publishers who have been generous with their permissions.

HARRY OVERSTREET
BONARO OVERSTREET

PART ONE

BEGINNINGS
AND DEVELOPMENTS

FROM ST. PETERSBURG
TO BUDAPEST

WHEN IT comes to understanding Communism—
and our own confusions and cross-purposes with
regard to it—we do well to move forward by going back:
back beyond the Bolshevik revolution of 1917 to the early
years of the century when this revolution was in the making.
For every item of world news in today's paper is a product
of history; and our reaction to it likewise comes out of the
past.

We can begin, then, with one landmark day which both
summed up "a long train of abuses" and anticipated tragedy
to come. On Bloody Sunday—January 22, 1905—the Tsar's
Cossacks were turned loose on striking workers in St. Petersburg. It amounted to that: to their being *turned loose*. More
than a thousand unarmed persons were killed, and twice that
number wounded. Russia was never the same again.

The general strike spread from St. Petersburg to every

major city. Mutiny flared in the navy. Peasants were stirred to revolt. Before the blood-soaked year ended, some 2,800,-000 persons had taken part in the rebellion. Lenin spoke with reason when he said that "the year 1905, the year of struggle, 'the mad year,' definitely buried patriarchal Russia." (1) *

What made Bloody Sunday so utterly senseless was that the strikers had not intended any resort to violence; nor had they been looking toward revolution. Their aims were specific and were embodied in a petition for "redress of grievances." They hated and feared the Cossacks and secret police; and experience had taught them to expect from their employers neither concession nor compassion. But they were loyal to the Tsar, whom they regarded as the father of his people. If only they could reach him, past the armed guards by whom he was ringed, and tell him the facts, they felt sure that justice would be done.

On January 22, therefore, with the Orthodox priest, George Gapon, as their leader, and with ikons carried before them, they converged—thousands of them, from all parts of the city—on the great square in front of the Winter Palace, to beg the Tsar to appear to them, listen to their leader, and judge their case.

Their petition asked five benefits: amnesty for strikers already arrested; basic civil liberties; a living wage; a gradual program of land reform; and universal suffrage. It followed, in brief, the line laid down by the Western democracies. But the manner of the appeal was pure Russian:

"We workers," the petition began, "inhabitants of St. Petersburg, have come to Thee. We are unfortunate, reviled slaves. We are crushed by despotism and tyranny. At last, when our patience was exhausted, we ceased work and begged our masters to give us only that without which life is torture. But this was refused . . ."

* Notes thus indicated are on pages 327–336.

And it ended: "Sire, do not refuse aid to Thy people! Throw down the wall that separates Thee from Thy people. Order and swear that our requests will be granted, and Thou wilt make Russia happy; if not we are ready to die on this very spot. We have only two roads: freedom and happiness or the grave." (2)

For all too many it was to be the grave. The Tsar did not appear. It is doubtful that he was even in the Winter Palace at the time. In any event, the Cossacks were turned loose on the packed crowd in the square—and Bloody Sunday took its place in history as the turning point beyond which the Tsar could do nothing to regain the standing he had lost in the eyes of the people.

When, later, he tried to make concessions, it was too late. What would, at the outset, have been more than enough to offer was by then too little. The workers replied, through their leader-priest Gapon: "We no longer have a Tsar. A river of blood separates the Tsar from the nation. Long live the fight for freedom!"

Lenin appraised the situation: found it much to his liking: "Events are developing with marvellous speed." And he amended the words of Gapon: "Long live the revolutionary proletariat! say we." (3)

This revolution of 1905 was suppressed. The Tsar was not deposed. Workers and peasants seemed, in the end, to be back where they had started from. A number of the significant revolutionary leaders were exiled—Lenin among them. Yet in spite of these outward appearances, Russia was not the same after the "mad year." Reforms were gradually instituted: reforms that started the lumbering nation on its way into the modern world, but that did not suffice to quiet the tides of unrest. Those who had seen political freedom almost within their grasp did not forget the vision. Old restraints and privations were no longer viewed as natural, but as imposed by an arbitrary regime. They were to be suffered until a new revolutionary situation could develop— but not for always. On this score, a myriad minds had been changed in the midst of struggle. Tsarism was on the way out.

What appeared to be on the way in was an order of life which would roughly approximate the one which had, over a period of several centuries, been developing in the West. The strikers' petition for "redress of grievances" seemed to forecast such an order. So did the attitude taken by many individual members of the aristocracy. So did the compassionate writings of intellectuals who, even as they portrayed the defeat of life, affirmed its inestimable worth.

This seeming groundswell of freedom distracted attention, however, from two determinative elements in the situation. One was the political naïveté and vague abstractionism which characterized many phases of the liberal movement in Russia: a movement which had developed *at the level of thinking,* but not *at the level of practice,* for the simple reason that Tsarism afforded no room for daily, trial-and-error democracy. The other element was a fateful division within the revolutionary forces of Russia with regard to the methods and goals of social change. This division had existed, with varying degrees of tension and acrimony, prior to 1905; but it had not yet become so sharply defined as to prevent a common front of struggle in that trial-run revolution. From then on, however, the cleavage became wider and deeper. On the one hand, there were those—comprising a number of different groups—who regarded the reforms which followed the uprising of 1905 as both a *proof* that parliamentary government could and should come next in Russia and as a *means* of working for its achievement. On the other hand, there were those who felt that this uprising had failed so completely that it had disproved, once for all, the efficacy of spontaneous, popular rebellion, the methods of gradual reform, and the goal of parliamentary government. This latter group were the Bolsheviks.

Fifty-one years after Bloody Sunday, in Budapest, "barricades hastily erected by Hungarian fighters presented a first obstacle to the Russian advance. The Hungarian Army, the National Guard and groups of freedom fighters, fought side by side against the advancing tanks." (4)

This was November 1956. Back of the events of that day were those of October; and further back, a mounting discontent with the rigid, Soviet-controlled regime in Hungary. In Budapest, as in St. Petersburg half a century before, those who sought "redress of grievances" had intended to stay within the law and induce change by peaceful means. But, like the striking workers, they had asked more than tyranny could give. They had asked for a kind of freedom that would inevitably point toward more freedom and the habits and attitudes that go with it.

On October 22, a number of student gatherings had taken place in Budapest, the most important of them at the Building Industry Technological University. There, "the students adopted a list of sixteen demands which expressed their views on national policy. . . . They included the immediate withdrawal of Soviet troops, . . . free elections, freedom of expression, the re-establishment of political parties, and sweeping changes in the conditions of both workers and peasants.

"Early next morning, the students' demands had become known throughout Budapest. Witnesses speak of an atmosphere of elation and hopefulness." (5)

That evening—October 23—some of the students went to the Radio Building to try to have their demands broadcast to the people of Budapest. "A large crowd gathered at the Radio Building, which was guarded by AVH or security police. The students sent a delegation into the building to negotiate with the Director. The crowd waited in vain. . . . Shortly after 9 P.M. tear gas bombs were thrown from the upper windows, and one or two minutes later, AVH men opened fire on the crowd. . . . In so far as any one moment can be selected as the turning point that changed a peaceable demonstration into a violent uprising it would be this moment when the AVH . . . attacked defenseless people."

Word of what had happened was swiftly phoned to workers in outlying districts. They "seized trucks and drove into Budapest, obtaining arms on the way from friendly soldiers or police, or from military barracks and arms factories." (6) By midnight, the Radio Building reported clashes throughout the city.

After that, it was too late for governmental concessions—inadequate and too long delayed—to mean peace so long as Soviet troops remained on Hungarian soil and a puppet regime in power. As the struggle was renewed with the coming of fresh Soviet forces, and as it spread to the provinces, more and more of the freedom fighters—workers, civil police, soldiers, students, mature intellectuals—reached a state of mind where they might well have paraphrased the words of Gapon: "We no longer have a government. A river of blood separates the government from the people. Long live the fight for freedom!"

How did it happen? By what perverse logic did the unfolding history of fifty years lead from St. Petersburg to Budapest: from the workers petitioning the Tsar, and being shot down, to the students petitioning the puppet Communist regime in Hungary, and being shot down?

It is to questions of this type that we shall seek an answer in this book: questions that have to do with the nature of the new tyranny—the Communist tyranny—which has come in the wake of the old; and which has strangely come where the tides of unrest have been those of a seeking for freedom.

In spite of the seeming parallelism of events in St. Petersburg and Budapest, this new tyranny, this new dictatorship, is, we know, very far from being a duplication of the old. It has an *ideological* thrust toward the future which Tsarism, seeking only to preserve the past, wholly lacked. It is *totalitarian* to an extent not conceived of by anyone—ruler or ruled—prior to the twentieth century. It is *international* in a sense which undercuts—and contradicts—the developing internationalism to which a myriad liberal minds around the world have long been devoted. It has introduced a concept of *revolution* so different from our Western concept that we mislead ourselves when we use the familiar word as though it applied to both types. Most strangely of all, it is—as Tsarism never was or could have been—a form of *absolutism* which has, like a magnet, drawn to itself millions of people who have sought to set men free.

We know these facts; and yet we do not know them. For at each stage of history, during these past fateful decades, our Western minds have tended to project upon Communism judgments not relevant to it: judgments carried over from the Tsarist era; judgments born of social and economic conditions in our own country; judgments that have reflected a host of made-in-America partisanships and antagonisms; judgments that reflect our common underestimation of *ideology* as a social force; judgments that have stemmed from a moral code which we have been unable to believe that the Communists have rejected—even though they have stated again and again that they want no traffic with it.

Because this book is not simply about Communism, but about it *as a force for our own minds to grapple with,* we have to ask not only how a new tyranny has succeeded an old, but where we were in our own thinking when the foundations of world Communism were being laid: in 1905; and later, when the Bolshevik revolution took place. Where have we been in our thinking since then—during the long succession of events that have turned Lenin's *coup d'état* of 1917 into a far-flung movement which now exerts totalitarian control over 900,000,000 human beings and which has its outpost Parties in all the countries of the world?

America itself was in no placid state around the turn of the century. After a long period of unregulated and incredibly rapid expansion—industrial and urban—we as a people were reacting sharply to the consequences of lopsided change. The two decades from 1890 to 1910 were, in terms of social ferment, unlike anything that had gone before them.

Big business was becoming bigger; and government—armed with its new weapon, the Sherman Anti-Trust Laws —was making sporadic efforts to keep it within bounds. Acute labor unrest was pointed up by the Homestead strike against Carnegie Steel, in 1892; the Pullman strike, in 1894; and the anthracite-coal strike, in 1902. Financial panic swept the country between 1893 and 1897, and again in 1907. Growing discontent among farmers expressed itself in the formation, in 1892, of the Populist Party—which demanded unlimited coinage of silver, postal savings banks, graduated income tax, and government ownership of railway, telephone, and telegraph lines.

On another front, Americans were taking stock of political processes, with an eye to both the control of abuses and the enlargement of political functions. The political machines of the big cities were being exposed to public scrutiny by dedicated journalists; and a broad movement was under way to make government more directly responsible to the people. Thus, in 1902, Oregon introduced the initiative and referendum; and in 1908, made all elective officers subject to recall. Wisconsin, in 1903, passed the first direct-primary law.

A parallel movement sought to make government the ally of the people against both big business and the hazards of accident and unemployment. Maryland, in 1902, enacted the first state workmen's compensation law; and 1903 saw the beginnings of a rapid, widespread movement among state legislatures to limit the factory hours of women and children. Both radicalism and reform, on the political-economic front, bred new parties and new organizations.

During the decade from 1890 to 1900, most of the ferment came from the efforts of the "have nots" to make their collective weight felt—through labor agitation and grassroots political parties. The language of protest was often Marxist; the tactics were those of mass pressure; and the aims ranged from reform to revolution. The extremist elements in this ferment were to form the nucleus, later, of the left wing of the Socialist Party; and in 1919, of the Communist Party in the United States. The moderate elements remained right-wing Socialists or moved over into the progressive wings of the major parties.

Up to the turn of the century, the disturbed conscience of American "haves" expressed itself chiefly in efforts to relieve suffering. But more and more individuals who were not themselves in need, shocked by the misery they witnessed, began to inquire into social and economic conditions. Thus, in the early 1900s, our country began to swing into one of the most dynamic periods of muckraking and reform in its history.

Labor unrest drew the attention of many liberal members of the owning class and they wanted to know what lay back of it. There were books to tell them: Veblen's *Theory of the*

Leisure Class, for example, which found a reading public far larger than its author had anticipated. Also, there were speakers to tell them: George Gunter, talking on "The Sweating System"; John Graham Brooks, on "A Living Wage" and "Why the Trade Unions Formed"; and Samuel Gompers, on "Strikes." In the field of economic theory, speakers talked again and again about Karl Marx, William Morris, Robert Owen, Lord Shaftesbury, and John Stuart Mill—and audiences ready to listen seemed to have sprung full-grown from the American soil.

The types of people who made up these audiences were, on other fronts, concerning themselves about slum clearance and city planning, settlement houses and residence hotels for working girls. They made note of how many persons were physically unfit and took up the struggle for pure-food laws and public-health services—an effort which culminated, in 1906, in the passage of the federal Pure Food and Drug Act.

They saw that legal abuses were flagrant: and again set themselves to learn and to act. Those were the years, for example, when Judge Rosalie Whitney was telling the public about "Fighting Legal Battles for the Poor"; when Judge Ben B. Lindsay was telling "What the Children's Court of Denver Stands For"; and when Thomas Mott Osborne was voicing his great plea for prison reform in "Experiences at Sing-Sing" and "Human Nature behind Prison Bars." They were the years, also, of the struggle for women's rights: not simply the right to vote, but legal and property rights.

For the most part, this dynamic liberalism stayed within the tradition of evolutionary change by democratic means; and it measured each project by the yardstick of the American dream. Characteristically, it focused on the individual: the morally responsible individual, who could not remain indifferent to exploitation and suffering; and the needy individual, whose human powers were being wasted and whose human rights were being flouted. For the enlargement of individual influence, it relied on voluntary association.

We must note, however, that a new concept was also, in those years, wedging itself into the minds of many liberal "haves"—often without any recognition on their part that it was at a far remove from the democratic concept. We might call it *scientific utopianism*. It was—in a variety of forms—the concept of manipulating mankind into a better society than the "masses" could be trusted to achieve for themselves. Born of the excitement and promise of physical science, such utopianism held a strong appeal for many whose good will toward men far outran their respect for the average human being; who were at odds with religious orthodoxy; and who were more profoundly moved by the vision of a perfect society than by the workaday drama of man's awkward grappling with one problem after another.

While they still "believed" in democracy, these utopians were most responsive to doctrines of the well-ordered State— which invariably turned out to be doctrines of the elite. They looked toward happiness for the many designed by the well-endowed and well-disciplined few; and specifically by the few who would learn to work wonders with the material resources and methods of science. Some among them invested their hope in eugenics and the breeding-out of the unfit; others idealized "the efficient life" and "the efficient society." Among them, also, was a fair number who would, in years to come, feel the tug of an elite Party—a "revolutionary vanguard"—which Lenin, in Russia, was even then organizing in the name of Marx's "scientific socialism."

It was this America of ferment and deep economic cleavages, of angry mass movements and stand-pat resistance to them, of big business becoming bigger and government assuming new functions, of dynamic liberalism and utopian visions, which in 1905 received the news of Bloody Sunday. It was this America which twelve years later was plunged into a world war it had never expected to witness—much less take part in; and which it translated into a war "to make the world safe for democracy." It was this America which reacted to the Russian revolution of February-March 1917; and then, after months of vast confusion, to the Bolsheviks' November (October) *coup d'état* and Russia's headlong plunge into civil war.

What Americans did at that time—Americans who ranged across the whole spectrum of political-economic opinion— was chiefly to project upon events in Russia *the feelings and attitudes which had been fostered in them by developments and partisanships in this country.* Among those who took sides, for or against the revolution, few were schooled in mind or emotion to move out of the Western frame of reference and appraise Communism in its own terms. This was as true, for the most part, of those who talked the language of Marxism as of those who detested this language. Not more than a handful—if that many—had any intimation of the fact that they were witnessing from a distance the arrival of a new form of social organization: *a totalitarian dictatorship.*

The America which emerged from the First World War was not, we know, simply a continuance of the prewar America. It was, on many counts, profoundly different in temper and outlook. The wave of dynamic liberalism had largely spent itself. When the United States refused to join the League of Nations, when wartime profiteering was brought to light in an atmosphere of postwar depression, when isolationism and Harding's "normalcy" became the order of the day, liberalism tended to subside into quiescence or to turn into disillusionment. As depression yielded to dizzy speculative prosperity, disillusionment itself took two forms: an attitude of "debunking," largely divorced from social action of any kind; and what we might call an "expatriated" idealism—an idealism, that is, which withdrew its hope for human betterment from the institutions of American democracy and invested it elsewhere. The idealism itself, however —even when it chose the Soviet Union as its homeland— was a product of the Western tradition. In the overwhelming number of cases, it invented out of the materials of this tradition the "Communism" to which it dedicated itself; and this "Communism" bore slight resemblance to that which Lenin had established and Stalin was consolidating in the Union of Soviet Socialist Republics.

Somehow, this has tenaciously continued to be the situation—through years of depression, war, and cold war. It has continued to be the situation not only with the persons attracted to Communism *as they have conceived it to be*—and then disillusioned by its realities—but also, by and large, with the persons who have hated and feared it. While an increasing number of individuals have come to know, by responsible study or direct experience, exactly why they regard Communism as a gigantic threat to human well-being, these are still very far from being a majority among the anti-Communists. The majority, it would appear, are still inventing the Communism to which they are opposed: fashioning it out of what they have hated and feared in the American scene. We must judge this to be the case by the lack of precision with which they apply the term; and also by the manner in which, time and again, they start talking about Communism and end—as though they were still on the same subject—talking about unrelated American issues and movements which arouse their ire.

In recent years, however, there are signs of change: signs that knowledge and an interest in knowing have begun to replace many of the ignorances and fictions which have long confused us and set us against one another. Perhaps this feeling of change comes chiefly from the fact that the number of informed individuals in certain groups has vastly increased: scholars who are devoting themselves to the study of Communist theory and practice and to the dissemination of what they learn; ex-Communists who have come to know the character of the Party at first hand; persons who have struggled to counteract Communist influence in groups to which they have belonged; persons who have had official reason to acquaint themselves with the inner workings of the world Communist movement.

Yet most of us still have our job of learning cut out for us: our job of coming to grips with the hard realities of Communism. This is, in fact, a threefold job. The first is learning the basic nature of this strange force—its ideology and the tactics and stratagems which derive from this. The second is making our own nation and the free world into an effective *whole* with reference to the problems posed by Communist expansionism—while keeping all our legitimate endemic differences within this wholeness. The third job is working out our own creative commitment with regard to the future of mankind.

TWO

THE THEORY BEHIND THE SYSTEM

WHEN THE Bolsheviks seized power, in 1917, they seized also—as exclusively theirs to interpret, apply, and defend against deviation—the "scientific socialism" of Marx and Engels. This they expanded into the "science of Marxism-Leninism"; and thus equipped, set themselves to build a new society from scratch—on a foundation of "infallible" theory, not on a foundation of cumulative human experience. Further, they undertook to make this society not one among others but, by world revolution, the archetype of all human society.

Thus there has come about one of the strangest situations imaginable. We, today, who turn to our daily papers to find out what the current Communist leaders are doing—or proposing that we do—cannot read what is written between the lines unless we have some grasp of Marx's "scientific socialism."

By Marx's day, Western humanitarianism had done its work well enough so that countless individuals felt both compassion and guilt when they saw fellow human beings reduced to misery and saw no way to set matters right. Yet no institution, religious or secular, seemed ready for an all-out attack on exploitation and poverty. Many persons, therefore, of good mind and conscience were emotionally "at large." They went their way as lonely reformers. Or they joined one or another of the small, zealous groups which were organized, dissolved, and reorganized along the margins of the established order.

By Marx's day, again, capitalism had brought the production of material goods to a point where, for the first time in history, a decent standard of living for all began to seem within human reach; and it had bred a new type of worker. Exploited though he was, this worker did not look at his world with the eyes of serf or slave. He was beginning to see himself as possessed of rights; and himself and his fellow workers as possessed of power.

What capitalism had not done, however, was to prove that it could or would produce economic justice. The workers' every gain, it seemed, had to be won *not through the capitalistic order but in spite of those who controlled this order.* Thus, paradoxically, the vision of a better future was the product of a system which seemed stubbornly set against delivering this future. Under these circumstances, many persons began to look for an alternative system on which to focus their hopes.

In physical science they saw unlimited promise. Yet, as often as not, they saw science treated as a mere adjunct of industry. Scientists themselves, moreover, preoccupied with segments of the physical world, sought no directive role with regard to broad human affairs. Even science, then, was disappointing to those who saw it as capable of great social ventures but as either held back from these by reactionary forces or simply holding aloof from them.

Enter, Karl Marx—with what seemed like a creative fusion of humanitarianism and science. What Marx did, in effect, was to "prove" that while the going order could never rectify its own faults, its accomplishments need not be lost. These, with the dross all washed away in revolution, could be lifted up to a higher level where their intrinsic promise would be fulfilled.

Marx was a man consumed by what appeared to be humanitarian anger. Also, he was a man with a theory—*dialectical and historical materialism*—which seemed to bring all reality within one frame. This theory, for those who accepted it, both took the guesswork out of history—past, present, and future—and guaranteed a happy ending to earth's long story of injustice. Finally, Marx was a man with a revolutionary program—*scientific socialism*—in which, because it was "scientific," countless persons felt they could invest hope and effort to some clear end, with no danger of being let down.

Marx dated all history from the point where mankind, itself a material part of a material universe, took a fateful step from which there was no turning back. To secure material necessities, men set up a system of production rooted in private property; and within this, a division of labor: a "class" system. On the one hand, there were those who owned the means of production; on the other, those who did the work.

Once human beings were related to one another within this system, they produced, moreover, not only material goods but also a "superstructure" of institutions and moral codes which "of necessity" reflected class relationships at the level of material production. While legal and political institutions expressed and enforced the will of the propertied class, moral and religious systems rationalized their privileges and fostered in the workers a voluntary compliance.

As Marx saw it, the process which was thus started would follow one certain course—and could not be diverted from it. Society would be ever more sharply divided into the exploited "masses" and the exploiting few. The latter, because they owned the means of production, could dictate the terms and conditions of labor; and they could impose unemployment and destitution upon those who tried to talk back. Also, they could compel the workers to produce a "surplus": goods not to be used by the owners, but to be marketed by them.

In this advantageous position, Marx insisted, the *capitalists* —owners of capital goods—would never feel that they had enough. With "unlimited avarice," they would exact more and more "surplus" effort from the workers, for the sake of profits, and they would pare wages down to the level of bare subsistence, for the sake of saving money. They would never voluntarily yield up one iota of wealth or privilege; nor, until this "inexorable" trend had run its course, could they be resisted. The workers could not resist. Neither could the petty bourgeoisie nor the intellectuals; for these would gradually be absorbed into the two major classes. Some few would rise into the propertied class. Most would sink into the proletariat. In either case, they would then share the fate of their class. The rich would become richer; the poor, poorer. It was thus, according to Marx, that capitalism had, by a predetermined course, come into being and then produced rich factory owners and impoverished masses.

Marx arrived at this version of history—which he called "scientific"—by imposing upon events and institutions, with all their variables and complexities, a dialectic which the philosopher Hegel had developed to account for the progression of *ideas* from lower to higher levels.

Hegel's conception was that every line of thought—every

thesis—when once started, goes too far. Its own unfolding logic brings it to a point of exaggeration where, instead of revealing further truth, it becomes false. At this point, it is confronted by its *antithesis:* its logical opposite. Out of the clash of thesis and antithesis comes a new *synthesis:* an idea which embodies the essential truth of both, but which is qualitatively different from either, being on a higher plane of reality. On this plane, it becomes a *thesis*—and the process goes on. . . .

As a logician, Hegel carried this pattern through to its fulfillment in a final perfect synthesis, Pure Reason—which he took to be the basic form of reality. Marx, as a materialist, had no room within his frame of reference for Pure Reason. What he did with the dialectic was to apply it to events and institutions in such a way that he coerced all past history into the "trend" noted above—and then projected this trend "inexorably" into the future. Thus he made it predictable, with "scientific exactness," that under capitalism the exploitation of workers must in time reach its intolerable extreme: where wages would be at the bare subsistence level, but where profit-hungry owners would still demand a marketable "surplus." With a glut of goods and no buyers, a matured productive system would be brought to a halt—by a lag in the pattern of class relationships. At this point, the dialectic of history would be fulfilled in revolution: in the "expropriation of the expropriators."

The workers would seize the means of production; and the whole "superstructure" of ideas and institutions that had enforced and rationalized the power of the owning class would crumble—to be replaced by one reflecting the new order. Socialism would now be established—but not yet Communism. Exploitation would end. But the State, as "dictatorship of the proletariat," would still have two coercive functions to perform. It would have to see to it that each person got a just return for his work; and it would have to defend the new order against counter-revolution. Eventually, however, all reactionary elements would have been liquidated or "educated," and world revolution would have taken place—now in one country, now in another, as capitalism matured. Thus, the working of "inexorable law" would usher in Communism. The State, no longer needed, would "wither away"; and in a "classless society," each would produce according to his ability and receive according to his need.

It was Marx, the revolutionary, who named as "infallible science" the formula thus worked out by Marx, the dialectician. For while the theory could not, in any scientific sense, be *proved*—least of all the projection into the future—it had to be *believed*. The workers of the world had to be so won over by it that they would act on it, without proof— and thereby bring its "proof" into being.

Marx, we must note, was his own first convert. He so firmly believed in his "economic interpretation of history" that he published it as conclusive and scientific before he even started to look for corroborative evidence. Only when Engels urged him to strengthen the appeal of his formulation by providing proof did he give belated attention to the fields of economics and history: that is, to what was actually on record as having happened in the past.

We know from his letters to Engels that what was thus on record disappointed him. Search as he would, he could find only one instance of any such dialectical change as he had pronounced universal: that from feudalism to capitalism. Even here, it took a careful playing down of some facts and playing up of others to make the ambiguous record fit the "conclusive" theory. Yet he made it fit—and worked this one instance to the limit.

The fact is that Marx was not trained as a scientist but

as a philosopher; and he was, moreover, temperamentally unfitted to be a scientist. His taste was for all-embracing concepts proved "true" by their inner coherence; not for hypotheses about segments of reality, these to be tested by accurate reference to the objective world. He had, also, a highly unscientific tendency to impose rigid *either-or* patterns upon the fluid complexity of life. People were *either* exploited *or* exploiters. There would be *either* total overthrow *or* no significant change. *Either* capitalism *or* communism would prevail. Most seriously, his intellectual assurance made him high-handed not only toward every critic of his theory but even toward "uncooperative" facts. The former, he set himself to "kill by epithet." The latter, wherever possible, he ignored.

On his first trip to England, for example, he expected to find the workers, in this most advanced industrial country, ripe for revolution. His theory prescribed their being so. Instead, he found them intent upon reforms within the going system: legal reforms and the building of trade unions. Judging by the record, he did not, at this critical testing point, re-examine his theory. Instead, he turned his back on these English workers and sought out a German group—a London branch of the "League of the Just"—among whom he found both a more radical spirit and a greater respect for theory.

As time went on, and as he dug more deeply into his subject, Marx did, to be sure, make a token bow to various unpalatable facts; but scarcely more than a token bow. Thus, anthropology revealed that certain primitive societies, with characteristic systems of production, had antedated *division of labor*. There was no place for these primitive societies in Marx's "science." They ought never to have existed. Yet they had existed. Faced by this dilemma, Marx tucked them in as early exceptions to the developments covered by his "coercive laws." But he did not, in any true scientific sense, make room for them in his theory.

Again, fairly late in life, he conceded that capitalism *might*, in some countries—such as England and the United States —so develop as to bring about socialism without violent overthrow. He had to weigh this possibility because effective resistance to entrenched power was patently shaping up where he had "proved" it could not do so. But again, he merely *added* the possibility. He did not face its full implications for his theory. By thus acknowledging unpalatable facts and yet giving them little more than a "footnote" status, he passed on to future generations—and to the Communists—a theory both "infallible" and ambiguous, "scientifically exact" and full of contradictions and loose ends.

The analysis which Marx made of the economic order of his day was acute and useful—if taken in moderation. It drew attention to facts and problems that had previously been passed over or left half interpreted. This was his creative contribution. The tragedy is that he became the enemy of his own best insights. Not only did he give "uncooperative" facts less than a fair chance to put his "science" to the test; but he also turned his back on the dialectic where this might have saved his theory from becoming rigid. Having pushed the logic of his "economic interpretation of history" to that extreme point where, in effect, it became false, he would brook no *antithesis*. "Demolishing" all critics instead of weighing their criticisms, he refused to let his *thesis* meet the challenge of a corrective opposite. Thus, he denied it the chance to have its very genuine portion of truth "lifted up" into a higher *synthesis*—and made part of an ongoing study of social and economic process. He fixated it at the level of coercive dogma.

Late in life, Marx became so dismayed, apparently, at some of the interpretations put upon his work that he stated,

"I am not a Marxist." Yet it was he who shaped an "infallible" theory, furiously defended it, and called for revolutionary action in strict accord with its dictates. If, then, he was not a Marxist, he was the original maker of Marxists.

When the Communists took over Marx's "immutable science," *they equipped themselves with the most potent weapon ever devised for building and rationalizing a totalitarian dictatorship, and for fomenting unrest and ill will between man and man everywhere in the world.* In this unscientific "science," they have had at their disposal both the "infallibility" of Marx's dogma and its convenient ambiguities.

Its "infallibility" has served as a binding force to give world Communism its tenacity of purpose and "monolithic unity." From the time the Bolshevik Party was first organized, long before the revolution, Lenin ruled out all disagreement about theory as incompatible with "iron discipline." The new truth, moreover, must supplant the old; not merely exist side by side with it. Down through the years, the edict has held—not in the Soviet Union alone, but in all Communist parties.

Thus, for example, J. Peters, whose *Manual on Organization* helped to shape the Communist Party in the United States: "We cannot imagine a discussion . . . questioning the correctness of the leading role of the proletariat in the revolution, or the necessity for the proletarian dictatorship. . . . We do not question the correctness of the revolutionary theory of the class struggle." (1)

The passage of time has not made the CPUSA more flexible. In 1957, a major struggle took place within the Party on the precise question of whether or not more free discussion should be permitted—and the "revisionists" were defeated. Control is still firmly in the hands of those who, on matters of dogma, tolerate no breach of iron discipline.

The same holds true in the Soviet Union—and throughout the Communist orbit. It appeared, for a time, that Khrushchev would countenance a more "liberal" policy; but more recent events have not borne out this brief impression. The August 1956 issue of *Kommunist,* official organ of the Communist Party of the Soviet Union, carried an article which defined the limits within which a "clash of opinion" would be tolerated—and this would appear to be Khrushchev's view: "Of course there can be no compromise with views and pronouncements hostile to Marxism."

Again, the "infallibility" of the "science" gives every Communist a useful sense of superiority. The comrade who "knows" that history is on his side can despise rather than fear those who seek to control his conspiratorial activities; after all, they are living on borrowed time, doomed by "inexorable law." This sense of being on the side of the inevitable runs through the Party from top to bottom. The truculence of Khrushchev's manner repeatedly expresses his doctrinal certainty that the West is doomed; and this same certainty can be added to the ego of the most obscure comrade to even the score between him and a society by which he has felt undervalued.

Once more, this "infallible" dogma tells Communists what to see in every situation and how to interpret it. Thus, the USSR was able to announce "conclusively"—without weighing the evidence—that the Hungarian uprising was the work of reactionaries and Western imperialists; for Marx had specified the types of enemies who would always have to be dealt with during the "dictatorship of the proletariat." The United Nations Committee, however—having weighed the evidence—stated that the USSR was simply insisting "that all historical happenings must be viewed as aspects of the Communist conception of Marxism and of the class struggle, illustrating a permanent conflict between 'good' Communist and 'bad' bourgeois elements." (2)

Finally, this "infallible" dogma, which has seemed to fuse *science* and *humanitarianism* into one great whole—one truth and one program—has exerted a magnetic pull upon countless minds in non-Communist countries: minds that hunger to have life possess more meaning than they have found in it; minds that have yearned for a cause to which they could attach hopes and loyalties that have, for one reason or another, been, in Auden's phrase, "unattached as tumbleweed."

The appeal of Marxism-Leninism, in such cases, appears to be twofold. In a confused world, *dialectical and historical materialism* imposes one simplifying principle upon the recalcitrant and painful complexity of existence. More important still, *scientific socialism* invites people, in behalf of a great human future, and in the company of the "revolutionary vanguard," to run great risks. Yet miraculously these are not, in any final sense, risks at all. For the outcome is assured. Countless interim projects may fail, and countless individuals die short of the goal. But there is no ultimate risk of having labored in vain. Or so it seems to the believers— for as long as they continue to believe.

If the "infallibility" of Marx's theory has thus proved useful to the Communists, its ambiguities have been scarcely less so. These have given Party leaders a wide-open chance to maneuver. When a policy has proved unfruitful or has expended its usefulness, the persons identified with it can be charged with an "incorrect" interpretation of Marx—and forthwith purged. Rivalries among the power elite can be similarly resolved: to the victor belongs the privilege of defining the "correct" line and purging his rivals as "revisionists" or "deviationists."

Again, when a new strategy is called for, some justifying chapter and verse, clothed in ambiguity, can always be found. Both Lenin and Stalin thought of themselves as

Marxists; and both held rigidly to those tenets of the dogma which kept the world sharply divided into "two worlds": Communist and non-Communist. Yet both, also, made the most of Marx's ambiguities.

Thus, Stalin showed how useful these could be to a dictator bent upon forging a vast power state: "We stand for the withering away of the state. At the same time we stand for the dictatorship of the proletariat, which is the mightiest and strongest state power which has ever existed. The highest development of state power with the object of preparing the conditions *for* the withering away of state power—such is the Marxist formula. Is this 'contradictory'? Yes, it is 'contradictory.' But this contradiction is bound up with life, and it fully reflects Marx's dialectics." (3)

William Z. Foster, veteran theorist and strategist of the CPUSA, writes: "The first great source of the strength of the Communist parties in all countries is their scientific Marxist-Leninist theory. This is their brain stuff, their nerve system, their life blood. . . .

". . . This Marxist science makes clear the lessons of history, and it also lays bare the significance of current political developments. It explains the economic and political laws that have operated to bring about the rise of capitalism, and also the forces that are leading inexorably to the decay of that system and the establishment of socialism." (4)

That is a large order for anything called "science." Yet even larger is the following: "Dialectical materialism, the world-view of the Marxist-Leninist party, is a philosophical science which *generalizes all scientific knowledge*, discovers the universal laws of all development, the most general laws of nature, society and thought." (5)

Communist writings abound in such passages; and they are not idle words. They are regarded as literal statements about the *ideology* which animates the world Communist movement. The "science of Marxism-Leninism" could never thus have served Communist ends *if it had truly been science:* that is, self-limited in its field of research, responsible in its handling of objective evidence, and always subject to re-examination. But neither, we must realize, could it have served these ends *if Marx had not given it the aura of science.*

As an instrument of revolution—able to endow Communism with both fanatic zeal and strategic flexibility; able both to divide and confuse non-Communists and to draw in adherents from their ranks—it would be hard to find anything more potent than an "infallible," conveniently ambiguous "science."

THREE

THE MAN
BEHIND THE THEORY

IT IS doubtful whether any other movement in history can
match the record of world Communism on one score:
that of drawing people to itself through their urge to better
the human lot and *then losing them through disillusionment*.
When a movement sets an all-time high on this peculiar
count, there is something wrong with it.

There is no rubber-stamp reason, of course, for people's
having joined the Party; nor for their having left it. Rather,
there are reasons and reasons. For the time being, however,
we wish to focus on this one repetitive pattern of illusion
and disillusion, and to ask whether it has to go on—year
after year, with one wave of converts after another. Does
the illusion still have to run its course in so many individual
lives? Can it not be prevented, in the first place, by some
understanding of the spirit in which Communism was born
and the type of relationship between man and man that it
calls natural and necessary?

A great many ex-Communists have, by now, told their stories—a handful of them in print, the overwhelming majority in personal consultations with university research teams, ministers and priests, government agents, psychologists and psychiatrists, individual employers, labor leaders, Congressional committees, representatives of the American Civil Liberties Union, the Urban League, and other concerned groups. Whether they have chosen to speak directly to the public or to make their hard-won knowledge indirectly available, ex-Communists—in other countries as well as in America—have tried to map the psychological roads that took them into the Party and, after months or years, out again. One element comes closer than any other to being a common denominator in these multitudinous reports: namely, the individual's faith, when he joined the Party, that by throwing in his weight with the Communists, he could hasten the coming of a better world.

Most of these defectors seem to have accepted Communism, at the outset, as a system that could produce democratic results faster than democracy could—and that was more singlemindedly intent upon producing these. They had implicit faith in the Party's humanitarian aims, and saw these as supported by a coherent plan of action and a discipline that lifted each comrade above selfishness. This discipline, moreover, established an efficient "order of command" and did away with what they felt to be the slipshod bungling and corruption of the democratic process.

Disillusionment has signified, in the vast majority of cases, a rejection of ruthlessness and of the rigid monolithic practices of the Party—and of the Soviet State. What it has signified beyond this, however, differs greatly from one defector to another. For many, it has meant a definitive re-embracing of democracy—or a *conscious* embracing of it for the first time. For others, however, it has virtually meant ex-idealism: a retreat into strictly private concerns and a resolve never again to be "played for a sucker."

For yet others it has meant an "Ancient Mariner" burden of guilt. Those who became defectors as a result of Khrushchev's revelations about Stalin seem to be particularly haunted. They cannot forget the dead and tortured whose treatment they either refused to credit, at the time, or even condoned as "necessary," because the Party line required this. Many who similarly condoned the Soviet Union's taking over of the satellites, and who defected after the Hungarian uprising, bear a like burden.

Not even disillusionment, however, has ruled out in every case a lingering nostalgia for the lost vision and a sense that if the Communist movement could just get back to some fork in the road where it took the wrong turn, all might still be well. If it could get back to the fervor of the revolution, before Stalin's arrogant ambition had corrupted the movement. . . . Better yet, if it could get all the way back to the untarnished humanitarianism of Marx. . . .

Not only because this nostalgia exists, but because the Party is today framing new appeals with which to attract a new crop of the unwary, we ourselves need to go back to Marx—to appraise, as an object of faith and idealism, the man behind the theory.

Whatever else he did, Marx promised a most peculiar miracle. He promised that those who followed his way until they had made it the world's way would harvest figs from thistles. Out of implacable class hatred would come, not the usual psychological fruits of implacability and hatred, but a classless society in which men would live at peace. Out of the "dictatorship of the proletariat" would come, not the usual fruits of unrestricted power, but the disappearance of the very instrumentalities of power: the withering away of the State.

Marx never had a revolution at his disposal—though he repeatedly saw one as imminent. Thus, we do not know how he would have conducted himself at the point where abstract theory was turned into violent fact. We cannot conclusively say whether he would have acted like the *humanitarian* his followers credit him with having been or like the *utopian* he always denied being.

The distinction is basic. A genuine *humanitarian* grants an intrinsic worth to living persons. A *utopian*, on the other hand, tends to see living persons as expendable. If they stand in the way of a perfect future portrayed in a conclusive theory, they must be removed—for the sake of that ideal Man who is to inherit the earth. If they are obstacles, in short, they need not be treated as individuals. A *utopian* is thus inclined toward the dictatorial—no matter how much he may talk about the rights of the "masses." His tendency to talk about the "masses" is, in fact, a danger sign. A *humanitarian* is concerned about the chances that individuals have to live fulfilled lives; and no matter how many individuals may belong to one group or another, he still does not lump them as a mass.

If Marx had no violent revolution in which to reveal his character, he had his full quota of less dramatic chances to show how he felt about people and how he treated them when he had power at his command. We can turn, then, to these. For human attitudes need not be exhibited in some vast historic drama before we can dare to estimate their quality.

Marx was an angry man. The famous target of his anger was the raw, ruthless industrialism of his day. But he had also many lesser targets; and many that less deserved attack. No one who crossed him personally could escape. Significantly, moreover, the fellow theorists on whom he most mercilessly vented his rage were those who—hating the same exploitation that he hated—sought ways of evolutionary change: ways of altering relationships without "liquidating" human beings. Where these men were concerned, Marx did not stop with disagreement. To the extent of his not inconsiderable power, he demolished them.

This word *demolish* points to a peculiar quality of his anger: its apocalyptic character. Whether directed against an individual, an institution, or some philosophy that he despised as "idealistic," his anger tended to take on the quality of a final judgment which he, an agent of doom, hurled at the offender. We may not notice this quality if we judge him only by his attack upon the industrial order of his day; for so vast were the evils of this order that the only practical humanitarian might almost seem to have been the one who could pit against these a rage of cataclysmic proportions. No such matching of rage to object, however, can explain the destructive attacks which he launched against individuals whose only "crime against humanity" was that they had befriended him until they could do no more; and whom he then felt appointed to demolish *because they could do no more.*

His treatment of Arnold Ruge is a case in point. At a time when Marx was at the end of his resources, Ruge made him co-editor with himself of the *German-French Yearbook.* In this publication he was first able, in two articles, to lay the groundwork for his "scientific socialism." But the *Yearbook* was short-lived. It neither satisfied its backers nor could pay its own way. Ruge, no less than Marx—or more, since his had been the original stake—suffered from its demise. Yet Marx was enraged at him for not somehow digging up funds with which he, Marx, could be kept on in a job he was enjoying.

From that day, he never spared Ruge when he could harm him. Thus, when Ruge published, in a small German paper, *Forward*, a sympathetic article about a revolt of Silesian weavers, Marx found in it only one sentence with which he could disagree. Yet starting from this, he "annihilated" Ruge in an article of such length that its installments were carried in several issues of *Forward*. (With regard to the offending sentence, incidentally, Ruge was right; Marx wrong. Ruge had said that the weavers' strike, for all its valor, would have little effect: would soon be forgotten. Marx, in his answering blast, called Ruge an illiterate and a charlatan and "proved" that this very strike would mark the beginning of the communist revolution in Europe.)

His attack on Bruno Bauer was even more intemperate. Bauer, who had known Marx at the University of Berlin, tried to get an instructorship for him at Bonn, where he himself was teaching. He also proposed their becoming co-founders of a new publication, which he would initially finance. Neither plan materialized. Bauer himself was in an anomalous position: an atheist, he was teaching in a school of theology. Instead of securing the instructorship for Marx, he lost his own; and he had no resources, then, for the publishing venture either.

Doubly disappointed, Marx interpreted as a betrayal this inability to give the expected help. He never forgave or forgot; and, years later, found a chance to vent his full apocalyptic rage. On a shoestring, Bauer had started the *General Literary Gazette*. When it failed, after only eight issues, he was left impoverished. The eight issues, however, had come into Marx's hands. He was then working, day and night, to dig out of books on economics some factual proof with which to undergird his own already published theory. Also, he soon learned of Bauer's financial plight. Neither consideration halted him; nor, even, did Engels' protest at his disproportionate obsession with Bauer. Putting everything else aside, he took on the task of "demolishment." Before he had finished dissecting the eight issues and their unfortunate author, he had poured out three hundred and fifty pages: *The Holy Family: Bruno Bauer and his Associates*. Without permission, he then attached Engels' name to this, as co-author with himself.

Marx claimed human society as a province exclusively his to interpret, the human future as exclusively his to map out: *exclusively* his—for he did not easily tolerate any rival, as his contemptuous treatment of Lassalle and other possible competitors makes clear. In view of his staking out this particular province, we cannot pass over, as mere eccentricity, his readiness to see all who crossed him personally as fit only for annihilation. Hitler exhibited this same trait. So did Stalin. It is, in fact, a trait that seems inseparable from the character of the modern totalitarian dictator.

Neither can we pass lightly over Marx's consistent attacks on all who held to idealistic philosophies or who sought ways of social and economic change other than violent overthrow. In his disagreements with such thinkers, he did not stop where reason—to say nothing of generosity—would have called a halt. The destructive contempt which he poured upon their views suggests that his adherence to methods of overthrow was dictated as much by emotion as by logic.

Both Marx and Engels revealed in their letters yet further characteristics which cast doubt upon their being well qualified as architects of human society. One such characteristic was their seeming compulsion to "kill by epithet." Most people can refer to someone whom they dislike without having recourse to such terms as *swine, shark, imbecile,*

reactionary humbug, bombastic demagog. But for both Marx
and Engels such terms seem to have constituted the *ready
response:* that is, a response prepared by a chronic state of
mind in advance of any given situation.

Further than this, invective was, for Marx, a favorite
weapon of calculated attack. Thus, he wrote to Wedemeyer,
on March 5, 1852, "Your article against Heinzen . . . is very
good, both brutal and subtle." (1) He then went on to make
various suggestions which Wedemeyer should feel free to
use if he wished. Heinzen and other "democratic gentlemen"
could be called "ignorant louts" who "presume to yap out
their contradictions." Because they looked to gradual reform,
rather than violent revolution, they could be labeled as
"slaves of the bourgeoisie" and as "disgusting in their servi-
tude." When Communists, today, call those who oppose them
"human rats," "glib agents of Wall Street," and "stoolpigeons
of the capitalist police state," they have every right to think
of themselves as Marxists.

Another feature of the writings of both Marx and Engels
—striking in view of their being rated as humanitarians—is
their total lack of compassion toward those whom they saw
as slated for liquidation. They granted that, according to
their own theory, these were doomed, not by their individual
behavior, but by the "inexorable laws of history." Yet no
quarter was to be given them.

In a letter dated October 23, 1846, for example, Engels
told how, in a certain group, he had been challenged by
some followers of Grün to state the explicit nature of Communism. "I covered no more," he wrote, "than the particular
point at issue and, by positing community of goods, *ruled
out* peaceableness, tenderness or compassion toward the
bourgeoisie." (2)

In like spirit, Marx criticized the Paris Commune for being
"carried away by dreams of establishing supreme justice"—

when, to his mind, it should have proceeded with the "expropriation of the expropriators." It showed "unnecessary magnanimity," moreover: "instead of annihilating its enemies, it endeavored to exercise moral influence upon them." (3)

As for maneuvers: one letter from Marx to Engels sets a precedent for one of the most familiar of Communist tactics: that of usurping the policymaking function in a group by simply preventing anything's being done until most of the people, out of sheer weariness, have gone home. Marx, moreover, was applying this tactic against fellow Communists—and seems, from the tone of his letter, to have relished the experience.

He recounts how a certain subcommittee, during his absence, had adopted a "declaration of principles"—this to be submitted later to a general committee. When he read it, he was "really frightened"—for it savored of moderate socialism. Instead of stating his objections openly, however, he persuaded the subcommittee that the document might be improved by further editing.

When the subcommittee met at his house, two nights later, to do this editing, Marx was "firmly determined that if possible not one single line of the stuff should be allowed to stand." Therefore: "In order to gain time I proposed that before we 'edited' the preamble we should 'discuss' the rules. . . . It was an hour after midnight by the time the first of forty rules was agreed on. Cremer said (*and this was what I had aimed at*): We have nothing to put before the Committee. . . . We must postpone the meeting. . . . But the subcommittee can get together. . . . This was agreed to and the 'papers' left behind for my opinion."

Having thus stalled matters, Marx proceeded, not to edit the *declaration of principles*, as agreed upon, but to write a substitute: *An Address to the Working Class*. Then: "on the

pretext that everything material was included in this Address.
. . . I altered the whole preamble, [and] threw out the
declaration of principles. . . . My proposals were all accepted. . . . Only I was obliged to insert two phrases about
'duty' and 'right' into the Preamble of the Statutes, ditto
'truth, morality and justice,' but these are placed in such a
way that they can do no harm." (4)

After we have read enough of this type of thing—this
record of the vengeful and arrogant—we are fairly well
fortified against the belief that Communism took the wrong
turn only with the advent of Lenin—or of Stalin.

Marx is called a humanitarian because he took the side of
the working class. Yet even upon this class he imposed his
dogma: workers, too, were dolts and fools if they rejected
his theory; and he made it clear that when the revolution
came, no individual worker would be free to go counter to
the destiny of his class. This was not, to his mind, stating an
edict. It was simply pointing out an "inexorable law" of
nature. But it is all too easy for a man with a theory and a
taste for coercive methods to take on the peculiar role *of
enforcing natural law.*

Marx's humanitarianism is further brought into question by
his having had no trace of compassion, but only contempt,
for those who were really down and out—the *Lumpenpro-
letariat*—even though the very industrial system which he
condemned was well calculated to produce countless such
derelicts. These persons had dropped too low to amount to
anything in relation to the class struggle. So far as Marx was
concerned, then, they simply did not amount to anything,
had no human importance.

Humanitarianism involves more than taking sides. It makes
room in its reckoning for traits, good and bad, that are not
the exclusive property of any one class; and its concern ex-

tends even to "the least of these." It is all too easy for us human beings to take the "right side" for wrong reasons—for reasons of hostility that we learn to call those of justice. Once we are on the "right side," moreover, it is fatally easy for us to start pushing others around "for their own good"—and to turn toward those on the "wrong side" the measuring, waiting eyes of the avenger.

Because Marx had no revolution to work through, we cannot know just how much ruthlessness he would have countenanced—or enacted—for the sake of making events "prove" his dogma. But we know more than a little about his capacity for ruthlessness as this was shown forth in his personal relations and his writings. We know also how rigid and exclusive was the world which he conceived—with never room in it for the variousness of human viewpoints or for the people on both sides of any issue or any cause.

Further, we know that anyone who once starts to coerce human nature to make it conform to a theory—and particularly a theory which calls itself "scientific" at the same time that it promises figs from thistles—is likely to become a "coercion addict." For there will always be one more individual or one more group to be liquidated in order to get matters finally under control—and get mankind going toward utopia. This way dictatorship lies.

A young Hungarian writer, Istvan Vizinczei—now a refugee in Canada—tells how he and his associates, thoroughly indoctrinated with Communism, came first to detest the system and then, gradually, to repudiate the dogma. As a group of friends bound together by their love of writing and their sense of responsibility to both their craft and their country, they tried again and again to figure out where things had started to go wrong:

"... In political and philosophical debates that continued

far into the night we tried to find the reason for the dictatorship's horrors. At first we thought that the source of all evil was the Soviet occupation. Since Marxism (like all theories) contains a vision of all the noble things lacking in life, we thought that the fault lay not with Marxism but with the brutal dictatorship which did not want Marxists (it had killed or silenced the idealists), but traitors.

"In the fall and winter of 1951, I devoured the works of Marx and Engels to find out in what way the Stalinists and their Hungarian hirelings were falsifying Marxism. After combing through piles of books and debating endlessly, we were startled to find that there was no falsification; what was happening was just what had been evisaged, and the fine words about freedom were a varnish covering the realities of the system. For the essential nature of Marxism is centralization, a concentration of control over business, politics, art and society." (5)

What this young Hungarian writer discovered, many defectors from Communism in the free world have also come to realize. Many others, however, have stopped short of this discovery. Nostalgia for the lost vision has halted them. Feeling that if Communism could somehow get back to Marx all would be well, they themselves have not gone back to Marx to search out how his theory actually relates man to man.

Around the world, moreover, there are still those—no one knows how many—who may well prove to be fair game for Communism on its next round; for with their eyes fixed on the Marxian vision "of all the noble things lacking in life," they do not probe far enough to discover how ignoble the dogma is at the core.

We shall, later, be sizing up Marxism-Leninism and the Communist regime from many different angles. But as a start, we do well to come to terms with one psychological fact:

namely, that where tenderness and compassion are *ruled out,* no humane society can be *ruled in.* Marx never learned this fact. As a humanitarian guide, therefore, he falls very far short of that man among his contemporaries who could say, even in the midst of shattering conflict, "With malice toward none, with charity for all . . ."

In *The People, Yes,* Carl Sandburg ponders the question of what a father can properly say to a son when he sees him nearing manhood. What shall he tell him?

> " 'Life is hard; be steel; be a rock.'
> And this might stand him for the storms
> And serve him for humdrum and monotony
> And guide him amid sudden betrayals
> And tighten him for slack moments.
> 'Life is a soft loam; be gentle, go easy.'
> And this too might serve him." (6)

The Communists know that life is hard; and they are disciplined to be steel and rock. But they are forbidden to know that life is also a soft loam. They are forbidden to be gentle, to go easy. We in the West have not come as close, by any means, as we intend to come to the fulfillment of our own dream. The challenging glory of this dream, however, remains unsullied: it is that of our trying to learn how to fuse strength and tenderness—in human personality and social institutions.

FOUR

THE ROOTS OF CONSPIRACY

THE BELIEFS and principles we call ours represent a long cultural heritage. They embrace the Judaic-Christian religion and Greek rationality, Roman and British common law, the spirit of Magna Carta and eighteenth-century Enlightenment. Abstract science and the practicalities of industry play in them. So do the experiences of millions of people who have coped with the problems of staying alive on many different geographical and social frontiers.

What we thus call our Western tradition is by no means as neat a product of the human intellect as is the "science of Marxism-Leninism." But it is a richer product; and it has been *grown into.* Moreover, because it can never aim at the precision of a theory made whole and "perfect" from the start, it gives us room to move—and to be multitudinously at odds with one another at the same time that we are in agreement. Our own Constitution is symbolic of the whole. With all our differences, we can live together under it, generation after generation—and refer new questions to it, and try to grow up to it—for the paradoxical reason that no one can, once for all, state its full meaning.

The "science of Marxism-Leninism," in contrast, has no natural roots in the life of any people. It is an artificial implantation in the human scene: a "conclusive" intellectual construct imposed upon the vast inconclusiveness of reality. No one would ever become indoctrinated with it by his own efforts to solve problems or by his normal associations in the give and take of life. Lenin made this fact explicit when he said that while workers could, on the basis of their discontents, develop "trade-union consciousness," they could never thus become "conscious of the irreconcilable antagonism of their interests to the whole of the modern political and social system. . . . This consciousness could only be brought to them from without." (1) The task of bringing it "from without" to those who would never, on their own, arrive at a "correct" view is the endless preoccupation of Communists everywhere.

This is no teaching task to be carried on in fellowship with those who are teaching other points of view. Lenin's own phrase makes clear the reason: ". . . irreconcilable antagonism . . . to the whole of the modern political and social system." Wherever the Marxist-Leninist revolution has not yet taken place, the bringing of the doctrine "from without" is a venture in conspiracy. This is true whether it is pursued outside the law or within the letter of the law for illegal purposes.

The Communists seem so sure of themselves when they talk about their ideology—so ready with their arguments, so confident that history is on their side—that we are inclined, sometimes, to credit them with a strength beyond our own. What we easily overlook is the terrible intellectual and emotional poverty of their estate. When they cast off the whole

Western tradition—all that Lenin covered by those twin phrases of contempt, "bourgeois democracy" and "bourgeois liberalism "—they also cut themselves off from this tradition. Left with no roothold in the human past, they strain endlessly to put down roots in an abstraction. They talk and talk about their "infallible science," and refer to it every problem and policy, *because it is all they have.*

When they want a guide to action, they have no one to whom to turn except Marx and Lenin—or their accredited interpreters. When, in contrast, we are on the search for some insight, we can call the ages into conference. Amos and Euripides, Socrates and Epictetus and Jesus, St. Paul and Martin Luther, Erasmus and Voltaire, the Barons of Runnymede, John Milton and John Locke, Shakespeare, Galileo, Jefferson, St. Francis, and Abraham Lincoln: these, and others in multitude, we can assemble in mind and bid them —in an old New England phrase—"to sitt down close togither." We are free, moreover, to go outside our own particular tradition—to consult the Buddha, Confucius, Lao-tse, the Chinese poets, or whomever we may see as a likely source of insight.

The figures thus convened will often contradict one another. But why should they not do so? They will also agree. And at every intersection of their agreements and disagreements, we are invited to think for ourselves. At these intersections, moreover, such aspects of reality as none of them have taken into account have a chance to wedge in. This is what it means to have a *growing* tradition; not an "infallible" theory.

When we are tempted to feel that the Communists have an ideological strength which we lack, we do well to remember that it is they, not we, who are on constant guard against "revisionism" and "deviationism"; and who have tried to block all channels by which "bourgeois" influences might

reach the minds of the Soviet people. Significantly, moreover, when the agreement on cultural exchanges between
the United States and the Soviet Union was being worked
out, in the Winter of 1957–1958, it was the Communists, not
we, who shied away from any exchanges that touched upon
ideological matters. They were ready for exchanges in science, technology, agriculture, and various other fields. Here,
agreement *in principle* could fairly readily be converted into
agreement upon programs. But in any area that approached
the ideological, they would agree *in principle* only. They
halted on the safe side of program planning. All this seems
to add up to what was expressed long ago in a parable: we
can venture far more with our "ten talents" of cultural heritage than they can with their one.

Their defense of this "one talent"—the "science of Marxism-Leninism"—and their "irreconcilable antagonism" to the
whole tradition of the West have been expressed, through
the years, in four major ways. The first has been the totalitarian dictatorship itself—rationalized by the obsessive conviction that enemies are everywhere, within and without.
The second has been the Iron Curtain—behind which Communist Man could be created with minimum danger of corruption from the outside. The third has been the official
foreign policy of the Soviet Union—which has never been
other than a *war* policy, openly so or in disguise. The fourth
has been the worldwide practice of conspiracy. It is this last
which we wish to explore in the present chapter—reserving
the other three for later consideration.

Communist conspiracy is no game of cops and robbers. It
is a carefully devised method *for carrying on a one-way
traffic of ideas*. It comprises all the tactics and stratagems by
which the Communists take their "one talent" into non-
Communist environments everywhere without ever taking

it into the "open market places of the mind." In this conspiratorial undertaking, Lenin is their master.

Conspiracy was indigenous in Tsarist Russia. The feudal machinery of State made no provision for the instituting of change by the people themselves. Either, therefore, the people had to remain passive in the face of misery and injustice or else become conspirators. This same pattern has existed in many other times and places throughout history; and the story of man's hazardous advance could hardly be told without reference to it.

The Bolsheviks, in short, were not unique in being conspirators. The *brand* of conspiracy, however, which they practiced under Lenin's guidance was unique; and this has become the official Communist brand. As a Marxist, Lenin generalized his anger at Tsarist tyranny into an "irreconcilable antagonism" toward all "bourgeois" governments; and his will to remedy specific abuses into a worldwide program of revolutionary overthrow. In support of this program, he refined the Bolsheviks' original resort to conspiracy into a detailed science of conspiracy. This, he indicated, was to be utilized to the limit in all "bourgeois" countries: not simply in those which, like Tsarist Russia, lacked machinery for change by popular will. Where democratic machinery existed, so much the better: it could be exploited for conspiratorial ends. But it must never be regarded by any Communist as a *sufficient* machinery of change. It must never be made an excuse for letting up on conspiracy.

Around the turn of the century, when Bolshevism was in its beginnings, Lenin wrote that it "must become infected with intolerance against all who retard its growth." (2) Today, with a third of the earth's people under its domination, Communism is still "infected" with this prescribed intolerance; and it includes among those who "retard its growth" all who oppose its effort to extend its control over ever larger portions of the globe.

We have noted earlier Marx's proneness to *either-or* thinking. In Lenin, this trait was even more rigid. Thus: "Since there can be no talk of an independent ideology being developed by the masses of workers in the process of their movement, *the only choice is:* either bourgeois or socialist ideology. There is no middle course (for humanity has not created a 'third' ideology, and, moreover, in a society torn by class antagonisms there can never be a non-class or above-class ideology). Hence, to belittle socialist ideology *in any way*, to *deviate from it in the slightest degree* means strengthening bourgeois ideology." (3)

This Leninist view has never become dated. In September 1957, for example, it was thought necessary to warn Soviet scientists not to take too literally or too broadly Khrushchev's tactical bid for "peaceful co-existence." Writing in *Kommunist*, official organ of the Communist Party of the Soviet Union, A. Topchiev undertook to set straight those who showed signs of regarding themselves as free seekers of truth in the world community of science:

"Our scientists cannot and should not stand on the sidelines of the ideological struggle between communism and capitalism. Some scientific workers attempt automatically to extend to the field of ideology the slogan of peaceful co-existence of countries with different social-economic systems. The time has come, so they say, when we can permit ourselves such coexistence of the two ideologies. This is a profoundly mistaken conclusion. . . . Now more than ever, vagueness, neutrality, indifference to politics, which V. I. Lenin constantly opposed, should not be tolerated among us." (4)

It takes almost more of a mental wrench than we can manage to encompass this Communist view: this fixed assumption that man's innovating spirit can devise two, but never more than two, social-economic forms; and that these two have no common ground on which they can ever meet.

Not the least part of our problem, in this regard, lies in the fact that the divisive task which the Communists assign to *theory* is at a far remove from one of the basic tasks which we assign to our beliefs and principles—religious, political, legal, moral. While we expect these to move us to convinced action, we also expect them to civilize our "native cussedness:" to nag at our consciences until we outgrow our unredeemed egoisms and provincialisms. We think of them, in brief, as overspanning a multitude of differences, disagreements, and mutual dislikes; and as obligating us to seek ways of living together in spite of these. The Communists do not credit any such use of theory. When they encounter it, they treat it either as stupidity or as an astute form of deception. We, in turn, find it hard to credit their determined use of theory, *not to overspan or reconcile human differences, but to "prove" them irreconcilable.* This very incredulity of ours can prove hazardous—can put us off guard—whenever they make a surface, tactical pretense of wanting a "united front" or "peaceful co-existence." We jump to the conclusion that they are changing: putting behind them their old divisive use of theory. This, however, is one thing which they do not put behind them.

The three most dramatic factional fights in the history of the Communist Party of the United States, for example, have all had to do with precisely this issue. Jay Lovestone in 1929, Earl Browder in 1946, and John Gates in 1957 were all charged by the Kremlin—and thereupon, by the dominant element in the Party here—with having tried to make the "irreconcilable antagonism" between Communism and American democracy less absolute; and all three, branded as "revisionists," were forthwith purged.

The Communist ideology, we must realize, is divisive not because Stalin had an insatiable thirst for power, not because Molotov, in his international dealings, was a scowling recalcitrant. Nor is it made less divisive by the fact that Khrushchev smiles where his predecessors would have been more likely to frown. It is *divisive at the core* because it denies to the individual any significant role outside the class struggle, and because it flatly denies that any moral law transcends this struggle, binding together as human beings those whom economic warfare has put asunder. Lenin's blunt statement on this score is no less "correct" today than it was when he made it: "We say that our morality is entirely subordinated to the interests of the class struggle. . . . Our morality is deduced from the class struggle." (5)

Communist conspiracy expresses this basic aspect of the ideology—this division of mankind into two warring camps —with no truce, compromise, collaboration, or peace possible between them except as a temporary strategic measure. If we are going to understand Lenin's science of conspiracy, therefore, we must study it, not as a sideline phenomenon, but as an integral part of his science of class warfare.

The Bolshevik Party was designed from the beginning to operate both *outside Tsarist law* and *inside the law with illegal intent.* "Conspiracy," wrote Lenin, "is so essential a condition of an organization of this kind that all other conditions [the number and selection of members, their functions, etc.] must be made to conform to it." (6)

Clearly, a movement of this type could not be left to amateurs. It would have to be the work of people who would "devote to the revolution not only their spare evenings, but the whole of their lives." For by its very nature, conspiracy requires a "small, compact core" of "reliable, experienced, and hardened workers." It would not be possible to "give a mass organization the degree of secrecy which is essential for the persistent and continuous struggle against the government." (7) Within the movement itself, moreover, there must be "iron discipline." Freedom of discussion and criticism of basic dogma must be ruled out; for these would gradually convert the revolutionary Party "into a democratic reformist Party." (8) Thus in Tsarist Russia, around the turn of the century, Lenin laid down the precise rules which the American Communists, Lovestone, Browder, and Gates, in 1929, 1946, and 1957 respectively, were purged for having violated.

Specifically, for example, Browder was charged with attempting to have the CPUSA "discard basic principles of Marxism-Leninism and to adopt a bourgeois-liberal program." (9) John Gates, editor of the *Daily Worker*, had his fate sealed by an article in the September 1957 issue of the *Kommunist*, Moscow. The label attached to him was "pseudo Communist"—a term which, according to Khrushchev, applies to a person who advocates Marxist-Leninist theory without adhering to Communist discipline.

Lenin did not conceive of the hard-core Party as comprising the whole conspiratorial movement. As a "revolutionary vanguard," it must have at its command as many mass organizations as possible, with "the widest possible variety of functions." The members of these, however—"average people of the masses"—must not be left to chart their own course. For while they could put forth "enormous energy" and even sacrifice themselves for a cause, they would not be capable of revolutionary self-direction.

For one thing, while they would act on grievances that were part of their own experience, they would not devote themselves to a continuous search for facts and grievances that could be exploited. Therefore: ". . . we must have 'our own men' . . . everywhere, among all social strata, and in all positions from which we can learn the inner springs of our state mechanism." (10)

For another thing, even when the masses were aware of injustice and corruption, they could not be relied upon to interpret these "correctly." The professional revolutionary must move constantly among the people "to take advantage of every petty event . . . to explain to *all* and everyone the world-historic significance of the struggle for the emancipation of the proletariat." (11) Anyone who has studied the manner in which the Party in this country burdens every tension and conflict, however small, with a Marxist-Leninist interpretation knows exactly what this edict of conspiracy means in practice.

Finally, the masses would never, on their own, know how and when to effect a tactical collaboration with an enemy. Governed by "bourgeois morality," they would tend to gear their actions to their true feelings. The hard-core revolutionary, therefore, must determine the time and method of expedient collaboration with "bourgeois reformists" or with disgruntled elements of the ruling class. But such collaboration must never mean the Party's becoming simply an equal among equals. "The whole art of conspiratorial organization must consist in utilizing everybody and everything . . . and at the same time maintaining *leadership* over the whole movement." (12)

The relationship between the hard-core group and the mass organizations would, in essence, be that between the illegal and the legal aspects of the work: between activities which must, by their nature, be centralized and secret, and those which must, to serve their purpose, reach the largest possible number of people.

"The centralization of the secret functions of the *organiza-*

tion does not mean the centralization of all the functions of the *movement.* . . . The active and widespread participation of the masses . . . will benefit by the fact that a 'dozen' experienced revolutionaries, no less professionally trained than the police, will centralize all the secret part of the work —prepare leaflets, work out approximate plans and appoint bodies of leaders for each urban district, for each factory district and for each educational institution, etc." (13)

The purposes of conspiracy are clear-cut and specific. All activities, legal or illegal, must aim *to disorganize the old regime* and *to strengthen the forces of revolution.* The hardcore revolutionary must learn, then, to look at society in a peculiar way: with a constant eye to its weaknesses—points where it may be attacked. To this end, he must "have a clear picture in his mind of the economic nature and the social and political features of the landlord, of the priest, of the high official and of the peasant, of the student and of the tramp. He must know their strong and weak sides; he must know all the catchwords and sophisms by which each class and each stratum *camouflages* its selfish strivings . . . ; he must understand what interests certain institutions and certain laws reflect and how they reflect them." (14)

Such knowledge, used as a basis for agitation and propaganda, enables the revolutionary "to utilize every grain of even rudimentary discontent"; and his field becomes as wide as society itself: "Is there a single class of the population in which no individuals, groups or circles are to be found who are discontented?" (15)

Within this broad field, however, Lenin singled out three groups for special attention: the army, the workers, and the intellectuals. The army, as "the most rigid instrument of the old regime," must be infiltrated with a view to undermining its morale; for until the army has been made ready for defection and mutiny, so that it will refuse to obey the orders of its officers, the moment for decisive overthrow cannot possibly come.

Trade unions must, at all costs, be infiltrated; for both the workers as a "mass" and the unions as organized bodies have special roles to perform in furthering the revolution—and this in spite of the fact that the vast majority of the workers are "bourgeois" in mentality and will not realize how they are being used. As a "mass," the workers must bear the brunt of "strikes and street battles with the police and troops," and must put forth "concrete demands" around which professional revolutionaries can build programs of agitation and propaganda. The unions—because they are designed to train labor leaders and are, in effect, "schools of administration, schools of management"—must be turned into "schools of Communism." (16)

The intellectuals—whom Lenin called "the educated representatives of the propertied classes" (17)—must at least be "neutralized" and, wherever possible, must be won over as sympathizers and supporters—for there are two revolutionary tasks for which they are peculiarly fitted. One is that of destroying public confidence in the old regime, by keeping its weaknesses in the forefront of attention. The other is that of putting a foundation of *theory* under the spontaneous protest movements of the workers, so that, instead of being satisfied with specific economic gains, the workers will become dedicated to the overthrow of "the whole of the modern political and social system." The intellectuals, in brief, must make up for the fact that the "science of Marxism-Leninism" has no natural roots in the life of the people. They must *verbalize* into being attitudes not induced by experience and that even go counter to experience: attitudes that alienate the "masses" from their normal social environment and its institutions.

Lenin had no illusion that it could ever be easy to organize a movement of this sort: illegal and legal; hard-core and "mass"; intent to exploit the smallest grain of protest and to bring on total overthrow. Studying every practical means to its accomplishment, he had already concluded by 1901 that the key to effective organization lay in the Party press. Only through a newspaper of its own could the vanguard "concentrate all of the elements of political discontent and protest, and with them fertilize the revolutionary movement of the proletariat." (18)

Around the newspaper, moreover, there could develop a body of skilled revolutionaries who would not only be on tap for local activities but who would learn "carefully to watch political events, to estimate their importance and their influence on the various sections of the population," and to plan the most useful ways of exploiting them. Also, the practical problems attendant upon putting out the paper and distributing it would "create a network of agents of a united party."

The party, as Lenin visualized it—and later organized it —must be large enough to embrace the whole country; tempered enough to carry on its work "unswervingly" even in the most unexpected contingencies; flexible enough to avoid being drawn into open conflict with the enemy at the wrong time; "and yet able to take advantage of the clumsiness of the enemy and attack him at the time where he least expects attack."

Readiness for action must be constant; and no chance must be missed to persuade the "masses" to identify the party with their own welfare. Thus: "Today we are faced with the comparatively simple task of supporting students demonstrating in the streets of a large town; tomorrow, perhaps, we may be . . . supporting a movement of the unemployed. . . . The day after tomorrow, perhaps, we may have to . . . take a revolutionary part in some peasants' revolt. Today we must take advantage of the strained political situation." Tomorrow, in order to capitalize public indignation over some abuse, a boycott or demonstration might have to be organized. Only revolutionaries thus trained in action could, at the strategic moment, "issue the call for the decisive battle." (19)

These tactics and stratagems of conspiracy were first worked out to fit the conditions of Tsarist Russia; but Lenin himself passed them on to all Communist Parties in non-Communist countries. During the First World War, for example, he laid down the categorical rule that these Parties must be conspiratorial and treasonable. With respect to the governments of their various nations, in short, *they must take on the role which the Bolsheviks had held with respect to the Tsarist regime:* for "class struggle is impossible without dealing blows to 'one's own' bourgeoisie, 'one's own' government, and dealing a blow to one's own government in wartime means . . . high treason, it means facilitating the defeat of one's own country." Communists, however, must feel no qualms about being treasonable; for those who are opposed to treason "adopt the bourgeois, not the proletarian, point of view." (20)

After the revolution, when he was trying to spark revolution in the Western countries, he specified that all Communist Parties must systematically "combine legal with illegal work, legal with illegal organization." (21) He reiterated, also, what he had earlier set down for the Bolsheviks about the necessity for infiltrating the trade unions: "It is necessary . . . to agree to any and every sacrifice, and even—if need be—to resort to all sorts of stratagems, maneuvers and illegal methods, to evasion and subterfuges in order to penetrate the trade unions, to remain in them, and to carry on Communist work in them at all costs." (22)

With equal decisiveness, he instructed these parties in the tactics of strategic collaboration; the uses of "united fronts" and front organizations, the exploitation of reform movements, of civil liberties, and of parliamentary procedures. Thus, he made all Communists around the world heirs to his tactics and stratagems of conspiracy. They did not decline his legacy; and they have never since repudiated it.

We shall have occasion in later chapters to study the uses to which Lenin's legacy has been put—in countries ranging from the most advanced to the most backward. Here, however, we turn to that most gigantic fruit of conspiracy, the Bolshevik revolution.

FIVE

THE REACTIONARY
REVOLUTION

ANYONE EXCEPT the Communists might be embarrassed to have to keep a "proletarian revolution" going
for more than forty years by keeping the proletariat strictly
in its place. But the Communists are not embarrassed. For
neither Marx nor Lenin set any limit on how long it might
take first to induce and then to complete the world revolution; and Stalin pushed these events off into the remote
future without making them any less "inevitable." Hence,
the revolution can always be said to be running on schedule;
and the Party has all the time there is to fulfill its "historic
mission."

The "dictatorship of the proletariat" is ideologically slated
to span the entire era from the first instance of "overthrow"
to the coming of the "classless society." The Party, therefore
—self-appointed to enact this dictatorship—can exert, decade after decade, the most coercive control over the proletariat and everyone else without being under any theoretical

pressure to re-examine its own basic premises, to ask whether the interminable need for dictatorship does not suggest that it is enacting something quite other than the "true" will of the people.

On another count, also, Lenin exempted the Party from uneasiness about its own coercive role: he provided the rationale for a minority's claiming the prerogatives of a majority. In the first place, he conveniently redefined the term *masses:* "I would like to say just a few words about the meaning of the term 'masses.' The meaning of the term 'masses' changes in accordance with the character of the struggle. . . . During our revolution there were occasions when several thousand workers represented the masses. . . . When the revolution has been sufficiently prepared, the term 'masses' acquires a different meaning." (1) Such a statement leaves it wholly up to the Party—or the current dictator—to decide when "the revolution has been sufficiently prepared"; and until it has been thus prepared, the few can continue to "represent" the masses.

In the second place, Lenin ordained that a majority was not something which should determine either the course of revolution or the form of government to be established, but something *for the revolution to produce after it had been enacted by force:* " 'In order to win the majority of the population to its side, the proletariat must first of all overthrow the bourgeoisie and seize state power and, secondly, it must introduce Soviet rule, smash to pieces the old state apparatus, and thus at one blow undermine the rule, authority and influence of the bourgeoisie.' " (2)

In the third place, he simply dismissed the will of the majority as irrelevant: "The question is not one of numbers, but of giving correct expression to the ideas and policy of the truly revolutionary proletariat." (3) As for the character of the revolution itself: "The class which took political power into its hands did so knowing that it took power *alone*. That is part of the concept of dictatorship of the proletariat. This concept has meaning only when the single class knows that it alone is taking political power in its hands, and does not deceive itself or others with talk about 'popular government elected by all, sanctified by the whole people.' " (4)

This "class," moreover, did not pretend to embrace even all the workers or all who were exploited under the old regime. It was made up of the "vanguard of the toilers." When it needed support in order to achieve its aims, it would form "an alliance with the labouring and exploited masses of other classes." (5) *But it would share power with none.*

With this type of theoretical backing, the Party today need feel no embarrassment about exercising unlimited dictatorship over the people of the Soviet Union. Neither is it likely to feel any disturbing contradiction between its calling the satellite countries "people's democracies" and the all too obvious fact that they are ruled by dictatorial minorities. When Bulgaria was taken over, for example, in September, 1945, and converted into a "people's democracy," there were only 20,000 Communists in that country out of a population of 7,020,000; and when Albania was similarly taken over, in December of that year, the Communists numbered only 12,000 out of a population of 1,120,000. The *actual* rule, moreover, in all the satellites—as in Soviet Russia itself—is exercised by an exceedingly small subminority of the minority.

How did it come about—this "proletarian" revolution which has never dared to let the proletariat out from under its thumb? The answer to this question is as much a portrait of Lenin as it is a record of events.

Exiled by the Tsar in December 1907, Lenin was granted

political asylum in Switzerland. He did not again enter Russia until April 1917—at which time he promptly set himself to disrupt and bring to failure a month-old provisional government, born in revolution, which represented a far larger majority of the people than he and his Bolsheviks even claimed to represent.

Russia, between 1907 and 1917, was an almost perfect breeding ground for a popular revolution. As a result of the trial-run revolution of 1905, a quasi-constitutional system was belatedly established under Prime Minister P. A. Stolypin. Stolypin's rule—particularly at the beginning, when he hanged several hundred revolutionaries and insurgent peasants—was bloody enough to keep the seething spirit of revolution alive. His dissolution of the Second Duma and his narrowing of the franchise to favor the rich served a like purpose. On the other hand, the political and intellectual liberties he granted gave this same revolutionary spirit room to mature.

"Political parties were numerous and could organize their branches and hold meetings. There was a wide variety of political newspapers and periodicals. Individual issues were confiscated by the police if they incited violence or rebellion, but no attempt was made to prevent the expression of Marxist, Populist or radical ideas. Book publication was still more free." (6) Government by law, moreover, was rapidly replacing government by edict.

On the industrial side, progress was marked. "Production of coal in southern Russia more than doubled between 1900 and 1913; so did the production of iron between 1905 and 1913, while pig iron output almost doubled." In 1906, labor unions gained the right to organize, though not to strike. "Under Stolypin industrial workers were growing in numbers, and the proportion of skilled to unskilled was increasing fast. Russia was in transition." (7)

Lenin himself took stock of these changes from a distance and declared that Russia's development "along bourgeois lines" was marching forward with remarkable speed. He did not count this as a sign of progress, however, but as a victory for Tsarism and "philosophic idealism." In fact, he declared the years 1907–1910 to be "years of reaction," because of the strong trend toward the Western type of development and a resultant drop in revolutionary fervor. The years 1910–1914—which he called the "years of revival"—were more to his liking; for even while the "bourgeois" development con- tinued, the Bolsheviks reconstituted themselves as a hard- core party and pushed aside the more moderate Mensheviks. But they "would never have succeeded in doing this had they not pursued the correct tactics of combining illegal work with the utilization of 'legal possibilities.' " (8)

Had the First World War not taken place, Russia might have moved into the modern world by normal stages. The war not only halted progress but, after the first year, plunged the country into a miasma of defeat and famine. These con- ditions, added to old grievances and to the ineptitudes of residual feudalism, weighed the balance in favor of revolu- tion. A series of uprisings and demonstrations in February 1917 led, by the middle of March, to the abdication of the Tsar and the formation of a provisional government under Kerensky, a moderate socialist.

This was revolution; *but not Bolshevik revolution.* The provisional government, intent to unite the whole country, gained the immediate support of the largest single party, the Social Revolutionaries; and these brought with them the support of the village Soviets. The Mensheviks held aloof for a time. As orthodox Marxians, they were reluctant to col- laborate with any government which contained "bourgeois" elements. Later, however, they too gave their support—and with this, the support of the town Soviets. Even among the

Bolsheviks—then a small party—more than a few were inclined to follow the Menshevik lead.

The Communists have had more than forty years, now, in
which to represent the provisional government as both *reactionary* and *ineffectual*. Yet even with all the disasters of war
on its hands—and with the Bolsheviks, after the first month,
obstructing it at every turn—this government managed to
leave a record which not even the Communists' rewriting of
history has been wholly able to conceal or erase; and this
record tells *what type of government it was setting itself
to be:*

". . . a full political amnesty was immediately proclaimed . . . ; all national, religious and class restrictions
were outlawed; unjust courts were abolished and trial by
jury decreed . . . ; a complete system of equal rights for
women was established; exile, that most dreaded punishment
of tsarism, was banned as a punitive measure; unconditional
liberty of press, organization and assembly was proclaimed . . . ; new provisions were drawn up for the election of urban and local authorities, based on universal suffrage and proportional representation." (9) In addition,
Poland was granted its independence.

There is little here to suggest a return to tsarism; little to
suggest *reaction* of any sort. There is much, however, that
stands in striking contrast to Communism—whether under
Lenin, Stalin, or Khrushchev. Lenin himself said of this first
revolution of 1917: "In a few days Russia was transformed
into a democratic, bourgeois republic, more free—under war
conditions—than any other country in the world." (10)
Again, however, he saw this transformation, not as a welcome
form of progress, but as a threat to his own type of revolution, which was to be revolution not *out of dictatorship* but
into dictatorship. He instructed the Bolsheviks, therefore, to
make every possible use of the liberties granted by the

provisional government *in order to overthrow this government.*

Could the provisional government have succeeded? No one can be sure. It could not, certainly, have solved all the problems by which it was immediately confronted. Neither could it have done in a hurry that which has always to be long-range work for a free society: the achieving of a balance between rights and responsibilities. Moreover, it made its full quota of mistakes—leaving one group and then another dissatisfied. Yet the chief reason why these mistakes were disastrous was that the Bolsheviks missed no chance to exploit them.

Communists and Communist sympathizers, down through the years, have stressed the ineptitudes and weaknesses of this government. Yet Lenin reports that the Bolsheviks had to move against this "bourgeois republic and against the Mensheviks very cautiously, and the preparations for it were by no means an easy matter. We did not call for the overthrow of the government at the beginning . . . but explained that it was impossible to overthrow it *until* the composition and the mood of the Soviets had been changed. . . . Without such careful, thorough, circumspect and prolonged preparation we could not have obtained victory." (11)

Karl Kautsky—branded by Lenin as a "renegade," but commonly recognized as one of the most authoritative exponents of socialism (as against Communism) in this century —had this to say: "Had the Bolsheviks . . . agreed to a united front, Russia would have been spared the three years of civil war and the consequent horrible misery. Peace and freedom would have made possible rapid economic recovery and with it a speedy development of the working class. . . . *All this would have been possible without dictatorship, without terror, through the democracy of the workers and peasants.* To be sure, we cannot say with certainty that this

would actually have come to pass, but this was the only road
that offered a possibility of obtaining for the people through
the revolution as great a measure of liberty and welfare as
existing circumstances permitted. . . .

"This united front was rendered impossible by the insatiable yearning for power on the part of Lenin and other
leaders of the Bolsheviks." (12)

The provisional government was one month old when
Lenin returned from exile. Arriving in Petrograd on April
16, 1917, he immediately issued his *April Theses,* calling
upon the Bolsheviks to give no support whatever to the government. With "all power to the Soviets" as his rallying cry,
he set himself to undermine the reputation and authority of
the government.

"The point," he wrote, "is to make the task clear to the
party. An *armed insurrection* in Petrograd and Moscow
(with their regions), the conquest of power and the overthrow of the government must be placed on the order of the
day. We must consider *how* to agitate for this without ex-
pressly saying as much in the press." (13)

Among the Bolsheviks, some called his policy madness.
Most, however, followed his lead; for he reinforced the
doubts they already had about collaborating with a government which contained "bourgeois" elements—even though
these were minority elements. Stirred to similar doubts, the
Mensheviks began to withdraw their support. Around a
"core" of revolutionaries, Lenin was then able to rally an
ever increasing number of politically inexperienced but discontented workers and peasants, and also rootless soldiers
and sailors who had cut themselves adrift from the dis-
rupted armed forces.

He was strategically placed both to attract the disgruntled
and to put the government at a disadvantage. The government was in a responsible position; he, in an irresponsible

one. The government could not, in the nature of things, offer any full or prompt satisfaction of the workers' hunger for bread, the peasants' hunger for land, or the soldiers' hunger for peace. Lenin, on the other hand, could—and did—deal in unlimited promises: promises which the Communists, to this day, have never redeemed.

By July, Lenin felt secure enough to drop his slogan about "all power to the Soviets" and to call, instead, for the "dictatorship of the proletariat and the poor peasantry." This was more than a verbal change. The Soviets were true workers' organizations. Power vested in them would be broad-based. A dictatorship, in contrast, could be centralized. Power could be lodged—as it has been ever since—in the hands of the Party.

In September, General Kornilov attempted a counter-revolution which would have been as fatal to the provisional government as to Bolshevik hopes. The Bolsheviks claimed all credit for his not succeeding—much as the Communists are currently claiming, and stating in their history books, that Soviet Russia, with very slight aid from the allies, defeated Hitler. In the wake of Kornilov's defeat, peasant uprisings spread and the armed forces mutinied. The government, then, was helpless to restore order; and on October 25 (November 7, by the new calendar), the Bolsheviks seized power by a *coup d'état*.

Both the manner of this *coup d'état* and the events which followed point up once more Lenin's disregard for the will of the majority; and also the reactionary character of the Bolshevik revolution. Between April and October, the Bolsheviks had employed against the provisional government all those tactics of conspiracy which Lenin had earlier devised for use against the Tsarist regime. In the "revolutionary moment," however, they switched from *conspiracy* to well-planned *insurrection*. Authorities disagree about the respective roles of Lenin and Trotsky at this point. On some counts, it would appear that Trotsky was the master of insurrection and that Lenin, in this particular, was his apt pupil.

In any event, a *principle of insurrection* was made clear in 1917 which has ever since been part of the tactical knowledge of every Communist Party that exists in a non-Communist country. This principle was that success at the point of overthrow depends upon the revolutionaries' being able to endow their minority group with the effective strength of a majority. In practical terms, this was clearly shown to mean three things.

It meant, first, that the numerical majority must be so disorganized and demoralized *that no single group within it would be as large and as unified in purpose as the disciplined revolutionary minority.* A majority, in brief, that has been splintered by factionalism is, in effect, a collection of minorities; and no single faction is likely to have as clear a plan for resisting revolution as the revolutionaries have for bringing it on.

Second, it meant that the minority must be ready to execute careful, preconceived plans for taking over certain key posts within society—thereby making the majority dependent upon it; and also preventing this majority from being able to unite itself for action. Thus, the Bolsheviks took possession of the water works, telegraph offices, railway stations, and various public buildings. They recognized, in short—as Communists have ever since—the strategic importance of public utilities, media of communication, and means of transportation; and they demonstrated that a trained minority that has its plans laid, that can catch the public and government alike off guard, need not call on the "masses" to help take these over. Here, what counts is swift precision: not numbers. The "masses" would only get in the way.

In the third place, the *principle of insurrection* meant that the minority must concentrate its forces at points where "masses" would be an advantage, thus making them at that particular time and place a "majority." "To have an overwhelming superiority of forces at the decisive moment and at the decisive point is a 'law,' not only of military success, but also of political success, especially in that bitter, seething war of classes known as revolution." (14)

Thus, the Bolsheviks' *coup d'état* represented a calculated disregard of the will of the majority, not the enactment of that will. What was thus shown at the very outset about the nature of the revolution was heavily underscored a few weeks later by Lenin's breaking up of the Constituent Assembly.

No one had been more vocal than he in demanding, prior to his seizure of power, that a Constituent Assembly be formed by popular vote; and the date for an election had already been set prior to the *coup d'état*. Confident, apparently, that his Bolsheviks could swing this election, he went ahead with it—still proclaiming the importance and legitimacy of the Constituent Assembly. As it turned out, however, the Bolsheviks—even after their rallying of the discontented and their successful seizure of power—polled only 9,000,000 votes out of 36,000,000. The reactionaries polled 4,000,000. The other 23,000,000 votes went to the various liberal and socialist parties which had supported the provisional government. *No free election has been held in Russia since that date.* Nor was the Constituent Assembly permitted to function. When it met, on January 18, 1918, under duly elected leaders, Lenin's Bolsheviks, with armed force and the clamor of hoodlums, broke it up.

Again, there were Bolshevik dissenters. Five members of the Party's Central Committee (Zinoviev, Kamenev, Rykov, Nogin, and Miliutin) resigned, declaring publicly, "We cannot accept the responsibility for the disastrous policy of the

Central Committee, carried out against the will of an enormous majority of the proletariat and soldiers." (15) Moreover, eleven out of the fifteen members of the Council of People's Commissars issued a dissenting declaration, five of them resigning outright; six signing the declaration but remaining on the Council. Yet Lenin prevailed. With power in his hands, and armed revolutionaries to keep it there, he made no concessions—either to fellow Bolsheviks or to the popular will:

"They imagine," he wrote, in *The Elections to the Constitutional Assembly and the Dictatorship of the Proletariat,* "that serious political questions can be decided by voting. As a matter of fact, such questions, when they have been rendered critical by the struggle, are decided by civil war." (16)

Thus ended the revolution for which Russia had been prepared by history and hope; and thus began the Bolshevik revolution—Communism's "permanent revolution"—which sharply reversed the trend which events had taken between 1905 and 1917, and which imposed upon the people a dictatorship far more total than that of the Tsar.

On January 22, 1918, an article by Maxim Gorky appeared in *Novaya Zhizn,* Petrograd. This article has long been virtually unknown—and known least of all within the Communist orbit; for it was not included in the official and allegedly "complete" edition of Gorky's works put out by the State Publishing House of the Soviet Union.

There was good reason—that is, good Communist reason —for its being thus left out. The Communists would prefer its being left out of history altogether. By their standards, it ought never to have been written. Since it was written, however, the next best resort is to erase it as completely as possible from human consciousness. The article was a memorial to workers who had been shot down, at Lenin's command, by the "People's Commissars," because they had demonstrated in favor of the duly elected Constituent Assembly which had met four days earlier, on January 18, and which had been broken up by Lenin's troops.

As we read this article, we realize that it provides one answer to a question which we asked in the first chapter of this book: *By what strange logic did the unfolding history of fifty years lead from St. Petersburg to Budapest: from the strikers petitioning the Tsar, and being shot down, to the students petitioning the puppet government in Hungary, and being shot down?* Gorky's article locates one way-station on the long road from St. Petersburg to Budapest, and indicates that the "logic" which mapped this road was simply that of dictatorship: the "logic" of maintaining power at all costs.

"When on January 22, 1905," Gorky wrote, "the . . . soldiers, in obedience to the orders of the Tsar's government, fired on the unarmed, peaceful crowd of workers . . . members of the intelligentsia and laborers rushed up to the soldiers shouting: 'What are you doing . . . ? Whom are you killing? They are your brothers; they are without arms; they bear you no malice; they are on their way to ask the Tsar to look into their needs. They are not demanding but merely petitioning. . . . Think of what you are doing, you idiots!' . . . But the reply was . . . : 'We have orders. . . .' And like machines they fired into the crowd of people. . . .

"On January 18, 1918, the unarmed Petersburg democracy, workers and employes, demonstrated peacefully in honor of the Constituent Assembly. For nearly a century, the best Russians had dreamed of the Constituent Assembly as a political organ which would give the Russian democracy a chance freely to express its will. Thousands of the intelligentsia, tens of thousands of workers and peasants have died in prison and exile, have been hanged and shot for this dream. . . .

"*Pravda* lies when it says that the demonstration of January 18 was organized by the bourgeoisie, by the bankers. . . . *Pravda* lies—it knows that the '*burzhui*' have no reason to celebrate the opening of the Constituent Assembly. What is there for them to do among 246 Socialists and 140 Bolsheviks? *Pravda* knows that the demonstrators were workers. . . .

"Perhaps the *burzhui* rejoiced to see the soldiers and Red Guards tear the revolutionary banners out of the workers' hands, trample on them and burn them. But perhaps this did not make all the *burzhui* rejoice, for among them are honest men who truly love their people. . . .

"Thus on January 18 [the Bolsheviks] fired on the unarmed workers of Petrograd. They fired without warning, they fired from ambush, through cracks in fences. . . . Just as on January 22, 1905 . . . people asked those who fired: 'Idiots, what are you doing? These are your own brothers. . . .' And just like the Tsarist soldiers, these murderers replied: 'We have orders to shoot'. . .

"I ask the 'People's Commissars,' among whom there must be honest and sensible men, if they understand that in putting a noose around their necks they will inevitably strangle all Russian democracy, destroy all the conquests of the Revolution?

"Do they understand this? Or do they think: Either we hold power, or let everyone and everything perish?" (17)

SIX

THE REVOLUTION
BECOMES PERMANENT

LENIN DID more, in 1917, than overthrow the provisional
government in Russia. He injected into history the
"permanent revolution" which Marx had called for in 1850,
in his *Address to the Communist League*. Marx wrote this
Address in urgent haste; and it was dispatched from London
by special messenger, lest it reach Germany too late to influence the course of the revolution which he took to be imminent there. Yet sixty-seven years were to elapse, and the
theater of revolution to be moved to a country very different
from Germany, before his directives were to become the established policy of a Communist regime.

In the two-volume edition of Marx's *Selected Works* prepared by the Marx-Engels-Lenin Institute, in Moscow, a
footnote to this *Address* credits Lenin with being "the only
Marxist who correctly understood and developed the idea
of permanent revolution." Since Khrushchev is now staging

a well-publicized "return to Lenin," we do well to understand the kind of performance Marx intended this "permanent revolution" to be.

The German situation, Marx indicated, would require the Communist League to make temporary common cause with "bourgeois" democratic elements. The Communists alone, however, must determine the long-range course of events. Hence, even during the period of ostensible alliance, they must set themselves to defeat the policies and purposes of the democratic forces.

"The democratic petty bourgeois," he wrote, would "wish to bring the revolution to a conclusion as quickly as possible" —as soon as they had achieved most of their demands; for their attitude would be reformist rather than revolutionary. In contrast, "It is our interest and our task to make the revolution permanent." It must be kept going until "in all the dominant countries of the world . . . at least the decisive productive forces are concentrated in the hands of the proletarians." (1)

Both during the conflict and after, the proletarians must do everything possible to counteract the "bourgeois endeavors to allay the storm": that is, to restore society to a state of peace. The fervors and hostilities of revolution must be kept at high pitch. "Far from opposing so-called excesses, instances of popular revenge against hated individuals or public buildings that are only associated with hateful recollections, such instances must not only be tolerated but the leadership of them must be taken in hand." Moreover, "from the first moment of victory mistrust must be directed not against the conquered reactionary party, but against the workers' previous allies." (2)

Marx felt certain that the German revolution would end with the democratic "reformist" elements in temporary control. The workers would not be able, at the outset, to "pro-

pose any directly communist measures." But they could—
and must— "drive the proposals of the democrats . . . to
the extreme and transform them into direct attacks against
private property; thus, for example, if the petty bourgeois
propose purchase of the railways and factories, then the
workers must demand that these railways and factories shall
be simply confiscated by the state without compensation as
being the property of reactionaries." Again, "if the democrats themselves put forward a moderate progressive tax,
the workers must insist on a tax with rates which rise so
steeply that large-scale capital is ruined by it."

Here, then, are the Marxist aims, methods, and ethics
which, the Communists affirm, Lenin "correctly understood
and developed." The proletarians would not, Marx granted,
achieve "final victory" in their first stage of struggle—not
even by the methods he prescribed. But they would be
schooling themselves for the future: "Their battle-cry must
be: the permanent revolution." (3)

We can believe that Khrushchev does not want nuclear
war. But when he says that he wants "peaceful co-existence"
or "peaceful competition," we must remember that he has
gone out of his way to declare himself a *Leninist*. We can
conclude, therefore, that any kind of peace which he is ideologically free to want must be such that it can co-exist with
the "permanent revolution."

The precise role which Lenin assigned to his Bolshevik
revolution was that of sparking revolution in the advanced
capitalist countries. Beyond these, moreover, he looked
toward the backward countries of Asia—and saw them, too,
as ripe for Communism. These future revolutions—adding
up swiftly to world revolution—were to be both the *justifying fruits* of his own undertaking and the *supportive force*
which would enable him to keep the upper hand in Russia.

Thus, he wrote in 1920: ". . . if our international comrades now help us to organize a united army, no shortcomings will hinder us in the pursuit of our cause. And this cause is the world proletarian revolution, the cause of creating a worldwide Soviet Republic." (4)

Again in 1921: "The world historical change has been made. The epoch of bourgeois-democratic parliamentarism has come to a close. A new chapter in world history—the epoch of proletarian dictatorship—has opened. The Soviet system and all forms of proletarian dictatorship will have the finishing touches put to them and be completed only by the joint efforts of a number of countries. We have a great deal to do in this sphere." (5)

His followers have also had "a great deal to do in this sphere." Thus, M. Olgin, who helped to organize the Party in the United States: "There is a Communist Party in every country in the world. All of them work for the same end, and all of them adapt their activities to conditions existing in their country. . . .

"The Communist Party of the U.S.A. is thus part of a worldwide organization which gives it guidance and enhances its fighting power. Under the leadership of the Communist Party the workers of the U.S.A. will proceed from struggle to struggle, from victory to victory, until, rising in revolution, they will crush the capitalist state, establish a Soviet state." (6)

Khrushchev keeps presenting Lenin as an exponent of "peaceful co-existence." But Lenin made his own position—on war, peace, and "permanent revolution"—abundantly clear. Thus, in 1919: ". . . there are wars and wars. We condemned the imperialist war, but we do not reject *war in general*. . . . Of course not. We are living not merely in a state, but in a *system of states*, and the existence of the Soviet Republic side by side with imperialist states for a long time is unthinkable. One or the other must triumph in the end. And before that end supervenes, a series of frightful collisions between the Soviet Republic and the bourgeois states will be inevitable." (7)

This particular quotation is not simply one among many. It has become a kind of "shorthand" for the initiated. Again and again, where Party leaders have not wanted to spell out their full revolutionary intentions, they have employed the phrase about living "not merely in a state, but in a *system of states.*" It is a phrase that can sound innocent enough in a "peaceful" context. But every well-schooled Communist, the world around, can complete the quotation in his own mind —and know that the "permanent revolution" is still on the books.

This tactic in itself is good *Leninism.* For Lenin repeatedly specified that hostile intentions need not always be advertised: "To tie one's hands beforehand, openly to tell the enemy . . . whether and when we shall fight him, is stupidity and not revolutionariness . . . and those political leaders of the revolutionary class who are unable to 'tack, to manœuvre, to compromise,' in order to avoid an obviously disadvantageous battle are good for nothing." (8)

Peace, as Lenin saw it, was "a respite for another war"— while the "permanent revolution" went on: ". . . there is no *other* alternative: *either* the Soviet Government triumphs in every advanced country in the world *or* the most reactionary imperialism triumphs, the most savage imperialism . . . Anglo-American imperialism, which has perfectly mastered the art of using the form of a democratic republic.

"One or the other.

"There is no middle course." (9)

The tactics which Lenin recommended are "correctly" Marxian: "As long as you are unable to disperse the bourgeois parliament and every other type of reactionary institution, you *must* work inside them." But not in good faith.

Such work must *"prove* to the backward masses why such parliaments deserve to be dispersed." (10)

From his own experience, Lenin gave an example of how Communists should operate. In 1901–1902, he recalled, when he was on the Editorial Board of *Iskra*—the revolutionary paper—this Board, for strategic reasons, concluded "a formal political alliance with Struve, the political leader of bourgeois liberalism, while it was able at the same time to carry on an unceasing and merciless ideological and political struggle against bourgeois liberalism. . . . The Bolsheviks always adhered to this policy." (11)

On the international front: "As long as we have not conquered the whole world . . . we must know how to take advantage of the antagonisms and contradictions existing among the imperialists." (12) The antagonism "between America and the rest of the capitalist world" was one that he specified as ripe for exploitation: "America is strong, everybody is now in debt to her, everybody depends on her, she is being more and more hated, she is robbing everybody." In any such situation, the "practical task of Communist policy is to take advantage of this hostility and to incite one against the other." (13)

All this sounds very much like the Communist policy of the Khrushchev era; but it does not sound like "peaceful co-existence." In his Report to the Twentieth Congress of the CPSU, in February 1956, Khrushchev launched his "peace" campaign. Yet in that same Report, he made it clear that if force should prove necessary in order to fulfill Communism's "historic mission," then force would be used.

"There is no doubt," he said, "that in a number of capitalist countries the violent overthrow of the dictatorship of the bourgeoisie and the sharp aggravation of class struggle . . . are inevitable." Why are they inevitable? "Leninism teaches us that the ruling classes will not surrender their power voluntarily. And the greater or lesser degree of intensity which the struggle may assume, the use or non-use of violence . . . depends on the resistance of the exploiters." (14) The free world, in short, by surrendering without a struggle, can put an end to the "permanent revolution"; otherwise, it goes on.

Whatever policy our country may adopt for the period ahead, we should at least go into it with our eyes open: knowing that, in remarkable measure, Khrushchevism *is* Leninism, as it claims to be; but that Leninism is not, by any stretch of imagination, a doctrine of "peaceful co-existence."

All this adds up to an incredibly difficult psychological problem for ourselves and the other peoples of the free world. It looks as though we are going to have to be *simultaneously*—and for an indefinite period—in a state of both peace mentality and security mentality. This is what cold war means; and unless we can meet the peculiar demand that it makes upon us, we are all too likely to defeat ourselves—and fail our heritage.

We have to go ahead with our normal business of living —and of putting our social house in better and better order. To do this, we must be able to give to the job at hand the kind of concentrated and creative attention it deserves. Yet we have also to divide our attention. We have to be ready to do what is called for by the presence—and the zig-zag tactics— of a powerful adversary for whom "peace" is a nonshooting phase of "permanent revolution": a chance to find out experimentally whether the West can be isolated, divided against itself, and destroyed without unleashing a world war.

We have never before faced a problem just like this; and our reactions, so far, have tended to be those of a people caught off guard. We have been *incredulous*. It has not made sense to us that anyone—Communists or anyone else—would want war to go on and on; or would literally think that it had to go on all the way to world revolution.

Being incredulous, we have also been *indecisive*. Caught between the Communists' "peace-loving" words and their obviously hostile policies, we have not known which to treat as basic. Their dogma, we know, makes the hostile policies basic and the words merely tactical. Yet both our version of what makes sense and our moral code, which bids us give people the benefit of the doubt, impel us to treat the "peaceful" words as basic and the hostile policies as a hang-over of past fears. Hesitant and indecisive, we have brought about a peculiar state of affairs: one in which Communist "zig-zags"—approved by Lenin as a calculated means of moving ahead against obstacles—are repeatedly matched by zig-zags on our part that are merely tardy adjustments to their changed political line.

In the third place, we have been *edgy*. We have let Communism, and our mutual disagreements over what to do about it, get on our nerves when they might better have been on our minds. Admiral C. Turner Joy, Chief of the United Nations Command Delegation to the Korean Armistice Conference, has warned that the Communists have an uncanny power to drive their opponents into a state of acute frustration—and then exploit every ill-conceived word or act. Therefore:

"The team selected to conduct negotiations . . . should be of the highest available quality. . . . Clear thinking, rapid thinking, are the criteria to be sought. . . . You can be assured that the Communists will put in their first team. You can be assured *your* second team will not be good enough." (15)

Most of us will never meet Communists at a conference table. Yet they are not remote from our lives. For the whole psychological atmosphere of our time is one into which they have, by ways recognized and unrecognized, been injecting their ideology and their divisive influence for more than forty years. Perhaps, then, we can translate Admiral Joy's warning into personal terms: out of our own full range of attitudes and capacities, emotional and intellectual, we need to form a top-quality team for dealing with the problems of Communism in whatever guise we may encounter it. There can be no room on this team for the type of fear or of blind exasperation that takes itself out in irresponsible words and acts.

Finally, to a greater extent than we may realize, we have let the Communists, by their insistent propaganda, distort our image of ourselves. They have called us war-mongers and imperialists until we, wanting to be neither, have become half-persuaded that we are both. They have spotlighted every unsolved problem of our society until we—always sensitive about our imperfect fulfillment of our ideals—have lost our sense of proportion and of honest accomplishment in an orgy of guilt feelings. They have called us smug and self-righteous —which we are desperately afraid of being—until we have become self-conscious about showing any pride at all in our tradition or our present way of living. They have pointed accusingly at us while describing themselves as encircled by enemies until we almost feel that we are the authors of their "permanent revolution": if we had just been nicer to them, would they not by now, we wonder, have settled down as normal members of the world community?

It would seem to be high time for us to go to the record; for until we get certain facts straight in our minds, we will be vulnerable both to Communist misrepresentations and to the self-doubtings and guilt feelings these generate in us. As long as we are thus vulnerable, we can scarcely hope to achieve the balanced, creative fusion of peace mentality and security mentality required of us for the long pull.

Since the Communists are determined to present us to the world as war-mongers and imperialists, the first key fact for us to get straight is that they—not we—started the "permanent revolution." They do not see themselves as having started it. To their minds, it was started by *history*—their equivalent of *fate*. The pattern of this revolution—from its beginning to its ending—is implicit in Marx's *dialectical and historical materialism* and in the "science of Marxism-Leninism." The Communists are certainly responsible, however, for the enactment of this revolution; for they, not we, are the ones who believe that it has to be enacted. In its name, they have killed millions of human beings, exploited millions more in slave-labor camps, and brought 900,000,000 under the control of a totalitarian dictatorship.

More than this, they have created a world—*two worlds,* they call it: Communist and non-Communist—in which they are bound to be "ringed by enemies"; for they define as an enemy everyone not of their own persuasion. We might say that they exhibit an *ideological paranoia.* They attach the label *enemy* without regard to how people act. The one determining factor is where these people "belong" in terms of the class struggle. This theory of two worlds—and the two forever irreconcilable—is their ideological invention; not ours.

When the Communists enter into any form of collaboration with non-Communists, it is, by their own statement, for tactical reasons only. If it were for any other reason, it would be a mark of stupidity, weakness, or deviation. When we hope, then, that we can reassure them by making it clear that we want peace, we are acting within our frame of reference

—but not within theirs. They, within their frame of reference, could choose between two interpretations of our peaceful overtures. They could see them as signs of stupidity or weakness—in which case they would be tempted to press their advantage; or as a shrewd counterpart of their own "friendly" tactics—in which case they would be more on guard than ever.

We tend to be shocked every time the Communists, for no apparent reason, do a sharp about-face from friendliness to hostility, or vice versa. Yet what they thus do is wholly understandable in terms of the "permanent revolution." When we ourselves are in the midst of a war, we do not explain to the enemy every lull in the fighting or every sudden attack. What confuses us in our dealings with the Communists is that we have not declared war on them—no matter how much we may be at odds; but they have declared war on us. More precisely, Marx declared war on their behalf, and ruled out any armistice until after world revolution had ushered in the classless society. Lenin reaffirmed the declaration of war. The Communists, today, therefore—carrying on what was started long ago—feel no more obligated to tell us what their next move is going to be than we felt obligated, during the Second World War, to tell the Nazis where we would strike next.

From the peculiar fact that they are at war, while we are not, certain other facts derive. We, for example, think of the present acute state of tension in the world as abnormal. They think of it as normal—*because a war is in progress.* We think of negotiation as a process which should be entered into with the aim of achieving significant agreements. They think of negotiation as one form of wartime strategy—among many others. When they talk across a conference table, they can also talk *to the world;* and they may be able to maneuver certain limited agreements that will permit them to gain a new margin of time and space for other types of strategic undertakings.

All this does not mean that we should refuse to negotiate with the Communists. Our own beliefs call for our trying to achieve, even within the frame of "permanent revolution," the best possible approximation of peace—so that, in the greatest measure consistent with basic security, human attention, energy, and resources can be released for constructive ends. But *a working approximation of peace*—arrived at with our eyes open and our wits about us—is a very different thing from a *pseudo peace* which we accept as genuine until we are caught off guard by some new Communist offensive in the "permanent revolution."

If we did not start the "permanent revolution," neither did we start that peculiar current phase of it known as the "cold war." This, too, is a Communist invention—and no amount of propaganda to the contrary can change the record.

The agreements at Yalta and Potsdam have been violated by the Communists at every turn. It can be argued that the faith in which these agreements were signed—faith in Soviet Russia's peaceful intentions—was unrealistic: that it was fashioned out of Communist deceit, our own wish-thinking, and the attitudes bred in us by our wartime alliance with the Soviet Union. *But the agreements themselves cannot be made to support the Communist contention that we are warmongers and imperialists.*

At the Yalta Conference, in February 1945, it was agreed that the liberated peoples of East Europe would have restored to them the sovereign rights of which they had been deprived by the Nazis and would be free to form governments of their own choosing. *One month later,* Roumania, by the combined action of its internal Communist Party and Soviet troops, became the first of the satellites. In September of that year, Bulgaria suffered a like fate; in December, Albania. Hungary came next, in August 1947; Czechoslovakia, in May 1948; Poland, in January 1949.

The tactics employed in each country depended on the degree of "revolutionary preparation" which the local Party had achieved. But Stalin made no more than a token pretense that the regimes set up—every one of them subservient to the Soviet Union—represented so uncoerced a popular will that they could have maintained themselves without the actual or threatened presence of the Red Army. It is reported, in fact, that he said at Potsdam, in the summer of 1945, that a truly free election in any one of these countries at that time would have been anti-Soviet in its outcome—"and this we cannot allow." Thus, there came into being that Communist empire which Khrushchev, today, refers to as the "status quo," and which, he says, must be respected by the Western powers at any Summit conference.

The Potsdam Conference, in July 1945, dealt with the postwar disposition of Germany. The agreement there signed provided for the restoration of local self-government and the operation of democratic political parties. It also assured freedom of speech, press, and religion, subject only to the requirements of military security. That the present dictatorship in East Germany is a travesty upon this agreement goes without saying. Even as we write this chapter, the estimated number of Soviet troops still in the country—after the withdrawal of 41,000 in February 1958—is over 350,000; and the East German Communist Party is again, as so often, purging itself of "bourgeois liberal" elements unfriendly to the Soviet Union.

Public opinion in America—as in Great Britain—broadly supported the hope for peace which was officially expressed in the Yalta and Potsdam agreements. Throughout the war, the conviction had been growing—among conservatives as well as liberals—that the Communists were ready to temper their dogma of world revolution and concentrate on the building up of their own society. Thus, for example, an opinion poll conducted by Elmo Roper for *Fortune* magazine, in 1943, showed that 48 per cent of the group specified as "executives" were confident that Soviet Russia would not try, after the war, "to bring about Communist governments in other countries."

In March of that same year, Gardner Cowles, Jr., publisher of *Look,* wrote that Stalin "wants just what the United States wants—security and peace." *Life* devoted its entire issue of March 29, 1943, to "Soviet-American cooperation"—without which, the editors stated, "there can be no stable, peaceful world." As for the restrictive character of the Communist regime: "When we take into account what the USSR has accomplished in 20 years . . . we can make allowances for certain shortcomings, however deplorable."

Admiral William H. Standley, our ex-Ambassador to Moscow, told a group of New York businessmen, on September 15, 1944, "I feel confident that we are on the threshold of a postwar period of collaboration in the fullest sense of the word."

To round out the picture, Winston Churchill, after the Yalta Conference, expressed to the House of Commons his conviction "that Marshal Stalin and the other Soviet leaders wish to live in friendship . . . with the Western democracies. I also feel that no government stands more on its obligations than the Russian Soviet government."

These men—and others like them—were neither soft-headed nor "soft on Communism." They were simply part of a Western world that was acting in character: treating war as an abnormal state; assuming that others, including Stalin, saw it in similar light; and therefore taking protestations of peacefulness at face value—as Khrushchev, today, bids us take them. The grassroots equivalent of their attitude expressed itself, as soon as the war ended, in the typical American drive to "bring the boys back home" and to reduce to a minimum armaments and the armed forces.

In spite of the Communists' having taken over Roumania within a month after the Yalta Conference, it is sometimes argued that Stalin signed the agreements in good faith but was driven to violate them by "Western imperialism." The argument will not hold. The Communists staged their return to "permanent revolution" too soon—even before the end of the war.

This return was announced by an event which few Americans not trained to follow the zig-zags of Soviet policy even knew about—or would have known how to interpret. The May 1945 issue of *Les Cahiers du Communisme,* the theoretical monthly of the French Communist Party, carried an article by Jacques Duclos, violently attacking Earl Browder, then head of the American Communists. At the time, Duclos had just returned from Moscow. Thus, Party members everywhere—as his article was translated for their consumption —knew that the attack on Browder was official and that it marked the end of wartime collaboration with the Western allies. For Browder was the very symbol of that collaboration.

In its behalf—with Soviet permission—he had even changed the name of the Party in America to the Communist Political Association. *Without Soviet permission,* however, he had suggested that, even after the war, American Communists might work to achieve their ends by normal political means: those provided by our democratic institutions. This went far beyond the Communist theory of tactical collaboration. This was "revisionism" of the first order. Duclos lashed out at Browder for predicting "long-range class peace in the United States." After that, it was just a matter of time until Browder was out as top man and William Z. Foster—faithful Stalinist—was in; and until the Communist Political Association was again the Communist Party.

On the surface, this might seem nothing more than a factional fight. Below the surface, it was much more. During the era of collaboration, Communist Parties in countries that were at war with the Axis powers had been permitted by Moscow to support the policies of their own national governments. The Duclos article—as evidenced by the shifts which took place in consequence of it, not only in the Party in this country but also in other Western countries—tacitly withdrew this permission. We can say, then, with good reason, that the cold war dates from the publication of this article —*while the Soviet Union was still ostensibly allied with the West.*

Actually, this call to renewed hostilities did not come as a bolt from the blue. From the moment that the tide of war had turned, so that Hitler's eventual defeat seemed assured, there had been signs—scattered but significant—that the Communists were ideologically "rearming." Throughout the spring of 1945, the Soviet Press had carried items to the effect that strong "fascist elements" in the capitalist world would still have to be dealt with after the war and that the military strength of the Soviet Union must still be regarded, therefore, as a chief bulwark against fascism and imperialism. Further, the Party press had said far more about the importance of bilateral treaties that would separately bind the countries of East Europe to the Soviet Union than about the importance of any worldwide organization of the United Nations variety.

We must note, also, that the actual signing of the United Nations charter, in June 1945, did not divert the Soviet Union from the theory and practice of the cold war. Mikhail Kalinin, for example, prominent member of the Politburo, stated at a conference of Communist Party secretaries, in August 1945 —just as the war with Japan was drawing to a close—that "even now, after the greatest victory known to history, we cannot for one minute forget the basic fact that our country remains the one socialist state in the world. You will speak frankly about this to the collective farmers. . . . Only the most concrete, most immediate danger, which threatened us from Hitlerite Germany, has disappeared." (16)

Even more significantly, Molotov, speaking on November 6, 1945, declared that "as long as we live in a 'system of states' . . . our vigilance regarding possible new violators of peace . . . must not be relaxed." His speech was not openly belligerent toward the West. He made a token bow to the United States and Great Britain as "peace-loving" nations. But every knowledgeable Communist, the world around, could complete his "system of states" quotation: ". . . the existence of the Soviet Republic side by side with imperialist states for a long time is unthinkable. One or the other must triumph in the end. And before that end supervenes, a series of frightful collisions between the Soviet Republic and the bourgeois states will be inevitable." (17)

In later chapters, we shall wish to explore the Communist charge that we are "war-mongers" and "imperialists," and also the peculiar problems imposed upon us by the fact that all negotiations with the Communists must take place within the frame of that "permanent revolution" which Marx declared long before the birth of the Soviet Union, which he declared when our own Constitutional government was only sixty-three years old.

Here, we must count it enough to remind ourselves once more of a basic difference between our viewpoint and that of the Communists. We think of war as an abnormal interruption of peace. We think of it as confined within a span of time that is bounded by a declaration of war and an armistice. We think of it, in short, as *terminable*—and therefore want to get it over and done with. The Communists, however, think of it as simply one phase of an *interminable* struggle.

The most painful and difficult lesson we are having to learn, today, is that no one party to a conflict in which whole value systems are at stake can safely regard it *as over and done with* if the other party regards it *as still going on*. What has taken place since the Second World War is different in circumstance, but not in essence, from what Marx visualized as happening after that German revolution which he anticipated in 1850. He predicted, we recall, that the "democratic bourgeois" element—being reformist and not revolutionary—would want to bring hostilities to an end as soon as possible. The Communist League, however, must not allow this to happen: "It is our interest and our task to make the revolution permanent." His further edict is also worth recalling: ". . . from the first moment of victory mistrust must be directed not against the conquered reactionary party, but against the workers' previous allies." (18) If we hold this Marxian edict in mind, we may be less inclined to feel guilty under the repetitive charge that we are warmongering imperialists. We have not been cast in this role because of specific things we have done during the past dozen years—even though our policies may often have been confused and shortsighted. We were *ideologically* cast in it, a long time ago.

As for treaties signed and broken, we must again take stock of a basic difference of viewpoint. Having signed these treaties in good faith, we feel that the Communists, by violating them, have clearly manifested bad faith. But they have never conceived of good faith as possible between

Communists and non-Communists. *Bad faith,* therefore, is an equal impossibility. The signing of a treaty across the division line prescribed by the Marxist-Leninist version of the class struggle is an act of expediency. The breaking of it is also precisely that—and nothing more.

We may well remind ourselves, here, of a speech made by Zinoviev, president of the powerful Petrograd Soviet—and one of Lenin's right-hand men—on February 2, 1919: "We are willing to sign an unfavorable peace with the Allies. . . . It would only mean that we should put no trust whatever in the bit of paper we should sign. We should use the breathing space so obtained in order to gather our strength." (19)

The permanent revolution goes on. We cannot stop it by this specific policy or that; for it is not our view of the "inexorable law of history" that keeps it going. Within its frame, however—so long as we remember that we *are* acting within its frame—a great many constructive things can be done. Once we understand the task that our security mentality has to take on, our peace mentality can find sufficient —and magnificent—work to do. As part of our own briefing for the job ahead, we turn now to a study of that historic instrument of revolution, the Communist Party as conceived and created by Lenin.

SEVEN

LENIN'S PARTY

LENINISM IS "Partyism." Marxism is not. Marx, to be sure, called for "an independent, secret and open, organization of the Workers' Party." (1) But the Party never became for him a major preoccupation. Lenin converted Marx's doctrine of revolution into *a doctrine of revolution as engineered by a certain type of Party*. All his writings, we might say, elaborate a single theme: the Party's character as the "highest form of class organization of the proletariat" and its role as "revolutionary vanguard."

Always, as we noted in Chapter Four, he visualized the Party as *professional:* as made up of persons who would never take their minds off the problems and stratagems of revolution. Its relationships to other groups must always further its own ends and never threaten its hard-core identity. It would collaborate where collaboration was expedient, or set group against group where doing so would pay revolutionary dividends. It would infiltrate groups and set up within them, for reasons of agitation and propaganda, its own "fractions."

Sometimes these would work in secret. Again, they would swing into the open—to lead a strike, for example, in order to get the workers to identify the revolutionaries with "selfless" courage in behalf of the exploited.

The Party would issue calls for "mass" protests and demonstrations. When it needed middle men to distribute its revolutionary wares—without the source of these being known—it would work through front organizations. *But it would never share with anyone its "vanguard" role.*

Such a Party was, for Lenin, the one fit instrument of revolution; and revolution was the one means of achieving significant social change. Thus, his logic led him to one of the strangest conclusions in history: namely, that all hope for human betterment rested with an elite Party "hardened" to foment revolution by conspiracy and violence.

He acted on this logic not only before the revolution, but after it; not only during the civil war that followed the revolution, but after it. The Party—now renamed *Communist* —was literally the only type of organization through which he knew how to get anything done. Moreover, his own sense of achievement was identified with it—and had no other roothold in society. Thus, after a lifetime of "Party thinking," he saw it as obvious, in 1920, "that only this class-conscious minority can lead the broad masses of the workers." (2) This meant in practice that Marx's "dictatorship of the proletariat" was translated into dictatorship by the Party.

"The proletariat," Lenin declared, "needs state power, the centralized organization of force, the organization of violence, for the purpose of crushing the resistance of the exploiters and for the purpose of *leading* the great mass of the population—the peasantry, the petty bourgeoisie, the semi-proletarians—in the work of organizing a socialist economy." (3) In whom was this vast power of state to be vested? "Our Party is a government party, and the decision the Party congress arrives at will be binding for the whole republic." (4)

History holds no parallel for what thus took place. *The most expert wrecking crew ever devised was, overnight, given absolute power not only to "expropriate the expropriators" but also to build a new social order.* Lenin himself assigned it this double task. To his mind, the proletariat— which, in practice, meant the Party—could achieve its aims "not by restarting the old machinery of state power, but by *smashing it to atoms* and not leaving a stone of it standing (heedless of the howls of the panic-stricken respectable citizens . . .). It must then create a new state apparatus, an apparatus which is adapted for the dictatorship of the proletariat . . ." (5)

How did Lenin ever come to the point where he could count it logical to assign to a wrecking crew so vast a job of social construction? To answer this question, we must go back to before the turn of the century and make a quick survey of certain key events through the years.

Lenin first moved out of obscurity in 1895 when, in St. Petersburg, he managed to unite a number of small, ineffective Marxist groups into one "League of the Struggle for the Emancipation of the Working Class." He was promptly exiled to Siberia. The League, however, continued to function. It stimulated the textile workers' strike, in 1896, for a 10½-hour day; and inspired the forming of similar Leagues in other cities. In 1898, with Lenin still in exile, nine of these Leagues met in Minsk and founded the Russian Social Democratic Labor Party: the Social-Democrats, for short.

Returning from Siberia, in 1900, Lenin found this Party in existence, but without program or proper leadership. He thereupon set himself, together with Plekhanov and others, to establish an illegal paper on an all-Russian scale: *Iskra* (*The Spark*). This paper was to serve as a "collective organizer." Almost from the beginning, it became the vehicle for his brand of Marxism: Partyism.

Lenin's writings of this period record the "character shaping" of the Party to which he later entrusted not only the revolutionary *coup d'état* but the building of the new social order. This Party was to lead the "masses," but must not practice "broad democracy"—which, under existing circumstances, would be *"nothing more than a useless and harmful toy."* The Party's principle of organization must be "strict secrecy, strict selection of members and the training of professional revolutionaries." Discipline must be by the purge. This would instill in the comrades "a lively sense of their *responsibility";* for they would know that "an organization of real revolutionaries will stop at nothing to rid itself of an undesirable member." (6) Its operational code would recognize *"in principle* . . . all means of struggle . . . all plans and methods, as long as they are expedient." (7)

From this period, also, we can date certain of Lenin's attitudes which had later consequences. Thus, he became involved in a long controversy with the "Economists," who held that organized proletarian activity should be economic only—limited to forming trade unions and working through these for the satisfaction of demands. Lenin, opposing them, took a stand which was to become his permanent stance: namely, that workers must be made to want the *total overthrow* of the existing order; and that, to this end, trade unions must be under the *political* tutelage of a revolutionary Party. Otherwise, trade unions would become "reformist" and would deteriorate into "an instrument of bourgeois democracy."

He urged that trade unions be supported in both their

economic struggle and in their struggle to win legal status. Significantly, however, his reason was a *Party* reason; not a *trade-union* reason: ". . . in the long run, the legalisation of the working class movement will be to our advantage." Trade unions could become a "very important auxiliary to political agitation." But to this end, it would be necessary "to guide the nascent trade union movement in the direction the Social-Democrats desire." (8)

Thus, by 1900, Lenin was already treating the workers' movement as an appendage to the Party. We need scarcely be surprised, then, that after the revolution it came naturally to him to reduce the workers' own organizations to virtual puppets and to institute dictatorship by the Party for the "true" benefit of the workers.

Another important turn-of-the-century group was the "Legal Marxists." Holding fast to Marx's dialectic, they contended that the maturing of capitalism and parliamentary democracy must precede the proletarian revolution—to prepare the workers for the exercise of power. This was the "inexorable" course of history. *In theory,* Lenin still agreed with this orthodox view. But he was already becoming restive within its confines and seeking some Marxian loophole through which he could, as it were, make a dash for revolution. His restiveness is shown by the frequency with which he expressed, side by side, ideas that bound him to Legal Marxism and ideas which showed his intolerance for the very processes upon which the fulfillment of such Marxism depended.

Thus, in the *Draft Programme* for the Social-Democratic Party, in 1902, he espoused a truly democratic constitution: one that would establish a legislative assembly representative of *all groups* and that would grant full civil liberties and full legal safeguards *to all persons.* Yet the same document shows his seething readiness to liquidate the capitalists:

"Russian Social Democracy sets itself the task of laying bare before the workers the irreconcilable antagonism between their interests and the interests of the capitalists . . . and of organizing a revolutionary class party." (9)

The normal methods and institutions of democracy, moreover, he regarded *as something to be exploited for revolutionary ends;* not *as something to be respected for their own contribution to human welfare.* "Hannibals of Liberalism" was his term for those who sought progress by gradual means. "Revolutionaries, of course," he wrote, "will never abstain from fighting for reforms . . . *if* they will serve to strengthen the attack." They will, however, appraise "every reform from the point of view of the general revolutionary struggle." (10)

Similarly, he regarded parliaments *as useful to revolutionaries* under certain circumstances, but *as basically contemptible.* Since he felt thus even around the turn of the century, we need not be surprised at his later breaking up of the Constituent Assembly; or his readiness to say, after the revolution, "Parliamentarism is 'historically obsolete.'" (11)

The further Lenin moved away from Legal Marxism, the further he moved into Partyism. Ever more conclusively, the Party became for him the instrument for short-cutting the dialectical process. As Archimedes, having discovered the principle of the lever, once declared, "Give me a fulcrum, and I will move the world," so Lenin—far less scientifically —declared, in effect, "Give me my kind of Party, and I will move the world into Communism."

The second Congress of the Social Democrats, in 1903, was an angry Congress—the bone of contention being the proper character of a revolutionary party. Through session after session, the arguments raged until, in the twenty-second session, the Party split into Bolsheviks and Mensheviks.

Lenin, heading the Bolsheviks, held fast to his demand for a "narrow" party of professional revolutionaries. The Mensheviks—who included most of the Legal Marxists—favored a more broadly based party: one that could bring into being the "transitional" institutions of capitalism and democracy.

Even after this split, the two factions often worked for the same cause; and for several years, individuals shifted back and forth between them. But each new crisis underscored their differences; and these were conclusively pointed up by the Revolution of 1905. Both expected this revolution to succeed; and both—anticipating the overthrow of the Tsar —indicated the type of postrevolutionary regime they hoped to set up.

The Mensheviks remained orthodox Marxians. Lenin, however, had at last found his way to forsake Marxism and yet hold on to it. Marx's pattern, he declared, was correct. But time had run out: it was historically too late for Russia to embark on the long line of development which had been followed by the Western powers. Nor did it need to do so. Instead, by taking a short-cut to the "dictatorship of the proletariat," Russia could serve the unique historic function of sparking, all across Europe, one orthodox Marxian revolution after another. These revolutions in more advanced countries would, in turn, give Russia time to catch up, historically, without the new regime's being overthrown by counter-revolution.

The Tsar, however, was not deposed in 1905. The revolution, as we have noted earlier, succeeded only in inducing various reforms. Lenin—a brooding and angry man—entered upon his long exile in Switzerland. There, turning over and over in his mind the reasons why the revolution had failed, he became ever more determined to build an elite Party. For as he saw it, the mistake in 1905 had been to place too much trust in the workers' own organizations and in liberals and Mensheviks—whom he now catalogued as "agents of the bourgeoisie."

For every socialist party in Russia, the period between 1907 and 1917 was an era of bad feeling: of mutual recrimination and angry factionalism. What concerns us here, however, is simply that every split and every purge within the Bolshevik ranks left the residual organization more nearly what Lenin felt a Party should be. By 1917, there was no group outside of this hard-core Party in whom he placed any confidence whatever or with whom he had any established ties. It was on the books, therefore, that the power which the *coup d'état* placed in the hands of the Bolsheviks would not be shared: not with the Soviets; not with any other party. The new order—involving the fate of millions upon millions of persons—was to be shaped *by no one* except Lenin's wrecking crew.

As time went on, and the civil war continued, the tendency was to make the Party still more "narrow." Lenin's constant anxiety appears to have been that a growth in numbers would be a threat to "monolithic unity." Hence, those who joined were almost automatically suspect. By 1921, he was ready to say, "In my opinion, of the Mensheviks who joined the Party after the beginning of 1918, not more than one hundredth part should be allowed to remain in the Party, and even then, every one of them who is allowed to remain must be tested over and over again." (12)

Lenin made the character of the new regime explicit. It was a dictatorship; and dictatorship "is iron rule . . . quick and ruthless." This fact he elaborated again and again: "The revolutionary dictatorship of the proletariat is a power won and maintained by the violence of the proletariat against the bourgeoisie, power that is unrestricted by any laws." This he declared to be "a truth that is as plain as noonday to every class-conscious worker."

Again: "The scientific concept 'dictatorship' means nothing more or less than unrestricted power, absolutely unimpeded by laws or regulations and resting directly upon force. *This* is the meaning of the concept 'dictatorship' *and nothing else*. Keep this well in mind." (13)

The weapon of the dictatorship, he specified, was to be the power of the state: "The state is an organ or machine for the exercise of force by one class against another. As long as it is a machine for the exercise of force by the bourgeoisie against the proletariat, the only slogan for the proletariat must be to *smash* that state. But when the state becomes proletarian, when it becomes a machine for the exercise of force by the proletariat against the bourgeoisie, then we shall be fully and unreservedly in favour of a strong state power and centralization." (14)

What about the people in general? One aim of the class war, Lenin indicated, would be "to demonstrate to the non-proletarian toiling strata . . . that it is better for them to side with the dictatorship of the proletariat than with the dictatorship of the bourgeoisie, and that no third course exists." (15) Basically, however, the response of the people was irrelevant: "People are crying out against force! But the proletariat justified and legitimatised force. . . . And we declare that the masses will starve until the Red Army triumphs." (16)

That was in 1920. For how long would such a dictatorship continue? Until the new regime had consolidated its power? Until the industrial potential of the country had been built up? Lenin's answer was unequivocal: "The essence of Marx's doctrine of the state is assimilated only by those who under-

stand that the dictatorship of a *single* class is necessary . . .
for the entire *historical period* between capitalism and a
'classless society,' communism." (17)

Here, then, was the product of Lenin's Partyism: a regime
in which the powers of life and death were held by a "narrow" Party: jealous of its prerogatives; wholly untrained in
the constructive aspects of the social process and conditioned
to think of *force* as the proper means of solving social problems; "unrestricted by any laws"; and committed to an
ideology which made living persons into mere trivia by
comparison with a remote "classless society." Given a set-up
of this kind, one thing that was bound to take place—and
that did take place—was that Lenin's list of those "who deserve only to be shot" became ever longer.

In 1918, he wrote, "There is still too little of that ruthlessness which is indispensable for the success of socialism, not
because we lack determination . . . but because we do not
know how to capture quickly enough a sufficient number of
profiteers, marauders and capitalists." (18)

By 1921, even those who had been co-makers of the revolution were "enemies" if they took issue with Party tactics or
decrees. The Kronstadt massacre is a case in point. Communists prefer to evade this subject; and when they must
speak of it, they talk about "counter-revolution." The facts,
however, are on record. The sailors and workers of Kronstadt had not only taken part in the revolution but had remained faithful to the regime through three devastating
years of civil war. Then, early in 1921, factory workers in
Petrograd went on strike—demanding fuel and bread; an
end to preferential treatment for privileged Communists; and
certain basic liberties. Lenin's answer was peremptory: they
could go back to work or lose their rations. After sending a
committee to determine the facts, and learning through this

committee that the strikers had been dispersed by force of arms and that no other response had been made to their demands, the Kronstadt sailors and workers declared their solidarity with the Petrograd group.

Significantly, they did not resort to force. On the contrary, through the columns of the daily *Izvestia,* on March 3, their Provisional Revolutionary Committee issued an appeal against any such resort: "The Revolutionary Committee is much concerned that no blood be shed . . . Comrades and citizens, do not suspend work! Workers, remain at your machines; sailors and soldiers, be on your posts." They knew what they wanted, and stated their case over the radio on March 6: "Our cause is just: we stand for the power of Soviets, not parties. We stand for freely elected representatives of the laboring masses." (19) Like the St. Petersburg workers of 1905, however, and the Hungarian students of 1956, they sought peaceful "redress of grievances." Their fate locates another milestone on the road from St. Petersburg to Budapest.

At 6:45 P.M., on March 7, Trotsky—then Lenin's commander-in-chief—opened fire on Kronstadt. The sailors and workers held their fire, at first; but soon were driven to self-defense. "We did not want to shed the blood of our brothers," they stated in *Izvestia,* on March 8, "and we did not fire a single shot until compelled to do so. We had to defend the just cause of the laboring people and to shoot—to shoot at our own brothers sent to certain death by Communists who had grown fat at the expense of the people." (20)

By March 18, it was all over. The Communists, "unrestricted by any laws," could chalk up another victory—this time over the proletariat. After Kronstadt came a reign of terror in Petrograd, with the Cheka exhibiting in full measure that ruthlessness which Lenin found "indispensable." In so far as they could manage to do so, they killed all whom the

Party held to be even remotely responsible for the uprising.

With reference to this orgy of bloodletting, the Communists used the word "necessary"—as they use it with reference to Stalin's later treatment of the kulaks and Khrushchev's slaughter of the Hungarian freedom fighters. But "necessary" to what end? The Petrograd strikers, on posters which they put throughout the city, had made clear what they were seeking: "First of all, the workers and peasants need freedom. They don't want to live by the decrees of the Bolsheviki: they want to control their own destinies." Among their demands were those with which dictators have been confronted time and again: "Abolition of martial law; freedom of speech, press and assembly for all who labor." (21)

The dictator's "necessity" is not the "necessity" of free people. It is simply that of preserving and consolidating dictatorship. Lenin made this quite as clear as had other dictators before him; and quite as clear as Hitler, Stalin, and Khrushchev have made it since. This fact is worth our remembering whenever the Communists, defending the morally indefensible, bring forth the word "necessary" and assume that it settles the issue.

Among those who knew Lenin and worked with him— even those whom he later expelled from the Party, even those whom he sent into exile—there is singular unanimity on one point: namely, that his pursuit of power was not motivated by personal ambition so much as by a fanatic conviction that he was an agent of "history." Having set himself to coerce all people and all social processes into validating a certain ideology, he started that which he could in nowise finish.

Determined to accomplish *by dictatorship* the freeing of mankind from exploitation, he ended by needing an ever more absolute dictatorship to keep the people from exercising or even demanding freedom. Even his closest friends, even the most dedicated of fellow Marxists, became "strikebreakers," "renegades," "White Guards" if they took issue with his edicts. Even the workers in their own organizations—as in Petrograd and Kronstadt—became "counter-revolutionaries" if they demanded either the rations or the liberties he had promised them.

Just as he had, down through the years before the revolution, cut the Party off from the tempering influence of each successive group with which it disagreed, so after the revolution, he progressively cut himself off from every dissenter. Desperate to accomplish what could not be accomplished by the means he was employing, he again and again issued edicts . . . and killed in their behalf . . . and reversed the edicts because they did not work . . . and killed in behalf of their reversal . . .

EIGHT

LENIN'S PROBLEMS
BECOME KHRUSHCHEV'S

THE ONE compelling reason, now, for us to study *Leninism* is that *Khrushchevism* is cut from the same cloth. It seems strange that it should be. Lenin worked out his early theories and stratagems when there had been as yet no Communist revolution anywhere; and his later ones in a state of desperate urgency—to prevent the collapse of his regime. Khrushchev has come to power in a vast Soviet empire and an even more vast Communist orbit. Soviet industry and arms—to say nothing of propaganda—are potent forces for the world to reckon with. Why, then, has Khrushchev brought Lenin back into the picture, not simply as revolutionary hero—which he has never ceased being for the Party—but as strategic guide for the post-Stalin era?

The answer appears to be that Khrushchev's policies are Leninist in character to the very extent that he is trying to solve, in their modern form, certain problems with which

116

Lenin wrestled in his time, for which he worked out "correct" solutions, but which he left conspicuously unsolved. Khrushchevism, of course, is by no means pure Leninism. It contains also a larger infusion of *Stalinism* than Khrushchev admits. Yet so far as certain problems are concerned, the Stalin era can almost be regarded as time out—not because the problems did not then exist but because Stalin did not really try to solve them. Instead, he put the lid on them by a ruthlessness which served his purposes to the end of his life but which no successor could have taken up and pushed to a further extreme. Khrushchev, therefore, in spite of empire and sputnik, is back where Lenin left off: doing business at the same old stand because it is still unfinished business.

Ever since the revolution, the Communists have subordinated all other domestic values to the building up of heavy industry. In behalf of such industry, they have virtually harnessed workers to the jobs; and, for the past dozen years, have harnessed the economies of the satellite countries to their own purposes. By political means, they have provided themselves with unlimited slave labor. In effect, the Party has said to the people, "Seek ye first the kingdom of material production and its efficiency, and all the rest will be added unto you."

This imperative has been a logical fruit of dialectical and historical materialism. According to Marx, the one definitive thing which could be said about man was that he was a "producing animal"—distinguished from other animals by his unique capacity to organize effort and resource for the satisfaction of his material needs. The Communists, then, *as Marxists,* have been "correct" in saying that if they could turn the Soviet people into high-level "producing animals," the rest would follow.

They have, now, their heavy industry and their nuclear science. This is their success story. The problems, however, which have taken Khrushchev back to Lenin for guidance are not those which material production can solve. Rather, this production has made them both more urgent and more difficult. Khrushchev's most acute problems, today—like those which Lenin faced in his time—stem from the fact that *nature had made man complex long before dialectical and historical materialism made him simple.*

They stem, in short, from qualities in man not covered by defining him as a "producing animal." Further, they stem from Communism's lack of any machinery save that of dictatorship or any theory save that of Marxism-Leninism for dealing with these stubborn surplus aspects of human nature. It was not merely as "producing animals" that the workers of Petrograd and the sailors of Kronstadt demanded freedom of speech, press, and assembly—only to be shot down by Lenin's troops. Nor was it merely as "producing animals" that the students and workers of Hungary demanded these same freedoms—only to be shot down by Khrushchev's troops.

Khrushchev can point with pride to sputniks in the sky. But some of the things which he cannot do on earth are fatefully significant. To take a few examples: he can neither permit people to question the dogma of Marxism-Leninism nor prevent their minds from harboring questions about it; can neither admit that the workers have no ownership rights whatever in the system which they theoretically own nor permit them, in the slightest measure, to act like owners; can neither permit an uncensored literature nor prevent the people from becoming bored with the official literature which is supposed to inspire them to "correct" thoughts and feelings; can neither admit that the Party bureaucracy is a new exploiting class nor prevent this bureaucracy from exhibiting that "unlimited avarice" with which Marx credited the capitalists.

For forty years, the Communists have assumed that if they could build machines enough, all would be well. Now they have machines enough to prove their own assumption untenable. Now it becomes increasingly apparent that they must build human relationships of a different order from any they have produced so far. Yet they are doubly handicapped in building these: by their own vested interest in dictatorship and by a Marxist-Leninist dogma which forbids their doing what must be done.

Every organized society finds human nature the toughest problem to solve. The more give a society has, however—the more elasticity in its customs and institutions—the better it can handle the pressure exerted upon it by this nature. No dictatorship has this kind of give. All dictatorships are rigid; for keeping human nature "in its place" is the very condition of their survival.

Totalitarianism is far more rigid than were old-style dictatorships. Because it claims dominion over every aspect of man's behavior—including those which even the Tsars left alone, as private matters—it has no give whatever: no points at which it can let people just be themselves. The pressure exerted upon totalitarianism by the unpermitted, unacknowledged aspects of human nature is, therefore, both constant and cumulative.

The problems, in brief, which continue to prevent any genuine stabilizing of the Soviet regime are generated at those points where psychological and social realities collide with the "science of Marxism-Leninism." Yet the Party cannot admit this. It still must turn for "correct" solutions to the very "science" which is the author of its problems; for this "science" happens to be the author also of the Party's own dictatorial powers—and these it has no will to limit or relinquish.

In the first place, the Communists have never been able to relate the "dictatorship of the proletariat" to the proletariat in any way that makes sense. From Lenin down, it has been "correct" to say that in Soviet Russia the workers are the owners. Lenin's revolution could not have been *Marxist* if it had not led to the workers' taking over the means of production. Yet it could not have been *Leninist* if it had not led to the Party's taking over these same means of production. Lenin "solved" this problem by assigning to workers *in words* a determinative role in the economy which they were forbidden, on pain of imprisonment or death, to try to *perform*. Thus, from the outset, the regime has had to uphold a gigantic falsehood.

The machinery for upholding it was promptly developed —and has never gone out of use. In 1921, the Kronstadt workers and sailors brought to light one of the devices: "The substitute Soviets manipulated by the Communist Party," they wrote, "have always been deaf to our needs and demands; the only reply we have ever had was shooting." (1) "Soviets" organized by the Party instead of by the workers; controlled trade unions; programs of forced labor; the issuance of work-books and domestic passports which virtually chained men to their jobs; secret police within the ranks of labor: all have helped to perpetuate both the fact of Party dictatorship and the fiction of proletarian ownership.

The outcome is common knowledge: Soviet Russia is a new class society. Its classes, as Peter Meyer noted in 1944, are *those who dispose* and *those who are disposed of*. The former are the Party bureaucrats; the latter, the theoretical owners, the proletariat. The bureaucrats "decide what is to be produced, and how and why; what prices, wages, bonuses and rewards are to be paid, and how social products are to be distributed." (2) The proletariat—mere appendages to the means of production—"must work, obey, and live in poverty."

More recently, Milovan Djilas—long a member of the Party hierarchy in Yugoslavia, but now in prison for speaking his mind—has said of the new class of bureaucrats: "This is a class whose power over men is the most complete known in history. . . . When the new class leaves the historical scene—and this must happen—there will be less sorrow over its passing than there has been for any other class before it. Smothering everything except what suited its ego, it has condemned itself to failure and shameful ruin." (3)

Khrushchev and the puppet leaders in the satellites still reiterate the fiction which Lenin prescribed: still assert, on every possible occasion, that in Communist countries the workers own all the means of production. They speak now, however, against a background of events which even they must recognize as spelling out a demand for new policies. These events began with the strikes in East Germany, in June 1953; and as they have since multiplied throughout the Communist orbit, they have suggested the coming of a new era: one in which unrest among the workers openly challenges the old fiction of worker-ownership.

The strikes in East Germany "could not happen"; *but did*. The Party's first response was dogmatically orthodox: they had been fomented from the outside. Thus, *Neues Deutschland*, in the issue of June 19, 1953, justified the crushing of the strikes by Soviet troops: ". . . it was necessary to inflict a decisive defeat on the Western war provocateurs. . . . Naturally it would have been better if the German workers themselves had repulsed the provocation. . . . But unfortunately large sections of the workers did not show the necessary highmindedness." Grudgingly, then, the paper admitted that the size of the demonstrations might point to some dissatisfaction with new work norms that had been set up.

A few days later, Premier Grotewohl, speaking to the Party's Central Committee, went a little further: "There were mistakes in our propaganda work. We frequently talked above people's heads without considering their wishes, hardships and worries. . . .

"Recently there was added to all this a partial deterioration in the living conditions of some categories of workers which aroused their discontent and over which we passed with insufficient arguments and phrases." (4) He could not, however, bring himself to admit that errors had been more than verbal.

In the end, all that the Communists could see to do was to impose new restrictions, and—even while denying that the people were desperate with hunger, and while refusing offers of food from the United States—to thank Soviet Russia effusively for a loan of $57,000,000 in foodstuffs, this to be paid off in East German manufactured goods: which is to say, paid off by inflicting new hardships on the workers.

How far this "solution" fell short of being any true solution is pointed up by events which took place more than four years later, in August 1957:

> BERLIN, August 11—The East German Communist Government resorted to a draft today to get workers to attend a farewell rally for visiting Soviet Communist Party First Secretary Nikita S. Khrushchev. . . .
>
> To make sure the East German workers attend they will be marched to the rally or will travel there in special trains, it was announced. (5)

Later reports revealed that even when the workers had thus, under orders, taken time out from the producing of machines to produce a requisite amount of applause for Khrushchev, the rally fell far short of being an enthusiastic demonstration. In spite of its commandeered volume, the applause rang hollow against the sullen silence of those whose bodies had been assembled to make a "mass," but who did not applaud—because their minds were still their own.

As Milovan Djilas has indicated, the Party cannot give up any of its power without having more taken from it; so it will hold on to all of it as long as it can. Yet the time has passed, it would appear, when the worker can be kept "in his place" by naked force. It was a queer moment in history, but perhaps a prophetic one, when the Hungarian freedom fighters, giving a new twist to an old Marxian phrase, begged the workers of the world to unite—against Communism.

If the Party's relationship to the workers is irrational, so likewise is its relationship to the Soviet Union's growing body of economic managers. These, of course, are Party members, many of them of ministerial rank. But they are set apart from the regular political bureaucracy by the fact that they are trained to organize and administer large-scale enterprises and want the chance to do so with maximum efficiency.

The Party hierarchy treats these experts well in terms of honors and material rewards. Yet there is mounting evidence that it also regards them as a sort of home-front enemy. The trouble is that those who have the know-how—like their counterparts everywhere—have a large investment of pride and satisfaction in a job well done, and not simply in the material rewards which accrue to them. These economic managers, therefore, are beginning to insist that in order to do their best work, they must have more to say about the over-all planning of industrial construction and production.

This demand makes economic sense. Yet for the political bureaucrats to yield up to these experts any portion whatever of their own power would mean that a first crack had appeared in the brittle structure of dictatorship; and cracks, once started, are unpredictable.

It may seem that these economic managers constitute for Khrushchev a type of problem which Lenin did not have to face. Yet Lenin not only faced a comparable problem but set a precedent for its handling. In order to get the services of trained administrators and technologists, he was willing to pay these "bourgeois" experts exorbitant salaries and bonuses —and even bribes—while the masses starved. But there was one thing he would not do: he would not let any vestige of policy-making power slip from the hands of the Party into the hands of these operating experts.

It appears that here again Khrushchev is walking in Lenin's footsteps. The way he reorganized the Soviet Union's pattern of economic management, in 1957, suggests how far he will go to keep the power of the political bureaucracy intact. Reorganization on a regional basis was clearly called for. As the Party organ *Kommunist* pointed out, it was absurd to have some 200,000 factories and 100,000 construction projects directed from Moscow. But the *type* of reorganization which Khrushchev coerced into being—purging Malenkov, Molotov, and Kaganovich in the process—does not seem to make any economic sense whatever: only political sense, Communist style.

In February 1957, the principle of economic decentralization was decided upon by a plenum of the Party's Central Committee; and an enabling resolution was passed which spoke simply of dividing the country into "basic economic regions." Most informed observers anticipated that this division would mean the setting up of some fifteen or twenty regions, each administered by a trained manager capable of integrating all the resources of the region into one productive unit. This would have meant an authentic advance in Soviet industry.

But Khrushchev's party mind appears to have sensed danger in such a plan; for it would have meant that most of these "basic economic regions," *each of them headed up by an economic manager,* would have overspanned a number of administrative units, *each headed up by a Party bureaucrat.* Khrushchev, we must conclude, was taking no chances on an arrangement which thus seemed to put the manager above the bureaucrat. In any event, after months of maneuvering and intra-Party struggle, he "corrected" one absurdity by substituting another: for excessive *centralization* he substituted excessive *decentralization.* The country is now divided up, not into fifteen or twenty "basic economic regions," but into one hundred and five "economic administrative units." Each area where a bureaucrat already held sway has been made into an economic unit as well. Each has its manager; but the danger implicit in his territory's being larger than that of the bureaucrat has been averted.

The propaganda machine never tires of showing the builders of the Soviet economy as uniquely happy—because they are not "lackeys of capitalism." Yet now that the Soviet Union has its own body of trained industrial managers, the Party seems bent upon converting them into lackeys of bureaucracy.

In yet another area the fruits of long irrationality are posing a major problem; and again it is a problem which, having been caused by totalitarian practices, cannot be solved by these. This is the area of relationship between the Party and the intellectuals and creative artists.

Lenin, as his early writings make clear, regarded persons of trained intellect and creative insight as necessary but untrustworthy: hard to discipline; stubbornly "bourgeois" in their individuality. While, therefore, he spread his net for the intellectuals, he also specified the use to which their minds were to be put when caught. An ideological system, he made clear, must have spokesmen who can handle *theory;* for only such spokesmen can convince all such groups as have grievances that these call for a particular type—a Communist type —of *political* solution. Intellectuals, in brief, must be won over and encouraged to use their brains to the limit—within limits defined by Party purposes. They were, in effect, to be turned into well-paid, superficially honored menials.

Stalin carried Lenin's policy to well-nigh incredible lengths, coercing trained and creative minds into ideological straitjackets and then commanding them to bring forth brain products in support of the regime. Thus, psychologists "discovered" human nature to be the very sort of thing which Party policies called for its being. Biologists promulgated a "correct" theory of genetics—since discarded. Writers, artists, motion-picture directors, and musicians were commanded to "inspire" the masses by works which conformed in every detail to the Party line.

Never in history has the creative, truth-seeking, sense-making spirit of man been so brazenly humiliated as under Stalin. Among countless instances of such humiliation, a few stand out as archetypes. Thus, Sergei Eisenstein, the noted Soviet film director, was called to account because he had not made a proper hero out of Ivan the Terrible—whom Stalin had decided to resurrect. Charged with having failed to portray this "hero" as "Ivan the builder, Ivan the creator of a new, mighty, united Russian power," and coerced into public "confession," Eisenstein, in a letter published in *Culture and Life,* wrote that all artists "must master the Lenin-Stalin method of perception of real life and history to such a full and deep extent as to be able to overcome all remnants or survivals of former notions."

Again, there was the case of Dimitri Shostakovitch, one of the most famous of Russian composers. The charge against him was that his Ninth Symphony was lacking in "warm ideological convictions." He, too, was harassed into "confession" and ended by stating that the "instructions of the central committee of the Communist Party head a new page in the history of Soviet art; they direct and inspire us."

Neither those who thus "confessed" nor the many who elected suicide or imprisonment were any real problem to the regime so long as Stalin's reign of terror could be sustained and made to pay dividends. Intellectuals and creative artists have now, however, become a major problem for Khrushchev.

Writers present a variety of problems. Because stereotyped literature is proving to be a wholly unintended "opiate of the people," boring those whom it is supposed to inspire, it has become necessary to lift the Stalinist lid enough to let writers produce books which the public will read. Yet as soon as the lid is even slightly lifted, the writers start pushing it off altogether.

Also, it turns out that even an author who deals with a "correct" topic and arrives at a "correct" conclusion can have a disturbingly "incorrect" influence if he handles his material *after the manner of a free writer*. Vladimir Dudintsev, author of *Not by Bread Alone*, is a case in point. Dudintsev is no counter-revolutionary—as he makes clear in the Introduction to the American edition of his book. Moreover, the particular type of bureaucrat against whom his book is directed is an approved object of attack. The trouble, however, is that his *characters come to life*. By the time he has told the story of one man—an engineer and inventor—and his struggle against one unscrupulous industrial bureaucrat, he has come close to indicting the whole Soviet system. For he has made all too real the play of favoritism, animosity, and sheer ignorance; and also the face-saving devices of rigged trials and Siberian exile. The public's eager response to *Not by Bread Alone* and the Party's castigation of it combine to make a real-life story quite as pointed as the one on which the novel is based.

On another score, also, writers have become a problem—particularly in the satellites. One vital by-product of revolt in both Poland and Hungary was the sudden bursting forth of pent-up creativeness. Writers, from poets to journalists, produced—or brought out of hiding—in a few crowded weeks an amazing literature of freedom. Typical of what they wrote are these few lines from one Hungarian poet:

> "Tyranny is in your food, your drink. . . .
> You smell it, taste it, warm or cold,
> Indoors or out, by night or day.
>
> Where there is tyranny
> There is tyranny only . . ." (6)

It is reported that when the revolt had been crushed, the author of this poem was thrust into an insane asylum—as a host of other writers were thrust into prisons and concentration camps, or deported to slave-labor camps in the Soviet Union. Yet the words are at large, and so are a multitude of others in similar vein.

Over and beyond what the writers said, however, was the fact that they moved so swiftly and surely out of silence into an expression of the spirit of freedom. Just as the revolt itself warned that the satellite empire is a powder keg, so the literature of revolt warned that the writers are waiting to speak: their minds have not been Communized. This is a type of warning to which the Party cannot be indifferent; it is too well schooled by Lenin in the fact that those who can articulate a cause are prime makers of revolution.

Increasingly, moreover, during the past several years, writers of the Communist orbit have been going beyond the rejection of tyranny to a new kind of humanism—or perhaps we might better say to a new affirmation of the *humane* element in man and society. The extent to which this trend is disturbing to the Party is suggested by the fact that the *Kommunist*, in its May 1957 issue, gave over a large part of its lead editorial to an attack on humanism. The tone of the editorial was curiously defensive. It declared "the struggle for the revolutionary transformation of society on Communist foundations" to be the "highest expression of love for human beings, of genuine humanism." Leninism, it said, "needs no sort of 'humanization,' nor any of the reforms proposed by the proponents of 'humanist socialism' "; and it made plain that what these "reformers" call for would amount to "a rejection of a number of the most important theses of Marxism-Leninism." "Petty-bourgeois humanism," it warned, is a "deceit, a mockery and muddling of the minds of workers and peasants in the interests of estate-owners and capitalists." (7)

Concerned as they show themselves to be, the Communists seem unable to decide on a literary policy. They waver between lifting the lid and clamping it down—with the current emphasis on the latter tactic. What they cannot do is to remove the lid. For doing this would bring the unthinkable to pass: it would mean that in an area essential to the making of "Communist man," totalitarianism had become less total.

Students, also, are turning out to be a problem. We are tempted to say that the Communists should have known they would become one; for in Volume I of the *Works* of Joseph Stalin there are certain telling sentences with which they must be familiar. Stalin wrote these sentences in 1901, in his native Georgia, when he was sizing up the various forces which were there combining to oppose the Tsarist autocracy; but they apply today in a manner which he obviously did not intend:

".... the students, being young intellectuals, are more inclined than any other category to strive for ideals which call them to fight for freedom"; and "at the present time, the students are coming out in the 'social' movement almost as leaders, as the vanguard. The discontented sections of different social classes are now rallying around them." (8)

In Hungary, students framed the petition for "redress of grievances" which sparked the revolt. In Poland, they show themselves tenaciously curious about the West, hungry for uncensored facts, and prone to exercise civil liberties whether or not these are officially granted. Within the Soviet Union itself, university students have started discussion groups without asking anyone's leave; and in these have shown a startling lack of respect for the regime.

Most widespread and most disturbing of all student attitudes, however, is *skepticism*. The challenge resident in this attitude goes deep. All Soviet institutions, down through the years, have set themselves to do a saturation job of instilling the Communist ideology—particularly in the minds of the young. Yet it turns out that the university students of this generation—brought up wholly under Communism, back of the Iron Curtain—are taking their place in the ancient, honorable, worldwide company of those whose minds ask unpermitted questions and hold unpermitted doubts. These questions and doubts, moreover, tend to focus on the ideology itself. Further than this, there is more than a little evidence that many professors—even among those who have done the Party's bidding—are not unhappy about their own failure to standardize the young.

At the Third Special Session of the Assembly of Captive European Nations, held in Strasbourg in April 1957, Sir Robert Boothby, member of the House of Commons, passed along a report that had come to him with regard to the widespread disaffection of professors of Marxism-Leninism in Poland: men who are choosing to resign "because they realize what nonsense they have to teach." He illustrated this general report with one specific story:

"A friend of mine the other day was in Warsaw. He is quite an eminent English statesman. . . . He was talking to a student in Warsaw and one of the professors was there too and introduced him. There were two or three students. Suddenly the students began to make a violent attack upon Marxism. The Professor looked a little disconcerted—rather surprised—and my friend turned to the Professor and said, 'Surely, Professor, these are rather strong sentiments coming from your students.' The Professor thought a moment and said: 'Yes. We have not succeeded in mis-educating them.'" (9)

At this writing, the Kremlin seems committed to the task of trying to make two incompatible policies look like one. It encourages artists, writers, and students to express themselves more freely; but warns that such expression must not lead toward "rotten bourgeois liberalism." An article in *Kommunist* has attempted to present this policy as both generous and firm, but has succeeded only in presenting it as the nonsensical end-product of an untenable relationship between the Party and the human intellect:

". . . the clash of opinion, on a foundation of Marxist-Leninist principles, must be thoroughly encouraged and developed. . . . Of course, there can be no compromise with views and pronouncements hostile to Marxism. . . . It must be remembered firmly that we are for peaceful co-existence of states with diverse social systems, but against peaceful co-existence of ideologies, since that would mean ideological disarmament. But this, we repeat, does not exclude the clash of opinion—of course within the framework of allegiance to the Party and Marxism—a clash in the course of which incorrect tenets and conclusions are rejected." (10)

Pointing up a singular paradox in the Soviet economy, Edward Crankshaw speaks of "a technical base so rich that it can harness the atom and girdle the globe, so poor that it has no talent to spare to mend a tractor." (11) In time, we must believe, the mending of tractors will become a skilled commonplace. There is no reason why it should not become so. Even when the tractors are mended, however, Crankshaw's statement may still be valid as a broad commentary upon the strength and weakness of Communism. Communist strength is in the spectacular—whether this be revolutionary *coup d'état*, sweeping five-year plan, vast public building, worldwide propaganda machine, or sputnik. Its weakness is in the area of the small and simple and ordinary: the area in which both common sense and creative wonder have their native habitat. Communism is the sort of system in which the leaders think nothing of making a three-hour speech or even a six-hour speech, but in which the most powerful bureaucracy in all history feels threatened when a handful of university students get into a free-for-all discussion of Marxism.

As long as the Communists can manufacture large-scale crises, and use these both to keep the world on edge and to justify a coercive control over the bodies and minds of their own people, they can lead from strength. They will not be able, however, to lead from strength once the outside world becomes clear about the fact that freedom's best ally is the normal human being's wish to lead a normal life. A free-world policy that took firm account of this wish—shared by the peoples of the Soviet Union, Red China, the satellites, and the undeveloped countries alike—would negotiate the Communists into a position where they had either to lead from weakness or else make room in their ideology and their policy for life at the level of unspectacular.

NINE

KHRUSHCHEV'S PARTY

K HRUSHCHEV'S PARTY is not yet defined in history, as Lenin's is. It is still in the making; and the maneuverings that attend its making are so ambiguous that it is hard to get the pattern clear. Today's interplay of forces, moreover, may be replaced tomorrow by some other combination—with a resultant shift in the over-all design of power.

These imponderables, however, do not make it unnecessary for us to explore what has happened *so far* in the post-Stalin era. The effort to take them into account is, rather, part of our basic lesson assignment: learning to move out of our Western frame of reference into the Communist frame when we are trying to interpret present trends within the Soviet orbit, or predict future trends.

The imponderables do not, in any case, comprise the whole picture. While Khrushchev's Party is not a finished product, and while unforeseen events may render it obsolete before it is finished, it has, *as of now*, a discernible character; and this character is a prime determinant of the Soviet policies with which we and other peoples around the world are having to deal.

For convenience, we can take as our starting point the Twentieth Congress of the Communist Party of the Soviet Union, in Moscow, in February 1956; and more specifically, the speech at that Congress in which Khrushchev downgraded Stalin and held up Lenin as the proper guide for the Party. With what we have come to know about Lenin—and Leninism—we can fruitfully make note of what Khrushchev, in his portrayal of him, chose to emphasize. For Khrushchev was not simply building up a hero to put on a pedestal. Indirectly, he was stating his own future intentions.

He could not have dared, at that time, to have stated them *directly* with any such force. When Lenin, in his day, resorted to the purge, he had the power and authority to define the "correct" interpretation of Marx and, in the light of this, the "correct" line for the Party to follow. When Stalin went in for his wholesale purges, he was similarly in a position to define "correctly" the "science of Marxism-Leninism"—and make his definition stick. But when Khrushchev purged the dead Stalin and began to move toward the purging of one rival after another, *his personal power was still to be consolidated.* Had he, at that time, set himself up as uniquely qualified to proclaim the "correct" line, in contradistinction to Stalin's "incorrect" one, he would simply have invited his own purging. But by speaking through Lenin, he could say exactly what he wanted to say.

When he catalogued Stalin's crimes, he did his best to get himself and his associates out from under a burdensome part of the past, though the points on which he *did not* repudiate Stalin—such as his liquidation of the kulaks and his building of the satellite empire—are quite as significant as those on which he did. But when he catalogued Lenin's virtues and insights, he was mapping the future. Khrushchev's Lenin has turned out to be the perfect "patron saint"—and strategic guide—for what has since become Khrushchev's brand of Partyism.

The Lenin whom Khrushchev portrayed was, first of all, a genius of "great modesty." (1) He "mercilessly stigmatized" every manifestation of the "cult of the individual." He "unswervingly" approved and practiced "collegiality of leadership." That is to say, collective leadership.

Khrushchev's speech, we will recall, was delivered in secret session; and broke on the world through the medium of a "leaked" copy published by our own State Department. The news of it was electric. Countless Western minds responded with hope and vast relief to his affirmation of collective leadership. They took it to mean two things which it quite logically would mean in our frame of reference: namely, no more one-man dictatorship and more room for differences of opinion.

In the Communist frame of reference, however, it meant neither of these things—as events since that Congress have made clear. For that matter, history even then held a warning that Khruschev's words should be read in a Soviet context. After Lenin's death, also, in 1924, collective leadership was established—and lasted exactly as long as it took Stalin to collect all the powers of the State into his own hands.

Just as Communism has devised no machinery other than the purge for correcting errors of policy or instituting a new policy line, so it has devised no machinery other than collective leadership for bridging the gap between a dictator who has died and the next dictator. Obviously, there is no provision for a leader's election by the will of the people. Neither is there any law of legitimate succession, as in a

monarchy. Nor is there even an informal but respected rule
that the old dictator can name his own heir. Lenin, we recall,
warned that Stalin was not, in his judgment, the best man
to follow him in power. But this did not prevent Stalin's
becoming the next dictator. In reverse, Malenkov was apparently Stalin's preferred successor. But while this fact
netted him a brief term as premier, it did not prevent
Khrushchev from first maneuvering him out of that position
and then purging him. *"Collective leadership," in brief, is
the Communist term for the interim condition which pre-
vails when no single leader is yet in a position to purge his
rivals.*

Every delegate to that Twentieth Congress must have
known—as Khrushchev did—that the only alternative to
collective leadership, at that time, would have been a cut-
throat struggle for power, with the outcome anybody's guess.
The mutual wariness which this knowledge engendered
would have guaranteed that the first person to be liquidated,
by the common consent of the rest, would have been the first
one to show signs, then and there, of aspiring to Stalin's role.

Thus, *only* collective leadership could give Khrushchev
what he needed: time and room to maneuver for power. The
success with which he has maneuvered—so far, at least—is
shown by the fact that during the first twenty-month period
after his speech, seven of the twelve major figures of the post-
Stalin "collective leadership" were downgraded or purged;
Pervukhin was demoted; Shepilov, purged; Kaganovich,
purged; Saburov, purged; Molotov, purged; Malenkov,
purged; Zhukov, fired as defense minister. The fall of each
represented a personal triumph for Khrushchev—and also
a further consolidation of the power which he was able to
command, by March 1958, in order to raise himself to the
status of premier as well as head of the Party.

It took Stalin far longer to achieve such power. As we

have noted, it was in 1924 that the post-Lenin "collective leadership" was established. Within its frame, Stalin and the Old Bolsheviks maneuvered for position; and because, year after year, no one could purge anyone else, a deceptive "freedom of discussion" prevailed—and was taken by many persons in the West to be a good omen. It was not until 1933 that the assassination of Kirov ushered in the period of the Stalinist purges. By 1938, most of the Old Bolsheviks had either been killed or sent to slave-labor camps; and one in ten among top-ranking officers of the Army had been similarly disposed of.

Khrushchev may or may not, with the passage of time, become a dictator of the Stalin type: so absolute in power that no one dares to cross him; and more and more prone to the paranoid ruthlessness which has been, throughout history, the disease of the absolute ruler who purges enemies until he sees enemies everywhere Khrushchev's fate as an individual does not, in any case, change the fact that so long as Communism does not provide for legitimate succession, Soviet history can be expected to alternate periods of one-man dictatorship with periods of collective leadership—the latter signifying no more in the way of democratization in the future than in the past.

There is nothing in the system, in brief, to prevent Khrushchev's becoming another Stalin. There are, however, several factors in the situation which argue against the likelihood of his becoming so.

The first is simply his age. Stalin became General Secretary of the Party at forty-three. Khrushchev's power was not equally consolidated until he was sixty-three. Thus, he does not have the time that Stalin had—either for maneuvering his way to absolute rulership or for developing the entrenched habits of mind that go with it. Nor is this all. At his age, he will not look as indestructible to either rivals or favorites as Stalin did. No matter what happens, he will, in a few years, begin to look exceedingly mortal to younger men: those who may feel that they can bide their time; those whose support of him may well be tempered by their wish not to be too obtrusively "labeled" in the eyes of whoever comes next.

There is a second factor, also, for us to take into account: namely, that Khrushchev's commitment to the Party as an instrument of power seems to be genuine. He is, therefore, far more likely to be a Leninist type of dictator than a Stalinist type. This would certainly seem to be the implication of his Twentieth-Congress speech in its references to both Lenin and Stalin.

Thus, he portrayed Lenin as a leader who "spoke with pride about the Bolshevik Communist Party," always respecting its vanguard role, and resolutely standing out against every attempt to belittle or weaken "the directing role of the Party in the structure of the Soviet State."

Moreover, "Lenin always diligently observed that the norms of Party life were realized, that the Party statute was enforced, that the Party congresses and the plenary sessions of the Central Committee took place at the proper intervals."

In contrast, Stalin was guilty of a "grave abuse of power" which did "untold harm to our Party." This abuse of power, according to Khrushchev, expressed itself in two ways: in Stalin's usurpation of Party powers in the area of policy-making; and in the repressive measures he took against fellow Party members, so that "many entirely innocent persons, who in the past had defended the Party line, became victims."

The closest Khrushchev came to denouncing Stalin's paranoid brutality *in general*—and not simply against Party members—was to say that "in regard to those persons who

in their time had opposed the Party line, there were often no
sufficiently serious reasons for their physical annihilation."
But Stalin's crimes *against the Party* made up the main
burden of his speech.

Khrushchev has put himself on record as strongly reject-
ing Stalin's type of one-man dictatorship. This statement
does not mean, however, that he has rejected one-man
dictatorship in practice. By purging rivals and dissenters
within the inner circle of the Party and replacing these with
his own men, he has progressively made it possible for
himself both to defer to the Party and to have his own way.
Lenin was the master of this type of dictatorship. Khrushchev has already proved himself to be an apt student and
disciple.

No sooner did he become general secretary than he began
to exploit the powers of office to maneuver his own friends
into key posts. Today, not only is the Central Committee
packed with his supporters but the Presidium also is dominated by them. Further still, he has negotiated persons whom
he can count on—as much as any dictator can count on
anyone—into strategic posts within the government apparatus. Thus, for example, General I. A. Serov, head of the
political police (KGB),* R. A. Rudenko, the Procurator-
General, and N. P. Dudorov, Minister of Internal Affairs,
were all closely associated with Khrushchev in the Ukraine,
the last two having been his subordinates there; and all three
are indebted to him for the power and prestige they currently enjoy. I. I. Kuzmin, head of Gosplan and first deputy
chairman of the USSR Council of Ministers, is similarly in
debt to him for his present position—he having been ele-
vated, on Khrushchev's word, from his former post as head

* Since the writing of this chapter, it has become apparent that a new
purge is in the making and that Serov, an erstwhile favorite, may be among
those who disappear into political limbo.

of the machine-making section of the Central Committee apparatus. One week after Kuzmin became head of Gosplan, moreover, the Supreme Soviet, on May 10, 1957, abolished altogether the State Economic Commission—which had not seen eye to eye with Khrushchev on economic reorganization —and made Gosplan the top economic planning agency of the USSR.

What all this adds up to is that, unless some unforeseen crisis develops, Khrushchev is not likely to feel the need of any more dictatorial power than the Leninist formula enables him to exercise; and at the present stage of Soviet development, this formula serves him far better than the Stalinist formula could. For it gives him a strong Party that he can command in his struggle against certain new "pluralistic" forces within the Communist orbit that are pressing for the relaxation of rigid controls: forces of worker discontent, managerial self-assertiveness, consumer wants, and intellectual nonconformity. The maintaining of a dictatorship is quite simply, today, more than a one-man job. Khrushchev is not in a weaker position than Stalin's because he has made it a Party job, with himself top man. He is in a stronger position. If he has against him the resentments of those whom he has purged and the ambitions of those who eye his power enviously, he also has on his side that which Stalin, going it alone, did not have: a vast bureaucratic network of persons who have a vested interest in his remaining in top place.

There is a yet further reason—again, barring some unforeseen crisis—why Khrushchev is not likely to become another Stalin. A one-man dictatorship calls for a constant resort to terrorism; and for the present at least, terrorism on a Stalinist scale is highly inexpedient—to be used only as a last resort for the maintaining of power.

This brings us back, once more, to Khrushchev's speech. Significantly, in that speech, he presented Lenin as a man of generous and humane judgment. Whatever history may say to the contrary, Khrushchev's Lenin "used severe methods only in the most necessary cases": only against "actual class enemies"; never against those who had merely erred. These, he patiently sought "to lead through ideological influence, and even to retain in the leadership."

Except in the case of Beria, who had made himself venomously hated as the head of Stalin's secret police—and who also knew much too much about the past of those who made up the new collective leadership—Khrushchev has not, to date, killed those whom he has purged. Carefully, instead, he has walked in the footsteps of the "humane" Lenin whom he created in his speech.*

While there is no record of his ever having made a protest against butchery—or of his having refused to take part in it while Stalin was alive—it seems probable that Khrushchev really prefers to dispose of rivals and "revisionists," where he can, without their "physical annihilation." But in any case, strategy now demands a new "mildness." For at this juncture of history, the success of his program depends upon his being able to get what he wants without conspicuous killing. His job, right now, is to create for world consumption the image of a Soviet Union that is a benevolent giant: a Soviet Union that should be feared only by the exploiters and imperialists.

There are, specifically, three groups of consumers to whom this image of a strong, beneficent, peace-loving Soviet Union must be sold. The first group is made up of persons in the West who must be persuaded to see hope in the Communist brand of "peaceful co-existence," and to help build up public opinion in its behalf. They need not like Communism or want its fur-

* What has gone on in the satellites, at his instigation, is another story.

ther spread. It is enough if their deep desire for a lessening of
world tensions makes them prone to wish-thinking and if their
judgments upon Communism are chiefly projections of their
own Western value systems and partisanships—so that the
"permanent revolution" has no reality for them. The second
group is made up of people in the backward countries who
must be convinced that their national independence is in
nowise threatened by their accepting Soviet aid and guidance. The third group embraces those leaders of "national
Communism"—specifically in Red China—who must be assured that the unity of the Communist orbit does not call
for their playing second fiddle to Khrushchev. These leaders
would be quickly put on guard by any Soviet dictator who
showed a Stalin-like ruthlessness in pursuit of personal
power; for it would be only a step from this to a Stalin-like
tendency to view the orbit as his personal province.

We in the West are strongly tempted to interpret any
vestige of Communist moderation—no matter how strategic
the reasons for it—as a sign that what we call extremism has
run its course. We must hold in mind, then, that after
Khrushchev had drawn his picture of Lenin as patiently
magnanimous toward erring Party members, he strongly
underscored the fact that this same Lenin could become,
when necessary, the ruthless avenger.

Lenin "demanded uncompromising dealings with the
enemies of the revolution and of the working class. . . . You
have only to recall V. I. Lenin's fight with the Social Revolutionary organizers of the anti-Soviet uprising, with the counter-revolutionary kulaks in 1918 and with others, when Lenin
without hesitation used the most extreme methods against
the enemies."

Thus Khrushchev kept intact, for his own use when
needed, that Communist rationale of terror which was first

set forth by Lenin: "We have never rejected terror on principle, nor can we do so." (2) Nothing, in fact, was more clearly spelled out in the Twentieth-Congress speech than that "enemies of the revolution"—translated to mean "enemies of the present regime or its policies"—were still very much outside the pale; and that to become "enemies" they still had only to be designated as such. What Khrushchev thus specified in words, in February 1956 in Moscow, he translated into action nine months later in Budapest.

There has been no time since he came to power, in fact, when he has not, in one way or another, been translating it into action. Terrorism does not express itself only in Stalinist orgies of killing. There are more ways than one in which a totalitarian dictator can make definitive the edict, "Do as I say, or else." Jail sentences are effective. So are policies that cut people off from the means of livelihood unless they toe the Party line. For Khrushchev, eager to sell his supposedly benign Communism to the world, these have been far more serviceable than mass executions—if only because they have been less conspicuous.

No one, perhaps, has felt the brunt of Khrushchev's brand of terrorism more decisively than have the Soviet writers. By mid-1957—after what seemed an interval of thaw—Khrushchev began to reaffirm, in ever more decisive terms, the Party's domination over the creative intellect of man. Heaping vituperation upon such authors and artists as had ventured to point up even minor shortcomings in the Soviet system, he described them as persons who "scavenge in garbage cans." Then came the edict: "We are against those who select from life only the negative facts and wickedly rejoice at this attempt to defame and blacken our Soviet ways." (3) There has been no further thaw. Instead, as in Stalin's day, one writer after another has been coerced into public "confession of error"—by the torturing prospect of no work to do, and therefore no means of livelihood, rather than by concentrated physical torture in a prison cell.

More than a century ago, Marx declared that capitalist employers held the power of life or death over the workers *because, owning the means of production, they could impose unemployment and consequent destitution.* But no capitalist or combination of capitalists has ever had, in this respect, a vestige of the power now held by the Marxist-Leninist one-Party State. Terrorism has many faces; and it is never absent where power is "monolithic" and edict is above law.

On one count, we must note, Khrushchev's position is strikingly different from Lenin's. He has at his command not simply the Communist Party of the Soviet Union and those in non-Communist countries around the world but also the compliant Parties of the satellites. Thus—to paraphrase a Leninist statement—he operates not only in a Party but in a system of Parties. The importance which he attaches to the puppet regimes is pointed up by the swiftness with which any "factionalism" within them is decisively checked and any voice "unfriendly to the Soviet Union" is silenced by the purge. It is also, of course, pointed up by his determination not to let the status of satellite countries be made a subject for discussion at any Summit conference. What Stalin willed him in the way of an empire, and of subservient Parties within this empire, Khrushchev intends to hold fast.

Just how subservient these Parties are to Khrushchev's will is shown by their prompt, uniform responses to his purge, in the summer of 1957, of Molotov, Malenkov, and Kaganovich. Considering the long services rendered to the CPSU by these three, the charges of "anti-Party" conduct and "factionalism" sound odd in the extreme. Molotov, for example, was already a leader in the old Bolshevik Party when, in April 1917, Lenin returned from his exile in Switzerland and launched his attack on Kerensky's provisional government. Yet when Khrushchev, in his drive toward power, maneuvered the purge of the three, every satellite regime accepted the "anti-Party" charge without, apparently, so much as a backward glance at the record or even the mildest show of skepticism.

Thus, the Albanian Party fell into line: "The Albanian Workers' Party, . . . all Communists, and the Albanian people, fully approve the decision of the Central Committee of the CPSU on the anti-Party and factional activity of the Malenkov-Kaganovich-Molotov group." The Bulgarian Party not only issued a resolution approving the Moscow purge but announced, a few days later, that it had purged three of its own leaders for "anti-Party" behavior and "factional activities." The Czechoslovakian Party declared that, in the interest of unity, "we unanimously welcome the condemnation of the anti-Party group." The Hungarian Party published a resolution that endorsed and "welcomed" the Soviet action because it "safeguarded the Party's unity and its political line of conduct." The Polish Party declared that the Moscow purge had effected "a new consolidation of strength in the socialist camp"; and the Roumanian Party not only hailed the ouster of the Moscow "anti-Party" group but both announced a purge of its own and issued a resolution stressing "unity of the Party." (4)

As a reminder that Khrushchev also has at his command the Parties around the world which Lenin first bound to the Soviet Union by the theses and statutes of the Third International, we might note in passing that the *Daily Worker*, on July 9, 1957, stated editorially: ". . . We view with the warmest sympathy the efforts of Soviet Communists to maintain inviolable the unity of the party which leads the 200 million Soviet peoples."

In all the celebrations that surrounded the fortieth anniversary of the Bolshevik revolution, one word was underscored time and again: *Partymindedness*. This word, it would appear, is Khrushchev's battle slogan; and with it he has tacitly declared war both on those who deviate from the Party line, as various writers have done, and those who, like the new economic managers, show signs of wanting to exercise a policy-making function within their own area of expertness.

To sum matters up, the CPSU of the Khrushchev era is decisively Khrushchev's chosen instrument of power. This Party—in spite of "collective leadership"—tolerates no differences of opinion and has taken no step toward internal democratization. In both theory and practice, it is a strictly Leninist Party, characterized by "monolithic unity," "iron discipline," and recurrent purges to insure the continuance of these. Further than this, it is—so far as the people are concerned—still acting the old "vanguard" role assigned it by Lenin. This means that it is still enacting totalitarian dictatorship and calling it the "dictatorship of the proletariat." To its Leninist strength, however, there has now been added the strength of Stalin's imperial legacy: the satellite Parties. Thus, under its deceptive "mildness"—and in no small part, because of this—Khrushchev's Party is the most potent instrument of internal dictatorship and world conquest yet to be forged in the Soviet Union.

PART TWO

THE PARTY
IN OUR MIDST

T E N

MOSCOW DIRECTIVES
AND THE
COMMUNIST PARTY U.S.A.

THE COMMUNIST Party U.S.A., founded in 1919, is, and has been from the beginning, a self-declared part of the world Communist movement. We as a people need to know *in what sense* it is part of this movement; and there is no better way for us to find out than to study both its past record and its current line. The two cannot be separated. The past record tells us how the Communists have acted, through four decades, with regard to certain problems that are still vital to us. The current line tells how, under conditions that now prevail, they work to advance aims that have not changed with the years.

As we study what the Party has done and is doing, we must seek an answer to one central question: namely, what has its record been on adherence to the Moscow line? The answer we work out becomes our best practical clue to what the Party is now setting itself to accomplish among us, and also to what we can expect of it, in the critical future, at every point where our American policy and that of the Soviet Union are at odds.

It goes without saying that no group in this country should have its basic loyalty or social philosophy judged by whether or not it is in accord with any given phase of American policy, domestic or foreign. Such policy must remain wide open to both criticism and renovating suggestion. We must note, however, that if our American policy has been far from infallible during the past forty years, so has that of every other nation.

If, therefore, one group in this country undeviatingly follows the line laid down by one certain foreign power—adjusting itself to every zig-zag of this line—we have reason to ask what the true status of this group is. We have all the more reason to be curious about this status if the foreign power in question is one that has repeatedly declared, in Lenin's words, its "irreconcilable antagonism to the whole of the modern political and social system" and has specified our country as the chief stronghold of the system to which it is opposed.

In May 1957, William Z. Foster—who has played a leading role in the CPUSA through most of its existence—wrote thus, in the Party journal *Political Affairs*, about the early relationship of the Party to the Soviet Union: "Manifestly, the fledgling Communist Party in the United States, as in other countries, was profoundly influenced by . . . the Russian Revolution and the newly organized Communist International; but especially it represented the historic Left wing of the Socialist movement in this country." (1)

It is historically true that the CPUSA drew most of its

initial members from the "Left wing of the Socialist movement in this country"—which long antedated the Russian
revolution. It is also true—as Foster states elsewhere in
the same article—that the "period of the formation of the
CPUSA, especially between 1919 and 1922, was marked by
one of the sharpest series of mass struggles in the history of
the American labor movement." Those who took part in
these struggles were not predominantly Communist. Then—
as since—the Communists were a small minority group.

It is the first part of Foster's sentence that seems to do
less than justice to the facts of the case: his statement that
the "fledgling Communist Party in the United States, as in
other countries, was profoundly influenced by . . . the Russian Revolution and the newly organized Communist International." Was that truly all there was to it: that the CPUSA,
as a "fledgling," was "profoundly influenced" by developments in Russia? If that were all, the matter could be
dropped—as a fragment of old history.

What Foster does not say, however, is that the "newly
organized Communist International" was, above all, an instrument devised by Lenin, not for "influencing" Communist
Parties in non-Communist countries, but for explicitly binding them to the Soviet Union and its cause. On this score,
there is nothing equivocal about the record.

The Third or Communist International—in compressed
abbreviation, the *Comintern*—was formed in 1919, with
Lenin as its architect. Defining the place of this Third International in history, Lenin said that the First International—
the International Workingmen's Association, which Marx
and Engels founded and which lasted from 1864 to 1876—
had "laid the foundation of the proletarian, international
struggle." The Second or Socialist International—1889–
1914—had "marked the epoch in which the soil was pre-

pared for a broad, mass, widespread movement in a number of countries." The Third—the Comintern—had "*begun to effect* the dictatorship of the proletariat"; and it had "a basis of unprecedented firmness" in the fact that the Soviet Union was already "enacting this dictatorship." (2)

No conditions of affiliation with the Comintern were laid down at its first Congress. Lenin did, however, specify what he took to be its five basic tasks; and two of these are of particular interest because they clearly imported into the program of the International, for the guidance of Parties around the world, certain Leninist edicts of conspiracy.

The first task was "to carry on all propaganda and agitation from the point of view of revolution as opposed to that of reforms"; but, as a means to this end, to utilize to the limit "parliamentarism and all the 'liberties' of bourgeois democracy. . . .

"*Secondly,* legal work must be combined with *illegal.* . . . The party which . . . does not carry on systematic, all-sided, *illegal* work in spite of the laws of the bourgeoisie and of the bourgeois parliaments is a party of traitors and scoundrels." (3)

A year later, in 1920, a second Congress of the Comintern was held in Moscow; and there Lenin spelled out the conditions on which Communist Parties might affiliate with the International. No Party that did not fully accept these conditions could become a member.

There were twenty-one conditions. Most of them had to do with how the Parties were to infiltrate and undermine the institutions *of their own countries.* Thus, one condition specified: "Persistent and systematic propaganda must be carried on among the armed forces, and Communist nuclei must be formed in every military unit. Mainly, the Communists will have to carry on this work illegally." Another called for similar action with respect to trade unions. Yet another prescribed the undermining, by constant propaganda and agitation, of both patriotism and non-Communist internationalism. In particular, each Party "must systematically point out to the workers that without the revolutionary overthrow of capitalism, no international courts of arbitration, no talk about reducing armaments, no 'democratic' reorganisation of the League of Nations will save mankind from new imperialist wars." Further than this, all Parties desiring to affiliate with the Comintern must make "a complete and absolute rupture with reformism"; and all must carry on their own publishing enterprises, legal and illegal, with these "entirely subordinated to the Central Committee of the party." (4)

One key condition, however, had to do with how the Parties must relate themselves, not to the various institutions of their own countries, but *to the Soviet Union:* "Every party desirous of affiliating with the Communist International should be obligated to render every possible assistance to the Soviet Republics in their struggle against all counter-revolutionary forces. The Communist Parties should carry on a precise and definite propaganda to induce the workers to refuse to transport any kind of military equipment intended for fighting against the Soviet Republics, and should also by legal or illegal means carry on a propaganda amongst the troops sent against the workers' republics." (5)

The Communist Party of the United States accepted all these conditions, without qualification, and by unanimous vote, at its own Second National Convention, in August 1920. This, then, was the profound influence which, according to William Z. Foster, the "newly organized Communist International" had on the "fledgling Communist Party in the United States."

We must note, moreover, that the Party did not stop being thus influenced when it stopped being a "fledgling." It continued its affiliation with the Comintern for twenty years; and when it withdrew, in November 1940, it did so, by its own statement, for purely tactical reasons. As reported in the *Sunday Worker,* November 17, 1940, it ended its membership "for the specific purpose of removing itself from the terms of the so-called Voorhis Act." This Act, which went into effect in January 1941, required any organization that was subject to foreign control and that was engaged in political activity in the United States to register with the Attorney General.

After directing and coordinating worldwide Communist activities for twenty-four years, the Comintern itself was dissolved in 1943—because Stalin, then needing a full military alliance with the West against Hitler, decided that everything possible must be done to lull the suspicions of the "bourgeois democracies" with regard to the revolutionary intentions of the USSR.

After the war, it could not possibly be revived in its old form, for the Soviet Union was no longer the only Communist country and could not, therefore, claim to be "the only fatherland of the international proletariat." (6) No matter how determined it might be to keep the satellites subordinate to its own will, it had to maintain, for world consumption, a strategic pretense that they were "liberated" and independent. Hence, it could not bind their Parties to itself by the old Comintern conditions. Neither, for even more obvious reasons, could it thus bind the Parties of Yugoslavia and Red China.

Stalin realized, however, that some way must be found to coordinate the activities of Communist Parties outside the Soviet Union—lest they go off on all sorts of tangents. Even within the orbit, there were dangerous (to Stalin) tendencies

to be countered. Communist countries were becoming involved, without Soviet permission or "guidance," in squab-
bles over territory; and, worse, some of them were showing
marked leanings toward the West. Thus, Yugoslavia and
Bulgaria were at odds over Macedonia, and Yugoslavia and
Italy over Trieste; and both Czechoslovakia and Poland
wanted to participate in the Marshall Plan—which the
USSR was determined to brand as a "war-mongering" imperialist policy.

In September 1947, therefore, at a convention in Poland,
the Information Bureau of the Communist and Workers'
Parties—or, again in compressed terminology, the *Cominform*—was brought into being. Its professed purpose was to
provide for "interchange of experience and voluntary coordination of action of the various Parties"; but its actual purpose, to judge by what has happened since, was to provide
the Soviet Union with a postwar instrument for making its
own aims those of Communist Parties everywhere.

Two landmark events took place at that first convention.
One was the founding of a journal; the other, the making of
a speech. The journal was *For a Lasting Peace, For a People's Democracy!* This was to be the Cominform's vehicle
for the "interchange of experience" among the Parties and
the "voluntary coordination of action." By 1953—the latest
date for which we have a figure—it was appearing, once a
week, in nineteen languages, and penetrating far more than
nineteen countries. This magazine did not formally obligate
any Party to adhere to any given line. Yet, so far as the
"monolithic unity" of the world Communist movement was
concerned, it enabled the Cominform to carry on from where
the Comintern had left off. For it served as both an authoritative ideological guide and a channel through which "correct" stratagems and tactics could be disseminated and kept

up to date. The chief content of the magazine was, we might say, an interminable, many-sided harping on one certain theme originally developed in one speech.

This speech was delivered by Andrei Zhdanov, who, together with Georgi Malenkov, represented the USSR at the 1947 convention. In it, he first drew the now "orthodox" picture of the postwar world as divided into two camps: the "imperialist camp" led by the United States; and the "anti-imperialist camp" led by the Soviet Union and "countries of the new democracy." He claimed that the United States was, through its "imperialistic" foreign policy, setting itself to dominate all the rest of the world, politically and economically; and to bring on an eventual war with the USSR. On the other hand, the Soviet Union was portrayed as patiently attempting, through every aspect of its foreign policy, to preserve peace and to bring about the co-existence, "over a lengthy period," of capitalism and Communism.

Describing what he called "a new alignment of political forces," Zhdanov defined the proper role of Communist Parties throughout the world as that of becoming "the leading force in the cause of drawing all anti-fascist, freedom-loving elements into the struggle against the new American expansionist plans for the enslavement of Europe"; and he urged that they "rally and unite their efforts on the basis of a common anti-imperialist and democratic platform and gather round themselves all the democratic and patriotic forces of the people." (7)

The description which Zhdanov there gave of the two "camps" has ever since been the cornerstone of Soviet propaganda; and all Communist Parties, with no apparent exception, have carried on the tasks which he "assigned" them. Stratagems and tactics have been constantly adjusted—to fit the different conditions in different countries and changing conditions throughout the world. From time to time, also, new subthemes have been added. Thus, for example, when the Cominform met in Hungary, in 1949, it not only underscored Zhdanov's analysis of the postwar world as "correct" but issued a specific new call to all Communist Parties: this time, "to organize and rally the broad masses of the people" in a united front for peace.

The CPUSA did not join the Cominform. According to William Z. Foster, it did not "deem it expedient at this time to affiliate with the Information Bureau." (8) In word and act, however, it has adhered to the line laid down by the Cominform—and appears to have "deviated" no more than have the affiliated Parties. The intention to follow the line was, in fact, made clear at the very outset, when the *Daily Worker*, on November 3, 1947, hailed this new type of Communist International as one that would strengthen worldwide resistance "to the program of imperialist expansion, intervention and war, of which Wall Street is the chief instigator."

With like fidelity, the speeches and resolutions of the CPUSA's Fifteenth National Convention, in New York City, in December 1950, repeated almost to the letter what had been said at the meeting of the Cominform in Hungary, the year before. They reiterated the charge that the United States was deliberately mapping a road to war, while the USSR had only peaceful intentions. The "fight for peace" was described in the exact terms used by the Cominform: as a "titanic struggle," a "cardinal task" of "particular urgency."

Not least, this Fifteenth Convention set in motion the prescribed effort "to organize and rally the broad masses of the people" in a united front for peace. Even though the

Cominform itself was dissolved in April 1956, this effort still goes on. Linked up with similar Communist efforts around the world, it represents the most complex and fateful program ever devised for persuading millions upon millions of people to apply labels that do not fit the facts and to convert their own legitimate peace-wishing into wish-thinking.

The very dissolution of the Cominform, we must note, was intended to facilitate the program which this body had previously initiated. It was not intended to terminate this program. The final issue of *For a Lasting Peace, For a People's Democracy!*—the issue of April 17, 1956—makes this clear. It states that the "peace" effort now calls for the forming of a united front that will embrace not only the Communist countries but also non-Communist countries that are seeking national liberation from "imperialism," and that will embrace, within each country, not only Communists but also Socialists and other working-class groups, and all who are interested in promoting peace. The Cominform—because of its all-Communist character—"no longer meets these conditions." It, therefore, must be dissolved—*to promote its own purposes.*

What the Cominform program has meant, through the years, here in our own country, is that we have been encouraged—by every stratagem and tactic the CPUSA could devise—to invest our deep hopes for peace in policies bearing the Soviet trade mark. Further—and again by the most varied stratagems and tactics—we have been encouraged to echo the Soviet charge that our own foreign policy has been "imperialistic" and "war-mongering": a charge not borne out either by the actual record of what we have done or by events on the world front. On many counts and many occasions, our policy may have seemed wavering, inept, uninspired and uninspiring: *but it has not been imperialistic or war-mongering.*

tain points across. An American flag must be in evidence; and, to draw the crowd, someone might ring a bell "announcing the meeting like a Town Crier." Party members would circulate the petition after the call for signatures— and would also take up a collection. Other members would be planted throughout the audience to start the question period off right.

It would all be very "American," very earnest, very stirring —and perfectly calculated to get people to sign the petition without reading it. No one *could* read it under the circumstances without holding up the parade: keeping others waiting. After all, the speakers had told what it was about; and, to reassure the hesitant, the petition carried, at the bottom, a quotation from Trygve Lie. This had been lifted out of an altogether different context; but it was so placed as to give the impression that the Secretary of the United Nations approved the document.

Guide[s] to Speakers were also issued. Always, these stressed two points. The first was that the speaker must know in detail the economic, racial, social, and ideological make-up of the shop or neighborhood and must tie up the "peace appeal" with "immediate demands" favoring the special interests or biases of the audience. The second was that the American government must be represented as a threat to world peace because it was enacting, through its foreign policy, the will of an "imperialist power-group"—commonly identified with Wall Street. Americans in general, however, were not to be charged with imperialist ambitions. They were to be carefully disengaged from their own government and merged with "the world's peace-loving peoples."

Open-air meetings; indoor mass meetings; door-to-door canvasses of whole apartment houses, whole blocks, whole communities: all these were part of the drive. Before long, the non-Communist circulators of the petition far outnumbered the Communists; and signatures were being collected in student groups, church groups, clubs, veterans' organizations, union locals, minority-group organizations, civic groups, business offices, factories. No likely source of signatures was neglected.

Finally, the lists—containing more than a million names and addresses—were sent into a designated post-office box: not to any address that identified the petition as of Communist origin. Thus was the Stockholm "World Peace Appeal" supported by Americans who knew only that they wanted peace; and thus, also, did the CPUSA come into possession of a vast and valuable mailing list, for use in connection with later "peace" and "amnesty" appeals.

This was a drive for *numbers.* It was coupled up, however, with on-going appeals related to the war in Korea. No sooner did the North Koreans invade South Korea, and categorically reject the United Nations' call for a cease-fire, than the CPUSA undertook to build up public opinion against intervention. Thus, for example, the *Daily Worker* of June 28, 1950—under a heading *Prevent World War III*—demanded "Hands off Korea! . . . Not a cent, not a gun, not a plane for Wall Street's puppet regimes in Korea, Formosa, Viet Nam."

Within a few days this line was rendered obsolete. On July 7, the Security Council set up a unified United Nations Command, under the United States—this action being subsequently endorsed by fifty-three member nations. Thereupon, the CPUSA shifted its tactics and settled down to a long campaign of alienating American public opinion from the war effort: the first war in history, we must note, in which the power of the United Nations to check a willful aggressor was being put to the test.

One appeal after another was directed toward youth.

". . . mankind needs no more white crosses 'row on row.' We want our youth to live, to grow in peace, love and happiness." Again: "More and more young Americans are saying they don't want to die 7,000 miles away in Korea so that Wall Street can make some more dough." (3) Or yet again: ". . . we must especially explain to the young people that war is not inevitable, and how the only way they can get an early start in life is to defeat the war-makers." (4)

But young people were not the only target. The relatives of men already in the service were subjected to an emotional barrage. Thus: "We wish we could grant the mothers of America their most fervent wish on this Mother's Day. One does not have to be a professional poll-taker to know that women of our country want one thing above all else—PEACE." (5) Letters were even sent to parents of prisoners of war, urging them—when the tide of war was going against the North Koreans—to write to their Congressmen, demanding an immediate cease-fire.

There was scarcely a group in our country that was not, in one way or another, converted into a target during the years of the Korean War and of the long negotiations that followed it. The Party even tied up the "peace issue"— wherever it felt that it could effectively do so—with its own fight against all efforts to restrain its activities: "The Communists are especially singled out for attack . . . because they are staunch fighters for peace against a ruling class gone war mad." (6)

The whole Communist drive which centered around the Stockholm "World Peace Appeal" and the Korean War holds a special warning for us today. For while this "united front from below" was Stalin's invention, Khrushchev is not only continuing it but giving it a post-sputnik emphasis. In speech after speech, he is declaring that the *peoples* of the world, including those in the Western nations, are "peace-loving";

but that the Western *governments*—in contrast to those of
the Communist bloc—are militaristic and imperialistic. By
a succession of dramatic moves, he has made his claim convincing or half-convincing to many millions of people; and
in our own country, the CPUSA is hard at the task of making
it convincing to Americans.

On another count, also, we must take stock, first, of Khrushchev's current line and then of a highly educative past
instance of our all being made a "target." The phrase which
Khrushchev more and more often teams up with "peaceful
coexistence" is "peaceful competition." This phrase tends to
ring a bell in our American minds. It savors of realism and
fairness: of putting openly to the test two opposed systems
that bid for the favor of mankind—"and may the best man
win."

Quite apart from Khrushchev's words, moreover, the world
situation calls for our competing with the Soviet Union for
the collaborative good will of peoples and nations. If we
fail thus to compete; if, in particular, we fail to help backward countries to help themselves, we let the future go by
default. We not only hand over to the Communists the un-
contested privilege of helping them but make it appear that
the "fine phrases" of democracy have no content: that they
mask a corroding unconcern about both human suffering and
human aspirations.

It would be sheer folly, however, for us to think that such
competition with the Soviet Union can be peaceful. Khrushchev has already made clear that he rates it as a nonshooting phase of the "permanent revolution." This means
that every positive policy we adopt, every creative program
we set up for cultural exchange or foreign aid, *will be declared by the Soviet Union and all Communist Parties
around the world to be a form of imperialism.* Following this

line, the CPUSA will set itself to alienate public opinion from all such policies.

We say this because the Party, ever since the launching of the "peace offensive" at the end of World War II, has been thus misrepresenting foreign policy wherever it has posed a competitive threat to Soviet expansionism. In short, the Communist line for the era of "peaceful competition" is already on record.

As a kind of Exhibit A, we turn to a *Speaker's Outline and Guide* on *The Truman Doctrine and the International Situation*. It was issued by the New York State Education Department of the Communist Party on May 20, 1947. Hence, it belongs to the period when American aid—military and otherwise—to Greece and Turkey was blocking the Soviet effort to convert these countries into satellites; and when the Marshall Plan was preventing an "economic vacuum" from developing in Europe.

We read, then: *"The Truman Doctrine* is the open declaration of a ruthless imperialist drive for world expansion. By claiming that terrible things would happen if we did not vote $400 million for Greece and Turkey by March 31, Truman tried to create an atmosphere of hysteria and emergency. It was an effort to stampede the American people into support of an imperialist expansionist policy under the pretense that we had to 'support free peoples' and 'stop Communism.'"

Again, we read: *"Political money-lending and relief* as a field of imperialist operation is almost completely an American monopoly." It is a means by which "American imperialism has plotted to make use of the fact that most of the rest of the world came out of the war needing help."

Communist speakers were instructed to take their lead from this outline in preparing for club discussions, speeches at open-air meetings and elsewhere, and full-scale lectures.

It was by no means, however, their only source of such a "correct" interpretation of American foreign policy. Throughout 1947, the Communist press devoted itself to undercutting the Marshall Plan.

Thus, for example, "The Truman-Marshall plans for world domination must increasingly render impossible peaceful relations with any nation; for even America's allies in imperialist aggrandizement are increasingly subordinated to Wall Street." (7)

And for mass consumption, in *The Daily Worker*, July 21, 1947, William Z. Foster declared, "The Marshall Plan is a scheme to place all of Europe in economic and political bondage to the United States."

Through the years since then, the line with respect to every positive aspect of our foreign policy has been unvarying. Thus, in 1952: ". . . Truman wants to take another $7,900,000 out of our pockets for a new phony 'emergency.' This time it is to rush our dollars to the munitions factories of West Europe; many of them controlled by Wall Street capital." (8)

And in 1957: "In reality, the Eisenhower-Dulles doctrine is a demand that Congress sanction Wall Street's plan to take over the role formerly played in the Middle East by British and French imperialism. This plan envisages ousting the British and French rivals of the American oil companies and using American men and money to halt the independence movement [of the Arab nations]." (9)

Significantly, moreover, in March 1957, an editorial in *The Worker* anticipated the failure of the London disarmament conference and specified the reason for this *even before it had taken place*. Conditions, the Editorial indicated, were so ripe for disarmament that "it would take considerable ingenuity to prevent an agreement." However, "the beneficiaries of the 40-billion-dollar arms program in our country" would be ingenious enough to prevent it, even though they would thus violate "the national need—for cutting taxes, preventing inflation and, most important, lifting the fear of atomic destruction." (10) The Soviet Union, in short, was absolved *in advance* from any blame for the failure of the conference.

All this propaganda simply adds up to the fact that, as we enter the era of Khrushchev's "peaceful competition," we do well to know by heart the line which the Communists will use in trying to alienate us from our own government— which, in effect, is also the line which other Communist Parties will use in trying to alienate the peoples of their countries from the United States.

The "peace offensive"—adjusted and readjusted to keep it in line with Soviet policy—has been with us for more than a decade; and the end is not in sight. Today, as in the beginning, there are countless Americans who have never been sized up *in person* as targets for Communist agitation and propaganda. But how many of us can say with confidence that we have never been even indirectly subject to—and responsive to—the Party's tactics of multiplied influence?

THIRTEEN

TARGET GROUPS
AND THE PARTY LINE

EVEN A ten-year "peace offensive" is a brief episode within the "permanent revolution." Just as this revolution goes on unceasingly, so there are certain groups that never cease to be targets—because of the roles assigned them by the "science of Marxism-Leninism." Five such groups are of prime importance—and the CPUSA has not neglected any one of these.

The first and most basic group is the working class. This is the class through which, according to Marxist ideology, capitalism prepares its own doom. It has, therefore, to be won over to the Communist cause; or, short of this, to be brought under the leadership of the "revolutionary vanguard."

One of the early slogans of the CPUSA was "Every Factory a Fortress of Communism," and the Party's effort to convert this slogan into reality has been one of the strangest dramas of our time. It has been a drama of united fronts, of the exploitation of labor's "immediate demands," of infiltration, and of strategic maneuvering to take over the leadership of the trade-union movement: first, in the American Federation of Labor, later in the Committee for Industrial Organization and the Congress of Industrial Organization.

Between 1921 and 1929, the organization which spearheaded the Party's work in this area was the Trade Union Educational League (TUEL). This was based on a united front of Left and Center forces in the Labor movement, with militant emphasis on the "vanguard" role of the Left. Agitation in behalf of specific "demands" was its chief stock in trade. Its driving aim was to replace craft unions by industrial unions—on the theory that industrial unions would make it easier to weld all the workers in a plant into one group under "vanguard" leadership and to infuse them with "class consciousness."

The CPUSA claims that within eighteen months of the formation of the TUEL, half of the organized workers in America—which, at that time, would have meant some 2,000,000—were endorsing its "central slogan" with regard to industrial unionization; and that it could command almost as strong support in behalf of three other major slogans: "For a Farmer-Labor Party," "Organize the Unorganized," and "Recognize Soviet Russia." According to William Z. Foster, "These broad mass movements of the TUEL quickly broke the previous isolation of the Communist Party and brought it right into the heart of the living class struggle." (1)

It did not long stay at the heart of this struggle. As we noted in the chapter on united fronts, the CPUSA was, in those days, far too obvious in its revolutionary aims and in its predatory will to control the labor movement. In 1923, a split with the Progressive forces—these led by La Follette

and Fitzpatrick—cost the Party much of what it had gained
in the way of mass support. But the TUEL continued to
function until the stock-market crash—and it claims credit
for having engineered many of the most bitter strikes of the
period. In 1929, the TUEL was reorganized as the TUUL:
The Trade Union Unity League. It was this organization
which made hay while the sun was not shining: while the
storm of depression swept across America. In 1935, however
—in line with the first of the "broad" united fronts, which
we have described in the preceding chapter—the militant
TUUL was abruptly liquidated; and *infiltration* became the
order of the day.

One of the most important and least known stories of our
era is the story of what took place in the C.I.O. between
1935, when the Party first made the organization a major
target, and 1949, when the anti-Communist forces, after a
long period of learning the score, expelled the Communist-
dominated unions. Because of having acted in this story,
organized labor in America has gone far toward making
every factory a fortress against Communism.

Was the CPUSA ever really a threat to the trade-union
movement and, through this, to our national security? The
facts, in careful and engrossing detail, have been put on
record in *The Communist Party vs. the C.I.O.*, a book by Max
M. Kampelman with an introduction by Senator Hubert H.
Humphrey:

"The traditional area of concentration for Communist
trade union activity has been the fields of transportation,
shipping, fuel, metal trades, and other industries vital to a
nation's economy. . . .

". . . The largest number of members which the Communist party has had in recent years is probably 70,000.
Assuming that of this number one-half belong to the unions
—and that would probably be an exaggeration—they would

have had a maximum numerical strength of .0024 of the 15 million labor union members. Yet at the height of this power drive within the C.I.O., they dominated 12 to 15 of the 40 international C.I.O. unions." (2)

That such strength could be consolidated by so few is an awesome testimony to the power of Lenin's tactics and stratagems. Yet the story, when followed to its outcome, is deeply reassuring: for it testifies to the counter-strength of the free trade-union movement. "The Communist infiltration of the C.I.O. was a direct threat to the survival of our country's democratic institutions. The C.I.O. victory over the Communist party was a significant victory for our nation. It was also a crucial defeat for the International Communist conspiracy." (3)

The struggle, of course, is not ended: a fact which the A.F. of L.–C.I.O. is being very careful not to forget. The CPUSA has by no means given up its effort to win over— or take over—the working class. As a Marxist-Leninist party, it cannot forgo this effort. But the frequency with which Communist writings refer to the American trade-union movement as corrupted by the "prosperity illusion" and as "bourgeois reformist" tells us that the Party knows the enormity of the set-back it has suffered at the hands of organized labor in this country.

A second permanent target has been the Negro community. It is a basic tenet of Leninism that an underprivileged minority group is ripe for revolution. All that is thought necessary to bring such a group into the Communist camp is to provide it with "vanguard" leadership and a "correct" interpretation of its problems.

From the early 1920s to the present, the Communist effort to win over the Negroes as a mass has been unceasing. No tactic or stratagem has been neglected; and both agitation and propaganda have been constant. The detailed record of this interminable drive can be found in William A. Nolan's *Communism vs. the Negro* (Chicago: Henry Regnery Company, 1951); in Wilson Record's *The Negro and the Communist Party* (University of North Carolina Press, 1951); or, in brief summary, in J. Edgar Hoover's *Masters of Deceit* (New York: Henry Holt, 1958).

The Communists claim "overwhelming success" for their work among the Negroes. This claim is itself a maneuver: an effort to instill fear in the minds of white Americans and thus to drive deeper the wedge of anxiety and prejudice between the races. In this secondary effort they have often succeeded far better than they have in their primary effort to win the Negroes. In this primary effort, they have largely failed.

As we study the record, in fact, we come upon a curious situation. Americans in general seem to believe that the Communists have made a profound dent on the Negroes and could, in a showdown, command a vast following among them. On the other hand, those who have actually investigated the problem—J. Edgar Hoover, the House Un-American Activities Committee, scholars like William A. Nolan and Wilson Record—are unanimous in stressing the tenacity with which the overwhelming majority of American Negroes have rejected the Communists.

The reasons for this rejection are part of the record. For one thing, the Party has all too obviously taken its commands from the Soviet Union. In 1928, the Comintern directed the CPUSA to build its work with Negroes around the slogan, *The Right of Self-Determination of the Negroes in the Black Belt.* American Negroes, in short, were to be treated according to a formula which had been devised to satisfy certain cohesive nationality groups within the Soviet Union. They were to be urged to form a "nation" of their own, this to comprise all geographical areas in which they were a numerical majority. The fact that such areas were scattered at random all over the Southern states was ignored. So, likewise, was the even more important fact that the Negroes themselves, except for one erratic splinter group, had not the slightest wish to form a nation.

There is ample evidence that the leaders of the CPUSA knew—or soon learned—that the Soviet formula did not fit the American situation. *Yet they did not protest the Comintern's ruling.* From 1928 to fairly recent years—when they were at last permitted to try an "American" approach to the problem—they kept at the unfruitful task of trying to "sell" the Negroes on wanting to be a nation.

A second reason for failure has been simply that the Party has exploited Negro problems instead of trying to solve them. One instance can here be made to stand for many. In 1948, in Georgia, three members of a Negro family named Ingram —a mother and her two sons—were convicted of having killed a white sharecropper, though evidence showed that the sharecropper had beaten Mrs. Ingram over the head with a rifle butt. Both the N.A.A.C.P. and the CPUSA launched fund-raising drives in behalf of the Ingrams. The entire sum which the N.A.A.C.P. collected went for legal defense. The CPUSA used its funds to prepare hundreds of thousands of leaflets that gave a "correct" Communist interpretation of the case. They further exploited the Ingrams in slogans for their May Day parade, and staged a "Free the Ingrams Week" in connection with a petition to the United Nations.

Such tactics have been standard. With variations, they have been employed in scores of cases where the Party has built programs around "immediate demands" in behalf of the Negro. Most Negro leaders have thus had ample chance to weigh the sincerity of the CPUSA—and have found it wanting. The N.A.A.C.P. acted on the basis of knowledge and experience when, in 1950, it "authorized its board of directors to revoke the charter of any chapter found to be Communist-controlled." (4)

A commanding reason for failure is one which the Communists seem unable to grasp. Yet it is luminously clear: the vast majority of American Negroes not only believe in democracy but want more of it; not less. The last thing they want, after their long effort to secure the full rights of a free people, is to find themselves under a totalitarian dictatorship—even if it is called the "dictatorship of the proletariat."

The third permanent target is the armed forces. Lenin categorically stated that the armed forces of a country must be infiltrated and subverted—emotionally disengaged from the going order and made ready for mutiny—before a "revolutionary situation" could develop. The Bolsheviks, we recall, did not attempt their *coup d'état* until the armed forces of the provisional government had been brought to the point of mutiny. All Communist Parties have accepted as "correct" both Lenin's edict and the Bolshevik experience. The CPUSA has been no exception. One of the conditions of affiliation to which it agreed when it joined the Comintern in 1920 was as follows: ". . . Every Party desirous of belonging to the Third International should . . . carry on a systematic agitation in its own army."

After the Sixth World Congress of the Comintern, in 1928, the CPUSA formed a special unit called the Joint Anti-Militarist Commission, or Armicom, made up of representatives of the Party and of the Young Communist League. Its job was to devise means of infiltrating, propagandizing, and agitating in the armed forces of the United States. It set itself the goal of establishing soldier and sailor "nuclei" in every post; and undertook to distribute literature designed to lower morale, undermine discipline, exploit petty grievances, and even incite rebellion.

Since then, each change in Party line, each united front, and particularly each "peace offensive" has been reflected in some concerted effort to influence the armed forces, their families at home, veterans, and the draft-age youth. In this era of cold war and "peaceful competition," we must note, the aim of all this effort has subtly changed. The Party no longer expects to bring about, within the foreseeable future, a true "revolutionary situation" in America: a situation ripe for *coup d'état*. What it does hope to do, however, is to bring about a psychological and practical weakening of the free world's defenses.

The fourth target is the youth group—because Marxist-Leninist dogma has always proclaimed that to win the youth for Communism is to win the future. The Young Communist League was, for more than twenty years—from 1922 to 1943 —the chief Communist youth group in America. Its wartime successor was American Youth for Democracy; and this, in turn, has had a cold-war successor.

What is most important for us to know, however, is not the names of these organizations but the nature of the Party's approach to our young people: the important thing is the manner in which it has sized up their strengths and weaknesses and set itself to exploit these. This kind of knowledge seems not to be ready at hand in any one book or in any one definitive report. It has to be dug out of Communist materials and out of an analysis of the countless "youth activities" the Party has sponsored. Articles for mass consumption in the *Daily Worker;* theoretical and policy-making articles in *Political Affairs* and in its predecessor, *The Communist;* study outlines prepared for use in Communist schools of "social science" and in classes for new Party members; a

multitude of reports in the non-Communist press on demonstrations and mass meetings which the Party has sparked
on and off college campuses: these are the materials out of
which we can slowly build a composite picture of the young
American as viewed through Communist eyes.

The picture we thus arrive at is a lopsided caricature; for
the only features possessed by this young American are those
which are presumed to make him vulnerable to "correct"
tactics and stratagems. Yet it is well worth our studying—if
only because it tells us what our young people must be
helped to understand about the Party's estimate of them
as targets.

What is he like, then, this "target" young person? He has
a consuming fear of war and is thus highly susceptible to
any "peace offensive." He knows and thinks too little about
the history and institutions of his own country to feel that
he has any personal stake in the present world struggle. He
blames the older generation for having mangled the world
and left to his generation a pretty complete mess. Not having coped yet with the complexities of economic and political problems, he feels that these could have been solved
long ago if those in power had put "human" values above
their own selfish interests. Thus, he is ready to believe that
America is in the hands of "war-mongering imperialists" and
"agents of Wall Street." Because he needs some focus for his
idealism, however, he is responsive to the idea that there is,
elsewhere, a system that has subordinated "selfish interests"
to a "selfless" concern about the human future.

He is highly susceptible to flattery—whether directed at
himself or his generation: "the future belongs to youth." He
craves the excitement of being in on something and will
move with the mass in any activity that is started. He feels
pushed around by the older generation and threatened by
social forces that he does not understand; and he can easily

be persuaded to convert this feeling into sympathy for a class that is portrayed as victim. Highly receptive to abstract ideals, he does not get much thrill out of piecemeal "reformism." Hence, he is vulnerable to well-placed insinuations that reforms are cautious, hedging, tepid, have no teeth in them: that they reflect, in brief, the "old age" of capitalism and "bourgeois democracy." Communism, on the other hand, with its bold vision and vast projects, is a movement that calls to youth.

The fifth of the permanent target groups is the intellectuals. Lenin, as we noted in an earlier chapter, assigned to intellectuals a specific task: that of putting a foundation of theory under the spontaneous protest movements of the "masses." He stressed also, we will recall, the necessity of so alienating the intellectuals from the going order that this will be left without spokesmen for its theories and institutions.

We have come to believe, as we have studied the attitude of the CPUSA toward sympathetic and unwary intellectuals, that it would almost rather use them in front organizations than draw them into the Party. This preference—if it truly exists—may reflect Lenin's judgment as well as the Party's own experience. Lenin, we know, rated the intellectual as *necessary*, but *unreliable*: highly resistant to discipline and highly susceptible to "bourgeois" considerations of "abstract morality and justice."

The record of defections would seem to prove that the CPUSA has had the precise type of trouble with its intellectual members that Lenin foresaw. Many of them have, to be sure, rendered it invaluable service; but even those who have been easy to capture have, in the end, been hard to handle and to hold. Most of them, having joined in illusion, have left in disillusion; and between joining and leaving, have infected other members with "revisionism" and "deviationism." As ex-Communists, moreover, they have been more than ordinarily dangerous to the Party; for, once disillusioned, they have tended to turn against it the very powers of analysis and interpretation that made them valuable to it.

In front organizations, on the other hand, intellectuals have often adhered to the line for long periods without becoming restive. For in such organizations, they can render limited, part-time service and are not asked to subordinate to the cause their whole life enterprise and their basic powers of self-determination. Nor are they close enough to the inner workings of the Party to feel the full impact of either its "monolithic unity" or its ruthlessness.

The Party's image of the intellectual, like that of the young person, is a caricature. For that matter, its image of *any* "target" group is so; for it is made up wholly of supposed vulnerabilities to the Party line, with all other individual and human characteristics disregarded. If we judge by the appeals that have been directed at him, and the causes in which he has been enlisted, we must assume that the "target" intellectual, as the Communist sees him, has at least the following characteristics:

First, he likes the kind of theory—preferably, scientific—that lets man put life in order and take charge of it. Where other factors are not unfavorable, this may be skillfully converted into a liking for the "science of Marxism-Leninism."

Second, he feels both undervalued by the power groups of his society and superior to them. Thus, the Communists argue, he is likely to respond to the flattery inherent in their needing his intellectual services.

Third, he has a "humanitarian" tendency to identify himself with the "people"—but at a distance. This makes him a pushover for any appeal that seems designed to better the common lot. Also, it makes him feel guilty about any advantages he himself has enjoyed—obligated to pay, somehow, for the fact that he does not "really work." The well-to-do intellectual has often proved peculiarly vulnerable on this count.

Fourth, he has a further guilty sense that, busy with his own affairs, he never does as much as he should for the cause. Hence, he is fair game for anyone who offers him an effortless way to do more: by signing a petition, lending his name as sponsor of a meeting, or becoming an honorary member of a board on which, he is assured, he will not be asked to do any work.

Fifth, he likes to "herd" with his intellectual kind and, in their company, to formulate and solve problems *in words.* The sense of mastery which he gains from this verbal engagement with life makes him, often, place more trust in his own judgment about politics and economics than his training would seem to justify. Also, it makes him deprecate the judgment of nonintellectuals. This trait, the Communists seem to have found, can be converted into a carping attitude toward our American culture in general and, in particular, toward almost any governmental policy; and, further, into a feeling that others—including Communists—who carp about these same things have something on the ball.

Sixth, looking out at the world from his "fortress of intellect," he sees himself, his group, and "humanity" as threatened by anti-intellectuals. The Communists have long since learned, in this connection, that the anti-intellectual who is also a vociferous anti-Communist is a prime maker of intellectual fellow travelers. Dean Inge, we recall, once defined a nation as a group of people held together by a common mistake as to their origin and a common dislike of their neighbors. The CPUSA has learned a great deal about the cohesive power of dislikes held in common.

Seventh—and finally—the target intellectual has a strong reluctance to admit error, particularly if in doing so he would have to admit the rightness of some group whose judgment he has been accustomed to deprecate. Hence, the Communists believe, he will, if challenged, continue to defend a stand he has taken long after he himself has come to doubt the wisdom of it. To see to it that he is challenged, then, with regard to any past affiliation with the CPUSA, or any active friendliness toward it, is to insure his going on the defensive. Often, it can be made to insure also his believing in the innocence of *all who are challenged by those who challenge him.*

These, then, are the five basic target groups specified in Marxist-Leninist theory: the workers; any underprivileged minority; the armed forces; the young people; and the intellectuals. Each group is doubly important: important because of what its active support would mean to the world Communist movement and important because of what its alienation would mean to our democratic culture.

In addition to these standard groups, however, the CPUSA has singled out certain other targets because of the place they occupy in the American scene. Of these, we must briefly mention three: veterans, poor farmers, and religious groups.

Communist propaganda aimed at veterans was first entrusted to front organizations. Since World War II, however, Party veterans have been urged to join the regular veterans' organizations. Immediately after the war, the CPUSA set up veterans' commissions, both at the national level and in most districts, and assigned these the task of coordinating Party work among veterans. At the same time, the *Daily Worker* began carrying a regular column devoted to veterans' affairs. Its stress upon "immediate demands"—for speedy demobilization of American troops stationed abroad; a servicemen's bonus; more housing for veterans—is typical of the whole program, which has been predominantly one of demands and pressure tactics.

We have before us as we write *An Outline for Discussion in All Clubs*—issued by the Educational Commission and Veterans Commission of the New York State Communist Party. It is called *The Veterans: Policy of the Communist Party*. Undated, it belongs by internal evidence to the period just after World War II. It emphasizes the fact, to begin with, that the veterans of the two world wars add up to 15,800,000. Then it has this to say:

"The veterans are not a class. Rather they make up a group of very mixed class composition (not united by a common class outlook, common economic motives). Therefore, their position will be determined by the policies and actions of one of the major classes: either the capitalist class or the working class. . . .

"The longer the veteran is out of service the more he realizes that his burning special problems are shared by millions of other vets. The longer monopoly capital delays the solution to these problems the more acute they become. Underlying the veterans' thinking is the realization that they must solve their problems quickly to make up for lost time."

Then it quotes William Z. Foster as saying, "The bulk of the veterans are democratically minded, but this in itself is not sufficient guarantee of a progressive policy on their part. These great masses of veterans must be organized and taught. Otherwise they can fall under reactionary leadership and be used as instruments by American imperialism."

The rest of the brochure undertakes to implement what is implied in these opening statements. Three lines of approach are indicated—all of them having in common a stress upon those "immediate demands" which hold the diversified veterans together as a self-conscious group. One approach is that of organizing new Communist and front groups to focus on veterans' problems. The second is that of infiltration: all Communists that are also veterans are instructed to join the standard veterans' organizations—preferably, the American Legion and the Veterans of Foreign Wars, since these are the largest groups; but also the American Veterans of World War II and, in the case of white-collar workers, the American Veterans Committee. The third approach is that of attracting veterans—both women and men—into a united-front coalition, the basic purposes of this coalition being set by the Party but never labeled as Communist. In addition to all this, Communist veterans and all veterans that have been drawn into coalition should be encouraged to act as a political pressure group in behalf of "immediate demands" and the "peace offensive." We can take this program as typical of the Communist approach to the veterans as a target group.

Where farmers are concerned, the targets are the poor. All prosperous farmers are classed with the exploiters. Again, the stress is on "immediate demands"—and many of these demands, as in the case of veterans and other target groups, resemble or even coincide with those that are being made by non-Communists. They have to do, for example, with crop surpluses, school-lunch and milk programs, taxes, interest rates, freight rates. What, then, is objectionable about the Communists' approach? Why are they not simply helping to get things done that need to be done?

To answer these questions, we need only contrast the way in which these demands are couched in the Communist press with the way they are couched in legitimate farm papers and magazines and in the programs of various rural groups. To do this is to get an education in why Communists—no matter what good cause they may seem to be sponsoring—

make very strange bedfellows for those who are trying to solve problems and extend opportunities by democratic means.

The Communist demand is recognizable on three counts. First, it is tied up with agitation in behalf of whatever foreign policy—and, in particular, whatever form of trade relations with the Communist bloc—the Soviet Union wants our government to be pressured into enacting. Second, it is tied up with unworkable schemes: schemes, for example, for credit at abnormally low interest rates; and for government guarantees against the foreclosure of farm mortgages. Thus, anything that is actually done by the government to help the farmer is made to seem niggardly by comparison with what is not done. Third, each demand is so handled as to magnify the state of crisis, to label capitalism as the enemy, to foment ill will between the poor and the prosperous, and to make class hatred seem the necessary dynamic of social change.

There is something peculiarly perverse about the manner in which the CPUSA has, since the war, made targets of religious leaders and religious bodies. Communism involves a repudiation of both the cosmology and the ethics of Western religion. That it does so is not a matter of argument. The fact is declared again and again in Marxist-Leninist theory and is expressed in policy wherever the Communists assume power.

During the first sixteen years of its existence, the CPUSA was open and aboveboard on this count at least. It fairly flaunted its contempt for religion and delighted to quote a certain sentence which Lenin wrote in 1905: "Religion is a kind of spiritual gin in which the slaves of capital drown their human shape and their claims to any decent human life." (5) Its leaders were frank in saying that no one could

be religious and also be a Communist; and that if, per-
chance, a person still "tainted" by religion should join the
Party, he would soon be freed from this "taint."

All this, however, belongs to the years when the Party
still thought it could induce, within the foreseeable future,
the type of revolution which Lenin had called for. With the
establishment of the first broad united front, in 1935, the
Party began to tone down its expression of antireligious
views; and it has since been overlaying these views with
ever thicker layers of pretense: with claims that its attitude
toward religious freedom is simply that of all liberal Americans.

What this drastic change chiefly reports is that the CPUSA
no sooner had contrived a broad united front that included
church groups than it began to learn the strategic value of
being able to tap—particularly in behalf of "peace" drives
and amnesty appeals—the vast reservoir of religious good
will. As an added confirmation of what tapping this reservoir
might mean, the Party had, in 1950, dramatic success in
getting religious individuals and groups to help circulate
the Stockholm peace petition. Since then, these have been
constant and favorite targets; for, the Party has learned, they
bring with them to any appeal, any mass meeting, any
"peace" drive, a peculiar "surplus value": the respectability
and authority of the religious tradition.

Here, then, are the target groups—and let him who has
never had a Communist missile aimed at him be the first
to reproach those who have.

FOURTEEN

THE PARADOX OF LEGALITY

IT SEEMS likely that we Americans will long continue to disagree about the extent to which Communist activities in this country can be or should be controlled by law. We do not disagree about their control, it can be assumed, in the case of provable subversion, sabotage, and espionage. If actions would be illegal if performed by a non-Communist, they are clearly illegal if performed by a Communist. Few persons would seriously argue otherwise. Few would argue that Communists are immune to legal control *because they are Communists.*

Yet even here the CPUSA, by its application of a double standard, has muddied the waters. While it held no brief for Nazi agents during the war, it has managed again and again to put Soviet agents in a different category. By nationwide appeals and propaganda campaigns, it has cast them as "martyrs." Thus, there has come about a most curious situation. Many Americans who would not deny that espionage should be controlled, and who would scarcely claim that Communists are too "nice" even to attempt it, have been unwilling to believe that it has existed *in any specific instance.*

In the case of each individual agent charged with espionage, such Americans have been inclined to accept the CPUSA's version—that the charge is a frame-up—and have scarcely bothered to weigh the evidence presented by our own government. For this evidence has been a matter of "cold" and difficult legalities, presented in the courts according to rules of evidence, while the Communist version has been brought to the targets' doorsteps—and to the thresholds of their minds—in the form of an "appeal" so couched as both to warm their sympathies and make them get hot under the collar. It has warmed their sympathies by presenting the Soviet agent as a victimized human being; and has made them get hot under the collar by a skillful relating of the case to their general anxiety about the state of civil liberties and their intense dislike of demagogues and "professional red-baiters."

Thus, many Americans have been moved to sign on the dotted line without noticing that the appeal "refutes" the whole body of governmental evidence by nothing more than a marshaling of emotion-laden stereotypes and irrelevancies. Characteristically—to take a few concrete examples—such appeals, and also the articles written in support of them, label the arrest of the agent as one more product of a "profascist reign of terror in the United States"; and dispose of the F.B.I. as "the department of frame-up headed by J. Edgar Hoover." Characteristically, also, they identify those who have "engineered" the arrest as belonging to the "antipeace forces." They declare that if this "victim" can be thus "railroaded," then any "militant worker for peace and democracy" who runs afoul of the "fascists" in this country "can be framed by the same forces on trumped-up charges."

The question of whether or not the Soviet agent has been guilty of espionage slips out of sight. What is substituted for it amounts to a statement that a democracy is employing "police-state methods" if it seeks to provide for the common defense by a legal control of totalitarianism's secret agents.

Actually, however, the problems that baffle us with regard to the legal status of Communist activities are not of this order. For no matter how much protest the Party may stir up in behalf of those arrested for breaking laws *which any person, Communist or otherwise, would be arrested for breaking,* the government will do what it has to do: namely, prosecute the case by "due process of law." All that the CPUSA can accomplish by its feverish campaign—and all, we must judge, that it expects to accomplish—is to fog the issue and to alienate a certain number of Americans from their own government. If it can do this, it can hope to have their residual anger and moral uneasiness about the case on tap for later use, in other connections.

The disagreements which we most need to explore have to do with the best way of handling, not persons identified as Soviet agents, but the Communist Party itself as it operates in this country. Here—to take one contrast—two men as experienced as J. Edgar Hoover and Senator Hubert H. Humphrey represent different viewpoints. While J. Edgar Hoover has been careful not to step out of his own province to trespass upon that of policy-making, he has analyzed, again and again—from the angle of law enforcement—the difficulties which would be created by outlawing the CPUSA and driving it underground. On the other hand, Hubert H. Humphrey, who conducted, during the 82nd Congress, the hearings on Communist infiltration of the labor unions, became, in 1954, the author of the Communist Control Act. While this did not go so far as to outlaw the CPUSA, it circumscribed the Party's activities and required a far more detailed accounting of these than had previously been required. With striking impartiality, the Communists have called both men *fascist-minded.*

There would seem to be a moral implicit in this contrast between the viewpoints held by two good men and true: namely, that when we disagree with one another on this matter of Communism and the law, we do well to look beyond our disagreement, at the complexity of the problem. It is not enough for us to indulge in what Eric Bentley has called "motive mongering."

The genius of the CPUSA has lain in its unique capacity to work for an illegal end by a variety of means many of which, taken separately, are within the letter of the law. To paraphrase a Marxian line of thinking, we might say that when enough of these lawful actions have been added up, a point is reached where *quantitative* change becomes *qualitative:* where the sum total of the lawful, viewed in the context of Party purposes and allegiances, becomes unlawful. Yet—and here is the paradox—there is often no precise statute under which it thus becomes unlawful. Thus, we find ourselves in a peculiar position: either, it appears, we have to let that which is illegal in its purposes and effects, but not in its immediate form, continue unrestrained; or else we have to run the risk that, by restraining it, we will curb the legitimate exercise of freedom as well as its illegitimate exploitation.

To take a concrete example of "lawful" illegality, we might return to a point which we touched upon in the preceding chapter: the Party's organized effort to disorganize the armed forces of the United States. Lenin himself knew and specified that what the Comintern demanded, in this connection, of all Communist Parties outside the Soviet Union was illegal; and that it would, in the event of war, be "high treason." Yet this, he indicated, was a "bourgeois" consideration by which no Communist should be deterred.

The CPUSA has not been deterred by it. Consistently, except for the period of war-time alliance between the Soviet Union and the Western powers, it has maintained an organization and a program specifically designed to undermine morale and discipline in the armed forces. Few Americans would doubt, we can suppose, that the Party's purpose in this has been illegal. But have its actions in behalf of this purpose also been illegal? In many cases—we have no way of knowing how many—they must certainly have been so. But in countless cases, they have not been. That is to say, as separate *actions,* taken out of the context of *purpose* and *plan,* they have managed to stay within the letter of the law while flouting the spirit of it.

There is no law against any American's expressing a derogatory opinion of our government's domestic or foreign policy. There is no law against a serviceman's griping about the chain of command, or the food, or the discipline, or the civilian public's lack of concern about whether the men in uniform live or die. There is no law against his surmising that the arms manufacturers are doing all right: not suffering at all from the world crisis. There is no law that forbids his wondering aloud why the government holds back from every peaceful overture made by the Soviet Union.

Moreover, there is no law that requires him to be accurate in what he says on any of these subjects. The government cannot sue a citizen for libel. The right to engage in unlimited, uninformed griping about our government is, we might say, implicit in the Constitution. If this right were declared obsolete, everything from smoking-car conversations to political campaigns would be so altered as to be unrecognizable; and the number of persons—in and out of the armed forces—who would be bound to sudden silence would roughly approximate the entire population of the country.

What, then, shall we say about the CPUSA's long-established tactics for undermining morale and discipline; and even, where strategically possible, for inciting to rebellion? Communist X says so-and-so about the fact that officers have it plenty soft; or that the administration in Washington wants a war to prevent a depression—and hopes a few million men will get killed, because dead men don't have to be supported on a W.P.A. program. But non-Communist Y may say more or less the same thing. Is there—in terms that can be legally indicated—any difference?

Hard as it may be to pin down in any individual case, there is this difference: non-Communist Y is speaking *his own mind,* or *his own mood;* Communist X is speaking *the Party line.* If this line changed, his "mind" or "mood" would change; or if it did not, he would be expelled from the Party. He, in brief, is saying what he has been told to say; and what he has been told to say has, in broad terms, come down through a chain of command that reaches all the way to the Cominform. Elsewhere in the armed forces, Communists A to Z are, like himself, on the lookout for discontents, grievances, and boredoms to exploit and are implanting similar views where they think these will be most likely to make non-Communists A to Z accept the Party line as their own opinion and echo it when they speak "their own minds" or "their own moods."

If we have any illusion that Communists A to Z are speaking as free individuals when they exercise their democratic rights, we need only remind ourselves of how some 55,000 Party members in this country "changed their minds" overnight when Hitler broke his pact with Stalin and invaded the Soviet Union. Up to that date, the CPUSA had urgently pressed the idea that the war against Nazi Germany was "an unjust, reactionary, imperialist war." (1) Abruptly, however, when Hitler moved into Russia, *The Communist* put forth a new slogan: "Defend America by giving full aid to the Soviet Union." (2) And the Education Department of the CPUSA circulated a brochure quoting Stalin to the effect that "the Second World War against the Axis powers, as distinct from the First World War, assumed from the very beginning an anti-fascist, liberating character, having also as one of its aims the re-establishment of democratic liberties." (3) Communists A to Z—in and out of the armed forces—realized suddenly that Stalin's view was precisely their own: that this was how they had felt about the war "from the very beginning."

Non-Communist Y, in brief, and Communist X may often seem to be doing the same thing: saying what they have a right to say, because it is what they feel like saying. But there is this difference: non-Communist Y is acting as a free individual; Communist X is acting, under orders, as a member of a conspiratorial organization. It is not easy to prove this in legal terms: not easy to prove that, on any given occasion, he is not simply speaking his own mind. It is not easy to pin down the fact that he, together with Communists A to Z, is helping to do a "saturation job" in the area of public opinion *while concealing his purpose in this regard*—and that the line which he thus "retails" never deviates from the Soviet line.

Years ago, Gerald W. Johnson wrote in the Baltimore *Evening Sun:* "Human ingenuity has never been able to devise a system of guaranteeing freedom to the wise and honest except by guaranteeing freedom for all; and freedom for the wise is so supremely important that it is worth the price of making the silly free, too." We have remembered this statement because it expresses a point of view which most of us as Americans profoundly cherish. It is in the spirit of this viewpoint that a great many anti-Communists have opposed all attempts to make any legal distinction between Communists and non-Communists in terms of freedoms to be exercised.

Yet does this viewpoint wholly cover the problem as we are being gradually forced to size it up? How would the above sentence sound to our minds and consciences if it read thus: "Human ingenuity has never been able to devise a system of guaranteeing freedom to the wise and honest except by guaranteeing it to all—including the conspiratorial; and freedom for the wise is so supremely important that it is worth the price of making not only the silly but also the conspiratorial free, too?" The question which we as a people are having to try to answer—and to which no one yet has found a satisfactory answer—is implied in this revised sentence. Can we find a way, consistent with liberty under law, of protecting ourselves against the Communist conspiracy while also preserving our freedom: the freedom of the "silly" no less than that of the "wise"—because the line between the two has always had a surprising way of shifting its position?

We who are not lawyers are not going either to frame the new provisions that may be called for or to judge their legal exactnesses. Yet we must bring to bear upon them minds that know the shape and complexity of the problem; and minds rendered humble enough by such knowledge not to import into the discussion stereotyped irrelevancies.

Ought we not, then, to begin by sizing up the attitude which the CPUSA has itself taken, through four decades, toward the law of our land and the Party's status with regard to this law? This attitude is not a matter of guesswork. It has been put on record many times over, by the Communists themselves.

The CPUSA is a Marxist-Leninist Party. It has never pretended to be otherwise. Its rigid adherence to the line has been confirmed many times over. Earl Browder, for example, when he was General Secretary of the Party stated the policy thus:

"In our approach to the masses whom we are striving to win, to organize, to mobilize for the revolutionary struggle, we always must be tolerant and patient, as well as stubborn and persistent.

"But . . . we must be resolutely intolerant with every deviation in theory, with every effort to revise Marxism and Leninism." (4)

Yet Browder himself was later removed from his top post —Moscow concurring—*because he did not adhere closely enough to Marxist-Leninist theory.* He was replaced by William Z. Foster, who seems never to have been charged with even minor "revisionism" since he first joined the Party in 1921. A decade after Browder's defeat, the CPUSA was again in turmoil, as we have noted in an earlier chapter; and again the "orthodox" element won out.

All this being so, we must, as a background for considering the legal or illegal character of the CPUSA's activities, pin down in our minds one basic principle of Marxism-Leninism: namely, that the government of any country is a "class" government, and that its legal system is a "class" system. No state, according to Communist dogma, ever defends the rights or promotes the welfare of *more than one class.*

Where the proletarian revolution has not yet taken place, the government is declared to represent *exclusively* and *by its very nature* the interests of the ruling economic class; and laws and courts exist solely to impose the will of this class upon the proletariat. Communist Parties in non-Communist countries must regard themselves, therefore, as operating under an "enemy" government which they will

eventually destroy. Meanwhile, only considerations of expediency, never a sense of having a stake in the going order,
must determine their relationship to it and to its laws.

The CPUSA has affirmed this concept of the State times
without number. Its most common "shorthand" expression
of it has been its endlessly reiterated reference to our government as "the agent of Wall Street." We usually miss the
ideological impact of this phrase because non-Communists
often talk in much the same way to express an exasperated
or disgruntled feeling that one or another administration in
Washington is too ready to do what "big money" suggests.
Thus, the phrase registers in our minds as a verbal equivalent
of the traditional American cartoon in which an overstuffed
financier holds the domed National Capitol in the palm of
his hand. In the Communist dictionary, however, the phrase
has nothing to do with disgruntled individuals or a particular
administration. It expresses, specifically, literally, and exactly, the Communist view of the relationship that exists
between the government and the ruling economic class in a
country—our own—where the revolution has not yet taken
place.

In the early days of the New Deal, for example, the Party
put out a variety of small pamphlets, selling for a cent or
two cents, which were designed to turn special groups—
workers, veterans, farmers—against Roosevelt's antidepres-
sion program, lest it succeed and destroy the "revolutionary
situation." One such pamphlet—*Farmers' Call to Action*—
contains a paragraph typical of both this particular effort
and the CPUSA's adherence to the dogma that our government is "the agent of Wall Street": "Coolidge and Hoover
openly carried through the dictates of Wall Street against
the toiling farmers. Hoover and the Republican Administration so aroused the wrath of the working people that Wall
Street needed a new face, one that would speak nicer words,

one that would raise new hopes and illusions, but behind which there would be hidden the same kind of program. Hence Roosevelt, the Democrat, was brought forth with many promises and the New Deal." (5)

The revolution, when it comes, does not aim to establish "liberty and justice for all." Lenin ruled out any such concept: "Ideological talk and phrasemongering about political liberties should be dispensed with; all that is just chatter." (6) What the revolution does is to *overturn* the social structure, so that the erstwhile exploited assume domination over the exploiters.

Here, again, the CPUSA has held to the dogmatic line. Striking evidence of how faithfully it has done so is found in various study-course outlines put out shortly after World War II. The Party's chief problem, at that time, was to "reorient" its rank-and-file members—and even its secondary leaders—with respect to the basic principles of Marxism-Leninism and particularly the class struggle. For these had been played down during the period of wartime alliance; and many comrades were showing themselves inclined to prolong expedient collaboration into "revisionism." The study-course outlines were part of a coast-to-coast effort at such "reorientation."

One of them—*Fundamentals of Marxism,* issued by the Educational Committee of the Los Angeles County Communist Party—can be taken as typical. In Lesson IV, *The State,* it indicated that "the dictatorship of the proletariat cannot be 'complete' democracy, a democracy for *all.*" Then, with an inserted quotation from Lenin's *The State and the Revolution,* it went on to say that "the dictatorship of the proletariat 'must be a state that is democratic in a *new* way —against the bourgeoisie.'" To underscore the point, it added a further quotation—from Stalin's *Leninism:* "Under the dictatorship of the proletariat, democracy is *proletarian* democracy—the democracy of the exploited majority based upon the restriction of the rights of the exploiting minority and directed against this minority."

The "exploiting minority," we must remind ourselves, is not defined in Marxist theory *by individual behavior that is exploitative*. Marx granted that many who would be liquidated when the revolution came would be wholly innocent of any personal misconduct toward their workers. They might even be persons who had tried to reform economic relationships for the benefit of the workers. But they would be "guilty" of belonging to the class that owned the means of production.

As for the legal system which the CPUSA visualizes for postrevolutionary America, William Z. Foster has written: "The civil and criminal codes would be simplified, the aim being to proceed directly and quickly to a correct decision. . . . The courts will be class-courts, definitely warring against the enemies of the toilers." (7) Such a legal system, in short, would *naturally* conduct trials as they have been conducted in the Soviet Union and the satellites, with no "hypocrisy" about "due process"; and all that we have cherished as the Magna Carta tradition would be destroyed as "historically obsolete."

When we have thus pinned down in our minds the relationship between the CPUSA's on-going and tactically varied program and the Marxist-Leninist theory of the State, we are in a better position than before to appraise the Party's forty-year record with reference to the law of our land and to understand the complex legal problems which our government—or any democratic government—faces when it tries to "provide for the common defense" against a resident Communism that exploits free institutions in behalf of the world Communist movement.

We can begin to understand, for one thing, that the Party, with regard to law, consistently lives by a double standard. When it condemns legal procedures in this country and approves those within the Communist orbit, it does not do so by reference to any embracing standard of justice; nor does it apply to the defendant in a case our customary standards of innocence or guilt. Both to the court and to the defendant it categorically applies "class" standards. Thus, a Communist defendant in a "capitalist" court is automatically "innocent"—whether or not he has broken the law of the land; and a "capitalist" defendant in a Communist court is automatically "guilty"—because even if it cannot be shown that he has broken the law of the land, he can be presumed to have "counter-revolutionary" intentions.

This fact of the double standard is all too often not clear to the individual who is asked to sign, for example, an amnesty appeal. He reads the words of the appeal and takes them to mean what they would mean about justice and injustice if he himself, with his Magna Carta frame of reference, used them in like context.

Countless instances of the double standard might be marshaled to show how it works; but we must content ourselves with one contrast. The July 1953 issue of *Political Affairs* carried a statement by the National Committee of the CPUSA on *The Rosenbergs: Heroes of Democracy*. It offered no evidence. It simply declared the case to be a "plot" based on "a fantasy created by the FBI"; and went on to say (pp. 3–4):

"The truth about the 'why and wherefores' of this frame-up must be brought to the labor movement which should be shown that behind the Rosenberg frame-up stood the worst enemies of all labor; that if the Rosenbergs could be framed 'as spies,' then any labor or militant worker can be framed."

A few months earlier, however, in the February issue,

Political Affairs had featured an article on *The Prague Treason Trials*, by Klement Gottwald, Chairman of the Communist Party of Czechoslovakia. Again, the stand was categorical. This time, however, those brought to trial *in a Communist court* were labeled as part of "the American fifth column" and the summary legal proceedings were praised for having put an end to "the murderous back-stabbing of this traitorous gang." To emphasize further the "correctness" of the trial, it was said to be like those which Stalin had conducted in the mid-thirties against "the Trotskyite-Bucharinite gang"—and which Khrushchev, in 1956, was to expose as having been frame-ups of the first order.

The CPUSA is not inconsistent in thus applying a double standard: not according to the Marxist-Leninist theory of the State. It is wholly consistent: it *never* bothers about objective evidence. Its verdict is reached, simply and directly, by reference to the "class" character of the court and the defendant. If we hold this pattern in mind, we have a key to a multitude of seeming contradictions in the Party's attitude toward law and government.

We have a key, for example, to the consistent inconsistency with which the CPUSA has taught its members how to flout the law, how to destroy the respect which the "masses" have for the law, and how to demand for themselves every legal safeguard.

Highly instructive, in this connection, is a pamphlet called *Under Arrest! How to Defend Yourself in Court! What to Do When Arrested and Questioned!* This pamphlet dates from the early years of the depression, when the Party thought that the revolution was in sight. It was drawn up by the International Labor Defense (ILD) and distributed on a mass basis, at five cents a copy, by the *Labor Defender*, New York City. The *Foreword*, explaining the reason for the publication, assumes the class struggle to be reaching a point of crisis and quotes Helene Stasova, International Secretary of the ILD, to the effect that it is therefore "necessary to follow the example of czarist times." Party members are instructed to study the pamphlet in detail and thus prepare themselves "to give leadership to workers on what to do when arrested and questioned, and how to defend themselves in the courts of capitalist class justice."

The pamphlet states categorically that the government's tactics in dealing with "class-conscious workers" will be those of terrorism and frame-up. The Party is instructed to get this fact across to the mass of workers *in advance of any particular struggle,* because "it is necessary to destroy the illusions that workers have concerning courts and court procedures generally. . . .

"The class struggle goes on in the court room as it does on the picket line, in the shops, and in the mines."

The worker must further be taught that "the real charge against him will not appear in the complaint. The worker is brought into capitalist courts only because of his working class activities, and the charge against him is only the legal frame-up of the capitalist courts."

After this Marxist-Leninist analysis of the "class" character of all legal procedures in the United States, specific instructions are given on how the "class-conscious worker" must conduct himself if he is arrested and questioned. No matter what he has done, he must never acknowledge guilt. He must remember, always, that the arresting officer is "a servant of the boss class" and an "enemy." Therefore: *"Give him no information of any kind whatsoever, either about yourself or your fellow workers, or any organization which you belong to, or in which you are interested.*

"Give no information in the police station where you are brought by the arresting officer and booked. . . . *And if*

*you are a foreign-born worker, no information of any sort, of
the date you landed, the name of the boat, etc."*

Beyond this, the Party member is told to make the courtroom his forum:

"Bring out the class issues at the trial. In most cases
the judge and prosecutor will try to evade the class character
of the case. . . .

"Expose the method of selecting jury-panels. . . . Make
a demand for a new panel. . . .

"Of course, the judge will deny this challenge. Yet this
motion will make a profound effect upon all present, especially the workers, before whom the court will at once stand
exposed as the bosses' tool for the suppression of the working class. . . .

"At the time of sentence, the judge or clerk will ask, 'What
have you to say why sentence should not be pronounced
upon you?' Take advantage of this opportunity. . . . Point
out that your 'crime' has been that you were fighting for
your class. . . . You should also state that workers expect
no justice in a capitalist court."

In order to provide a responsive audience for this "forum,"
Party members should not only be present in considerable
numbers wherever a "vanguard" worker is being tried but
should pack the courtroom with rank-and-file workers who
need to be "educated."

The pamphlet contains more than thirty pages of tight-
packed instruction—on how to stall legal procedures, create
confusion in the courtroom, plant strategic doubts in the
public mind, put forth the Marxist-Leninist concept of law,
"prove" the class bias of the court by statements which can
be disproved—if at all—only by long digressions, and, not
least, demand every right and safeguard provided by the
law of the land.

The only reason why such a "dated" document cannot be

relegated to the past and forgotten is that the methods it spells out have, with minor variations, been used to the limit in every court case down to the present where Communists have been defendants. Far from being obsolete, in fact, these methods have been continually developed and brought up to date. Nowadays, for example, members are encouraged to resign from the Party for the duration of a trial or a hearing in order to be able to swear that they are not members.

Unless we are willing to accept the Party thesis that no proletarian is ever guilty of a crime for which he can justly be brought to trial in an American court of law, we need to understand what judges are up against when they have to handle cases involving Communists. They are—in terms that have repeatedly been spelled out by the Party itself in the form of "instructions"—up against an organized conspiracy to obstruct legal procedures and to destroy public confidence in these procedures.

It is in the theory of the State, once more, that we find the rationale of one of Lenin's basic edicts: namely, that Communists in non-Communist countries must maintain both a legal and an illegal apparatus. They must be able to work in the open—through a legal Party, where this is allowed, and through as many fronts as possible—in order to give "vanguard" leadership to the masses and to "politicalize" their struggles. But also they must be able to work in the underground, carrying on activities that are patently outside the law of the land but that are called for by the long-range purpose and "monolithic unity" of the world Communist movement. Such double organization, Lenin specified, is necessary in any "bourgeois" country—which is to say, any "enemy" country—just as it was necessary for the Bolsheviks in Tsarist Russia.

The CPUSA has always—or, at least, since it first affiliated with the Comintern—maintained the requisite double apparatus. Between 1920 and 1935, it scarcely bothered to conceal its double character; for, during those years, it was always seeing the revolution just ahead. Thus, we have only to turn to early issues of *The Communist*—forerunner of *Political Affairs*—to read the record of legal and illegal organization. The October 1921 issue, for example, states without equivocation, "The center of gravity of our activities is not fixed. It is constantly shifting; sometimes in the direction of the legal organization, sometimes in the direction of the underground organization. This center of gravity is at all times determined by the ever-changing realities of the actual class struggle." (8)

An equally frank statement appears in the July 1922 issue: "A truly revolutionary [i.e. Communist] party can never be 'legal' in the sense of having its purpose harmonize with the purpose of the laws made by the capitalist state. . . . Hence, to call a Communist party 'legal' means that its existence is tolerated by the capitalist state." (9) The article then goes on to say that since the "legal" political party thus exists by "enemy" tolerance, the revolutionary cause can never be entrusted to it alone.

As late as 1934, the Manifesto of the Eighth Convention of the CPUSA said that, in view of the "growing danger of illegality," the Party must tighten its discipline, combat spies, and "insure the secret functioning of the factory nuclei."

Since 1935, however—because of "the ever-changing realities of the actual class struggle"—open acknowledgments of the underground Party are almost non-existent. Two factors appear to account for their having vanished from the Party press. The first is the increase in governmental controls. The second is the policy of broad united fronts. Each of these has in its own way recommended the Party's appearing to be a strictly legal organization.

In 1953, therefore, we find the National Committee of the CPUSA stating: "All Americans have every reason to be alarmed by this talk of a Communist 'underground.' Where else but in fascist countries is there talk of a Communist 'underground?'

"By 'underground' they mean any and all attempts to protect democratic rights from unconstitutional, illegal and undemocratic police state invasion. . . .

"What is needed is to abolish the secret political police in the U.S." (10)

This tone of high indignation has become fairly typical of the CPUSA in recent years. It has been employed to brand as a "myth" the Party's subservience to the Soviet Union. It has been employed to state: "The Communist Party . . . has never advocated, nor does it advocate today, the overthrow of our government by force and violence. . . .

"The slander of 'conspiracy' aimed against the Communist Party ignores the clear truth that the Party bases its opinions and acts on real social conditions, on the real needs of the people and the nation as they develop objectively in the real world." (11)

The tone of high indignation, however, does not erase the record. Neither does it conceal the fact that the Party is still in good standing with the Soviet Union—which is equivalent to saying that the underground is still in good working order.

The United States is by no means alone in having to cope with the problems attendant upon the legal-illegal operations of the Party. Every non-Communist country in the world faces the same problems—and deals with them as it thinks best. But no country has solved them.

In all Central American and many South American countries, for example, the Communist Party has been outlawed. This policy has markedly reduced the number of card-carrying members and also the Party's open contact with the "masses," but has by no means put an end to its activities. These have been carried on without interruption by the underground Party and by front organizations.

To go to the opposite extreme, the Communist Parties of France and Italy have been open and legal, enjoying all the prerogatives of normal political parties. Both, as a result, have large card-carrying memberships—the Italian Party being the largest in the world outside the Communist orbit. Their enjoyment of legal status, however, has in nowise reduced their antagonism to the going order or made them reluctant to exploit their privileges. On the contrary, these Parties have served as major outlets to the free world for each new Soviet line. We recall, for example, that it was Duclos, high-ranking French Communist, who was assigned the task of conveying to the Parties around the world the Moscow edict that war-time "Browderism"—collaborationism—was at an end. He was able to handle the task with maximum ease precisely because he could move back and forth through the Iron Curtain without restraint.

The plain fact is that the embracing problem eludes definitive solution. It is, as Nehru has pointed out to the Parliament of India, the problem of consistent Soviet intervention in the internal affairs of other countries by the device of having in these countries resident "native" Parties that do its bidding. Nehru was speaking about a particular instance: about the fact that the USSR's demand that Yugoslavia adhere strictly to the Soviet line was reflected in India by an immediate effort on the part of the Communist Party to disrupt that country's friendly relations with Yugoslavia. (12) What he said, however, goes far beyond a single instance.

It testifies to the fact that the whole non-Communist world has on its hands a problem that cannot be solved by any means yet devised, but that is going to have to be knowledgeably lived with for a long time to come. The point that Nehru made is one for us to recall to mind whenever the Communists insist—as they repetitiously do—that only the Western "imperialists" intervene in the affairs of other countries.

All this would suggest that when we exercise our "eternal vigilance" in behalf of liberty under law, we would do well to include the Communists among those who need to be watched. We would do ill to let them tell us the direction which our vigilance should take. This direction must be determined by our own democratic standards.

It suggests, in the second place, that a new tone of thoughtfulness and of honest perplexity is called for in our discussions—and mutual disagreements—about how and whether the activities of the CPUSA should be restrained by law.

The *Statement* of the National Committee of the CPUSA from which we have quoted above has this further word to say: ". . . it is impossible for any hysterical group of imitation-fascists to outlaw the ideas or the influence of the Communist Party." Ignoring the slur about "imitation-fascists," we can accept this as true. While we may achieve, in time, a far more seasoned body of legislation than we have at present for the restraint of conspiracy without the restraint of legitimate freedom, we will still not have outlawed "the ideas or the influence of the Communist Party." We as citizens, therefore, must equip ourselves to do *by understanding* what cannot be done *by law*. We must come to know the tactics of "legal" illegality too well to be deceived by them.

As for Communist "ideas"—perhaps our best safeguard,

here, is to realize deeply that as long as the CPUSA holds fast to the divisive Marxist-Leninist theory of the State and, in behalf of this theory, seeks to set class against class, it is *outside the law* whether or not it is proclaimed *illegal.* For no member of the Party can repeat in good faith the *Preamble* to that Constitution which we regard as the supreme law of our land:

"We, the people of the United States, in order to form a more perfect Union, establish justice, insure domestic tranquility, provide for the common defense, promote the general welfare, and secure the blessings of liberty to ourselves and our posterity. . . ."

This is a document for the overspanning and harmonizing of differences and disagreements, and for the affirmation of common stakes; not for the arbitrary dividing of mankind into warring classes.

PART THREE

WHAT ARE THE STAKES?

FIFTEEN

THIS SIDE OF THE PLANET

THE SECOND meeting of the Cominform, we recall, launched in 1949 that "People's Front for Peace" which still serves as the focal theme of Communist agitation and propaganda. It is instructive to explore, in the light of this fact, the 1949–1950 issues of the journal of the Cominform, *For a Lasting Peace, For a People's Democracy!* Before we have read far, we become aware that the journal is punctuated with a curious series of militant declarations. Emanating from Communist Parties inside and outside the orbit, and singularly uniform in tone, these are more than affirmations of friendship for the Soviet Union as the leader of the "peace forces." They are blank-check pledges to support the Soviet Union in the event of war.

It would appear, in short, that the journal of the Cominform was not, as it claimed to be, simply an organ "for the exchange of experience" among Communist Parties "fraternally" related to one another. It served a purpose remarkably akin to that served by the "conditions of affiliation" of the old Comintern. That is to say, it bound the Communist Parties of the world to accept *in advance* the thesis that the Soviet Union's cause in any future war would be so "righteous"—so unmistakably the people's cause—as to justify their working against the governments of their own countries, if need be, and serving *as extraterritorial outposts of the USSR.*

Such pledges of support, moreover, were peculiarly explicit and uniform in declarations from Communist leaders and Parties in the Western Hemisphere. Thus, we read, in the issue of March 15, 1949: "At its recent meeting, the Executive Committee of the Communist Party of Argentina declared that the Party would do everything to secure the victory of the Soviet Union if a third world war should break out. The Party called for an anti-imperialist front in the Western Hemisphere."

The same issue reports Dionisio Ensina, General Secretary of the Mexican Communist Party, to the effect that a common front would be formed in Mexico "in the near future, uniting all elements who are determined to oppose any imperialist war which the United States and Great Britain may unleash against the USSR."

A month later, in the issue of April 15, Cuba is brought into the picture by means of a quotation from Carlos Rafael Rodriguez, a member of the Party's Executive Committee. This declares that the "progressive forces of Latin America" must ally themselves with "the forces of the anti-imperialist camp, headed by its glorious vanguard, the USSR!"

Ricardo Fonseca, then General Secretary of the Communist Party of Chile, comes next, in the issue of June 1: "The people of Chile will never fight against the Soviet Union, the bulwark of peace and democracy, the defender of the oppressed and dependent peoples."

So the statements are added one to another. On August 4,

1950, the quote is from Eugenio Gomez, General Secretary of the Communist Party of Uruguay. He reports that the Party's Fifteenth Congress has "approved with great enthusiasm" a declaration adopted a month earlier by its Executive Committee. This "says that 'fighting against imperialism, we Communists will always, under all circumstances, be on the side of the Soviet Union.'"

Luis Carlos Prestes, General Secretary of the Communist Party of Brazil, says his say in the issue of September 1, 1950: "The Brazilian people will never take any part in any aggressive war and particularly in a war against the Soviet Union—the bulwark of peace and Socialism."

So much for sample statements from Latin America. The Communist party in Canada, however—the Labour Progressive Party—was not a dissenter. Its declaration is carried in the same issue as those of Argentina and Mexico: "We are fighting to prevent Canada from being drawn into war. That is why we are against Canada signing the North Atlantic military pact. . . .

"The Labour Progressive Party opposes the attempt of the imperialists to smash Socialism by war."

After reading enough such statements, we can scarcely help asking, "What goes on here?" One fact is obvious: namely, that when the Soviet Union cries havoc every time the Western nations set up a plan for mutual defense, it does so for reasons of agitation and propaganda, not for reasons of principle. For not only has it bound, or tried to bind, every nation in the Communist orbit to support it in the event of war, but it has similarly bound outpost Parties around the world—and more than a few of them in the Western Hemisphere.

A second fact is scarcely less obvious: the line set forth in the declarations of these outpost Parties is identical with that which has been made familiar to us by endless articles in the Communist press in the United States. The CPUSA, struggling to preserve its status as a legal party, does not now militantly declare that it would support the Soviet Union in case of war. It adheres to the line, however, on all other counts; and it dropped out of the Comintern, we remember, only to evade the provisions of the "so-called Voorhis Act."

The declarations made by Communist Parties of Latin America sound so much, in fact, like an echo of something we have heard before that they send us back to a statement made by Alex Bittelman, in 1935, when the CPUSA was less guarded in its words than it has since become: ". . . the Soviet Union is the only fatherland of the workers and toilers the world over, whose major international task is to seek the defeat of the enemies of the Soviet Union." (1)

We doubt that Bittelman would make that statement in public print today. But he himself is still a member of the Party and apparently in good standing; and the Party appears to be in good standing with the Soviet Union. It was so, at least, we must judge, in 1949–1950. For during those years, sixteen articles in *For a Lasting Peace, For a People's Democracy!* either commented favorably upon activities of the CPUSA or quoted directly from *Political Affairs* and the *Daily Worker*. Meanwhile, in 1949 alone, *Political Affairs* reprinted, in whole or part, six articles which had first appeared in the Cominform's journal.

To bring this picture of relationships up to date, we can note that William Z. Foster, in 1957, stated that "practically every Communist Party in the world now proclaims its own specific national road to Socialism," but then added this revealing sentence: "The XXth Congress of the Communist Party of the Soviet Union, in February of last year, put its stamp of approval upon this flexibility." (2) Thus, we can conclude that we still have in our midst the strange phenomenon of a Party which claims all the prerogatives of a normal American political party but which must have a Soviet "stamp of approval" upon its "independence."

When we ask, in short, "What goes on here?"—*here* being the Western Hemisphere—we can reasonably make two assumptions. The first is that the Communist Parties of North, Central and South America are unanimous in their basic allegiance to the Soviet Union—the CPUSA being no exception. The second—based on their own declarations—is that these Parties form a *network* of allegiance: or, as they put it, "an anti-imperialist front."

Even this much realization of what is going on may move us to pay unaccustomed attention to our own hemisphere. As a people, we have tended—when we have looked beyond our own shores—to fix our eyes on events in Europe and to feel "well informed" to the extent that we know what is taking place there. In recent years, we have begun to school ourselves to appraise, also, events in Asia, and even in Africa; and to get rid of certain emotional "blind spots" which have distorted our image of these continents. Yet we have largely continued to ignore our own side of the planet.

There seem to have been two curious and conflicting reasons for this neglect. On the one hand, we have felt that *all is well:* that our country is rendered secure within the hemisphere by the Monroe Doctrine and the common heritage and mutual friendship we have enjoyed with Canada. On the other hand, we have felt that *all is confusion:* that Latin American affairs are marked by so many cross currents, and are so prone to revolutionary change without notice, that it is scarcely worth while to learn today what may be obsolete tomorrow.

If we are not to pay, in the end, a disastrously high price

for our long indifference to hemisphere affairs, we must begin to realize that all is *not* well and all is *not* confusion. All
is not well because the Soviet Union has established what
we might call an anti-Monroe Doctrine, and has done so by
means of outpost Parties which elude all traditional controls.
All is not well, moreover, because our own lack of interest
and comprehension has tended to create in every Latin
American country—and even, to some extent, in Canada—
a vacuum to be filled by Communist agitation and propaganda directed against the United States.

On the other hand, all is not confusion. Every country in
the hemisphere is, through its discontents and political struggles, showing itself to be part of the most dramatic movement of our century: the world-wide movement of under-
developed countries into a modern state of independent
competence. If we have a sympathetic understanding of this
movement *anywhere on earth,* we can make sense enough
out of what is going on in our own hemisphere to make
order out of confusion in our own minds.

Communism in the Western Hemisphere, as in Asia and
Africa, is exploiting legitimate hopes and hungers; and is
trying, as in Asia and Africa, to condition the "masses" to
regard the United States as their archenemy. There is even
evidence, we might note in passing, that the sense of common stakes which is progressively uniting all backward
countries is inclining Latin American Communists to seek
guidance from Red China as well as from the Soviet Union.
While the basic line is set by the USSR, it appears likely
that Red China—because of its timely experience in organizing pre-industrial "masses"—may play an increasing role in
the training of leaders.

In the swiftly spinning world of the past dozen years, certain centripetal forces have pulled the countries of North,
Central, and South America into closer, firmer unity. Chief

among these have been a growing economic interdependence and a growing awareness of the need for mutual defense. At the same time, however, certain centrifugal forces
have tended to pull these countries apart. The instability of
various political regimes; a rapid growth in population; economic developments which, in many areas, have meant both
the breaking of old habit patterns and the emergence of new
hopes faster than they could be satisfied: all these have
created pressures, tensions, and frictions.

In particular, they have fostered in Latin America a growing resentment toward the United States. We are charged
with colonialism and imperialism; and certain of our past
and even present policies make us vulnerable enough to
these charges that we are blamed far beyond our guilt
when discontent is seeking an object, or misery an explana-
tion for its own being, or when hope is seeking a reason for
its own lack of fulfillment. We are blamed for all the factors
—native as well as imported—which have kept the Latin
American countries from developing their own secure patterns of political freedom and economic well-being.

The Communist effort can be briefly defined as an effort—
carried on jointly by all the Parties of North, Central, and
South America—*to dissipate the centripetal forces and in-
tensify the centrifugal forces in hemisphere relationships.*

Even though statistics have a way of turning into just so
much inert matter in our minds, certain figures here become
necessary. Without them, we cannot feel the size or sub-
stance of the "anti-imperialist front" which the Communists
are working to establish throughout the hemisphere. The
latest figures we have been able to secure date from 1956.
They must, therefore, be taken as approximate. Yet so far
as an understanding of the situation is concerned, they are
not, we think, outmoded.

In 1956, then, the population of South America was 45

million less than that of the United States. The *Communist* population of that continent, however, was 225,000—or more than ten times that of the United States. To put the matter another way, there was one Communist for every 500 persons in South America, as against one for every 9,440 in our own country—the membership here being, at that time, around 20,000. The figure we have for Canada—35,000—is disproportionately high because it embraces both card-carrying members and active collaborators. Taking the hemisphere whole—including the West Indies—Communist membership appears to have been in the neighborhood of 300,000.

Taking the hemisphere whole is a good key phrase for us to keep in mind; for it would be hard for us to find anywhere else on earth as many different countries bound into a cohesive pattern of Communist agitation and propaganda. All the Parties, for example, are working to infiltrate labor organizations and intellectual and student groups, to win key posts in transportation and communication industries—and, where these are important, in mining industries. All of them are trying to get a strategic hold on enterprises in which the United States has a vital interest of investment or need—disrupting these, wherever possible, by strikes and "protest demonstrations" and preparing to sabotage them in the event of war. All are portraying our foreign-aid programs as disguised imperialism, and joint plans for hemisphere defense as efforts on the part of the United States to "browbeat" weaker countries into pulling its chestnuts out of the fire. All, of course, are representing the Soviet Union as the "bulwark of peace and democracy."

In another sense, also, the hemisphere has to be taken *whole* as a theater of Communist operations. From the Arctic Ocean to the Antarctic the land mass stretches; and there is not a national boundary from north to south that can be definitely closed against illegal passage. Over this whole vast territory, moreover, only four major languages are spoken: English, Spanish, Portuguese in Brazil, and French in French Canada. Whether, then, his base of operations is in Canada or in Argentina, in the United States or in Mexico or in Paraguay, the Communist on an underground mission can say, in the words of the Ancient Mariner, "I pass, like night, from land to land."

This strategic *wholeness* of the hemisphere as viewed by Communist leaders is something for us to bring into the forefront of our minds whenever we are tempted to think that some 10,000 Party members in our own country—or some 3,000 in Bolivia, or 5,000 in Ecuador, or 1,000 in Guatemala, or 35,000 in Chile, or 40,000 in Argentina—are so vastly outnumbered by the non-Communists that they can do little harm.

Also, however, certain countries call for special attention. It is important for us to realize, for example, that Brazil is regarded by the Soviet Union as the leader of the Latin-American Communist movement; for this fact throws significant light on the intensity of the "anti-imperialist" drive in that country. Although the Party was outlawed there in 1947, it is currently estimated to have between 100,000 and 130,000 members. Active sympathizers, moreover, run to ten times this number. The program which the Brazilian Party adopted in 1954 has been specifically endorsed by the Soviet Union as a model for the Parties in other Latin American countries. The central thesis of this program is the need to establish "democratic fronts of national liberation" to combat United States "imperialism." Translated into non-Communist language, this means that the Party is setting itself to exploit native movements of both discontent and hope and to cast the United States as the one prime agent of misery and frustration.

Communist strength, in Brazil, is in organized labor—particularly in the large urban unions; and in front organizations designed to reach intellectuals, students, and women. Also, however, there is disturbing evidence that pro-Communist elements within the Brazilian army are large enough that they, together with guerilla forces commanded by the Party itself, would constitute a real danger in the event of national crisis.

The movement in Mexico likewise invites attention—if only because of the strategic proximity of this country to the United States and the virtual impossibility of really sealing the long border against a two-way passage of Communist agents and Communist-inspired materials.

Figures, here, become highly misleading. The Mexican Party was said to have, in 1956, some 5,000 card-carrying members, and to be directing the activities of some 15,000 persons through front organizations. Communist *strength* in Mexico, however, appears to be misrepresented rather than represented by these numbers. For some observers—persons not given to exaggerated judgments—estimate that the Communist and pro-Communist elements which might be fused by strong "vanguard" leadership would total more than 100,000; and an effort to build up such leadership is in progress. It appears, for example, that a group of Mexican Communists went to the Soviet Union in 1956 for intensive training; and that the Soviet Union has been stepping up, in recent years, both financial aid to pro-Communist groups in Mexico and guidance in the field of propaganda.

The temper of the movement is well indicated by a statement which was made by A. B. Magil, of the CPUSA, when he was heading this Party's Commission on Latin-American Affairs: ". . . the same winds are blowing in Mexico as elsewhere in Latin America—winds that bode no good for the master in the big house across the river." (3) We ourselves need to know the direction and force of these winds—in Mexico and elsewhere—and how they are being fanned by Communist agitation and propaganda.

Any movement that seeks to alienate Canada from the United States, and to sow distrust between our two countries, must be viewed with concern. The activities of the Communist party—the Labour Progressive Party—in Canada hold our attention, also, because they reveal with unusual clarity certain patterns that prevail throughout the hemisphere, wherever the Communists are at work. They represent a direct and concerted attack upon the centripetal forces—economic interdependence and programs of mutual defense—which tend to unify North, Central, and South America.

The key fact from which the Communists start their agitation and propaganda—in Canada, as in Latin America—is the simple and obvious one that the United States is, by all odds, the strongest country in the hemisphere. Starting from this fact, the Party works to implant and exploit the idea that *having strength* is equivalent to *taking advantage of weakness.*

Thus, every economic relationship is interpreted as one in which the United States, by open or disguised pressure, comes out on the long end of the bargain. Economic relationships in their totality, moreover, are interpreted as a means by which the United States gradually encroaches upon the legitimate sovereignty of other countries and usurps control over their affairs—exploiting their resources and reducing them to a state of dependence.

Programs of mutual defense are similarly interpreted. The degree to which Canada and the United States have, in recent years, united their defense efforts has caused some concern on the part of many Canadians who are by no means Communists. The basis of this concern is the fact that the joint plan for the defense of the "northern roof" of Canada calls for an unusual amount of activity, on Canadian soil, by armed forces of the United States.

Here, it would seem, the sheer practicalities of the situation have been the determining factor. In territory, Canada is the second largest country in the world. Only the Soviet Union is larger. A significant portion of this territory—virtually uninhabited—has become peculiarly vulnerable in the air age. Yet the population of Canada is so relatively small —about one-tenth that of the United States—that armed forces sufficient to defend this northern roof could not possibly be assembled. The term "wide open spaces" applies to Canada, perhaps, more accurately than to any other country on earth. For with all its vast territory, 90 per cent of the population lives within two hundred miles of the border; 60 per cent of it within the two provinces of Ontario and Quebec.

The basic interests of both Canada and the United States obviously recommend, therefore, a joint plan of defense. To call this plan *necessary,* however, is not the same thing as calling it, in all its aspects, *palatable;* and the Communists have set themselves to make it thoroughly unpalatable. One of the Canadian Communist leaders, Tim Buck, has set forth the line in sufficient detail for us to see exactly what it is: He states that the mutual defense efforts of Canada and the United States should be recognized by all Canadians as an effort on the part of the United States to establish military bases from which to launch an aggressive war against the USSR. He predicts that Canada will not only become an "occupied country" but will be destroyed by "rocket-borne atomic bombs" unless it becomes aware of the "imperialist" intentions of the United States and calls a halt to the mutual defense program. (4)

It is this Communist line, we might note, which gives meaning to the declaration of the Labour Progressive Party which we have already quoted from *For a Lasting Peace, For a People's Democracy!*: "We are fighting to prevent Canada from being drawn into war. . . .

"The Labour Progressive Party opposes the attempt of the imperialists to smash Socialism by war."

This general picture of Communists in action in the Western Hemisphere serves as a background against which we can locate in perspective many different items of news.

The winter of 1957–1958, for example, brought one report after another that the Communists were preparing to foment large-scale labor troubles throughout Latin America. On December 14, 1957, the President of El Salvador read to the people of that country a warning that a Communist plan "is to be undertaken in 1958 consisting of a movement of strikes, demonstrations of protest, and other actions of similar nature"—including, he anticipated, sabotage and assault. Shortly before that, the Minister of Government in Ecuador had issued a like warning that a "major Communist labor offensive" was being organized. To support his statement, he offered as evidence a "directive" which had seemingly originated with Vicente Lombardo Toledano of Mexico, leader of the powerful Confederation of Latin American Workers (CTAL). This "directive," he stated, was being sent to all labor unions and affiliates of the Confederation throughout Latin America; and it placed major emphasis on the acquiring of information about American enterprises and about transportation systems.

Items of a different but related sort also fit into the picture. As part of the current Soviet effort, for example, to disrupt trade relations between Latin America and the United States—and to divert trade to the Communist bloc—

we can take note of a Spanish-language broadcast which Moscow Radio beamed at Latin America in the spring of 1958. This broadcast pictured the recession in the United States as "inevitably" destined to become a major depression; and it warned that "U.S. monopolist circles" were planning "on unloading the burden of their economic difficulties onto the shoulders of their southern neighbors." Increased trade relations with the Communist bloc, on the other hand, "would enable Latin America to improve its present economic situation and free itself from economic dependence on foreign monopolies."

In August 1953, William Z. Foster published in *Political Affairs* an article called "The Explosive Situation in Latin America." In certain key sentences, this article both indicates the Communist line with reference to Latin America and—if we have our wits about us and our sense of values in good working order—poses a challenge to ourselves:

"Conditions are fast ripening in Latin America for a revolutionary, anti-imperialist upheaval. . . .

"During the past couple of years there has been growing a renaissance of the anti-imperialist, national-liberation movement . . . primarily directed against the leading imperialist aggressor, the United States. . . .

"One of the first necessities . . . is for the Left and progressive movements in the United States to get better acquainted with what is taking place . . . and then to make this information known far and wide among the masses. Here the Marxist press has the definite duty to act as the vanguard. . . .

"Our Party must realize what is happening in Latin America and fall into step with the vital mass movement which is there taking shape."

The Communists are not the only ones who "must realize

what is happening." Unless the rest of us can develop an informed and sympathetic awareness both of events and of the anxieties and hopes that inspire these, the Soviet Union actually may experience in the Western Hemisphere a dangerous measure of the triumph which it proclaims to be certain.

It need not experience this triumph, however. We have it within our power to effect a different outcome. Communism—unlike nature—does not "abhor a vacuum." It thrives on finding vacuums to fill. Wherever practical conditions and human hopes in Latin America have markedly changed, without our having changed our habits of thought and our political and economic policies, vacuums are created between the two. Only we can prevent these from becoming an asset to the world Communist movement; and we can do so only by so bringing our minds and policies into contact with Latin American realities that the gap is closed.

Most people in our own country, for example, still have little awareness of the extent to which the economic interdependence of North and South America is now *mutual*. Accustomed to think of the United States as virtually self-sufficient, they feel that Latin American countries need us more than we need them. This has become a dangerous illusion, as a few key figures may suggest. Between 1936 and 1952, United States imports of raw materials and manufactured goods increased by 70 per cent; but our imports from Latin America increased 140 per cent. Since 1950, trade between the United States and Latin America has averaged more than $3,000,000,000 annually *each way*. The United States has been absorbing 80 per cent of the copper output of Latin America, 70 per cent of its lead and zinc, 17 per cent of its crude oil, and more than 60 per cent of its wool.

Obviously, this trade has been vital to Latin America. But it has also been vital to ourselves. We have not bought these

products in order to "do good to" these "backward" countries. What we have bought has become an integral part of
our standard of living. If the Soviet Union is able to persuade South America that a diversion of its exports from
the United States to the Communist orbit would give it better safeguards than we have offered against "imperialism" in
general and the effects of "regression" in particular, where
do we plan to secure our future resources of necessary materials?

What holds good in the field of trade holds good, also, in
the area of mutual defense. The United States is obviously
much stronger than any one Latin American country; or
any combination of several. But does this mean that we
will know how to deal *with the South American continent
as a whole* if the Soviet Union is able to infect it *as a whole*
with its anti-Monroe Doctrine?

These are questions that call for realistic and creative answers. As we learn to come to terms with them, we will be
learning also how to bring about in the Western Hemisphere
a unity of freedom and of economic development good for
all the people on our side of the planet. Such unity, moreover—by what it would prove about the fact that freedom
and economic progress belong together—would be good for
the other side of the planet, also.

SIXTEEN

THE SHADOW OF EMPIRE

WHEN IT turns out that certain writings of Marx and Engels are either altogether suppressed in the Soviet Union or published only in an expurgated form, and that the essays thus censored are those in which the two authors dealt specifically with Russian foreign policy, the question *Why?* becomes insistent.

Why is Marx's tract, *Herr Vogt*, which he wrote in 1860 on Russian-Polish relations, not allowed at large? Why has a second essay which he wrote on the same subject seven years later been similarly withheld from the public? Why did Stalin, in 1934, act to stop the re-issuing of an essay on Panslavism which Engels wrote in 1890? One Russian-language edition of their *Collected Works* contained a number of such essays—some of them dating back as far as the 1850s. Why has this particular edition been withdrawn from circulation?

Marx and Engels were writing about Tsarist, not Soviet, foreign policy. They were making a highly critical analysis of the very regime which the Bolsheviks later conspired to overthrow. On what possible grounds, then, have the Soviet leaders found this particular series of their essays so unpalatable as to call for strict censorship? The logical—or psychological—answer is best expressed, perhaps, in an old proverb: *He who wears the shoe knows where it pinches.*

No proverb says that he who walks as though his foot were pinched draws attention to the shoe he is wearing. Yet this also is true. What Marx and Engels wrote about Tsarist Russia becomes interesting as a commentary on the Soviet Union precisely because the Soviet leaders do not wish it to be read.

Marx wrote, in 1853, "One merely needs to replace a series of names and dates by others and it becomes clear that the policies of Ivan III (who ruled from 1462 to 1505) and those of Russia today are not merely similar but identical. Ivan, in turn, only perfected the traditional Muscovite policy which he inherited from Ivan I." This policy—marked by "intrigue, corruption, and secret usurpation"—became, in time, that "of Peter the Great, and it is that of present-day Russia."

He went on, then, to say that Peter the Great was the real inventor of modern Russian foreign policy; and that he had attained this role by making two changes in "the old Muscovite method of unnoticed penetration and annexation." He had "removed the purely local flavor" of this method and applied it to wider areas; and, "by forging it into an abstract formula," he had raised the pursuit of power within given limits to "an attempt to gain unlimited power."

In 1860, in *Herr Vogt,* he wrote that the Russians "had heavily equipped the fortresses of Warsaw, Modlin, and Ivangorod under the pretext that they were needed to keep Poland in check. Their true purpose was the complete strategic command of the Vistula region, the establishment of a base from which to carry an attack towards the north, the south, and the west."

Seven years later, appraising Tsarist strategy with respect to Poland, he observed, "The policy of Russia is changeless. . . . Its methods, its tactics, its maneuvers may change, but the polar star of its policy—world domination—is a fixed star."

Engels, meanwhile, was declaring the objective of Pan-slavism to be the setting up of a Slavic empire under Russian domination. Later, in that essay of 1890 which Stalin was at pains to suppress in 1934, he analyzed the permanent character of Russian foreign policy. Among the methods which he declared to be basic to this policy were deceit, bribery, and the exploitation of disunity—often, after having fomented this in the first place. All seeming changes in policy he saw as tactical: mere surface adjustments to shifting conditions. (1)

The picture thus drawn is not a pretty one. It is the very kind to make Tsarism stand condemned as a system no less ruthless in empire building than in its treatment of proletarians and peasants. Why, then, have the Soviet leaders suppressed these essays? Why have they not said to their own people and the world, "This is the sort of imperial policy that once existed in Russia—and that exists no more"? The answer seems evident: This is the kind of imperial policy that once existed in Russia—*and that still exists.* In 1958 as in 1853, "One merely needs to replace a series of names and dates by others and it becomes clear that the policies of Ivan III . . . and those of Russia today are not merely similar but identical."

They are not actually identical, of course. But on two counts they are fatefully similar. First, the "old Muscovite methods"—intrigue, deceit, the exploitation of disunity after first fomenting it, unnoticed penetration, secret usurpation—are all Soviet methods likewise; and, more broadly, Communist methods. It would appear that Lenin, working out his tactics of conspiracy, was more opposed to Tsarism *as an enemy power to be overcome than to Tsarist methods for overcoming enemies and extending its power.* In the second place, old Russia's traditional objective—world domination —is the Soviet objective, also.

It is never proclaimed to be such. Ostensibly, the one aim is to establish world-wide Communism. Yet Lenin, Stalin, and Khrushchev have all translated the fact that the Soviet Union was the "first homeland of Socialism" into a demand that all Communists adhere to the policies it lays down. It is to the Soviet Union that the Parties around the world pledge their support in the event of war; and the unanimity of viewpoint prescribed for all the countries of the Communist bloc is always a Soviet-inspired unanimity.

It seems doubtful that Lenin ever recognized that, in setting up the Comintern, he instituted a new form of imperialism. To the end of his life, we can assume, he anticipated that as Communist Parties triumphed by revolution in country after country, they would be related to one another *as equals.* The Soviet Union, however, was the focus of his intense concern. If a revolution had actually come anywhere else—in Yugoslavia, for example—he would have found it as hard, we can believe, to turn a theory of equality into the practice of it as Stalin and Khrushchev have found it.

In any event, Stalin and Khrushchev have clearly shown themselves to be empire-builders. From the time that Stalin proclaimed the doctrine of *Socialism in one country* down to Khrushchev's latest feud with Tito, the right of the Soviet Union to extend its power by all expedient means and to demand from all Communist Parties and nations a basic subservience to its will has been made to seem a natural if not a "divine" right. All non-Communist territories, meanwhile, are regarded as subject to future conquest: by intrigue, by the exploiting of disunity, by unnoticed penetration, by secret usurpation, and by "peaceful competition."

In view of this dual conversion of "old Muscovite methods" into Soviet methods and the old Russian objective of world domination into a Soviet objective, what is it that makes Communism so different from Tsarism as an imperial force? The answer lies in the area of theory. The difference between the two is the difference between the "abstract formula" by which Peter the Great extended the pursuit of limited power into the pursuit of unlimited power and the "science of Marxism-Leninism."

Here, certainly, we are dealing with one of the strangest paradoxes of history: the fact that the qualities in Russian policy which Marx and Engels regarded as altogether dangerous have been made incomparably more dangerous than they ever were in Tsarist Russia by being fused with the "scientific socialism" of Marx and Engels. It has been this theory—with its professed aim of establishing economic justice and a classless society—which has made countless otherwise honest individuals willing to apply the conspiratorial tactics of Tsarism-Leninism in behalf of the disguised imperial aspirations of the Soviet Union. It has been this theory, likewise—with its rigid dogma of the class struggle and the dictatorship of the proletariat—which has enabled the Soviet Party-State to rationalize *totalitarianism:* the exercise of total power over the total human being and the total structure of society.

During the forty years of its existence, the Soviet Union has practiced six kinds of imperialism and is currently learning the skills of a seventh.

The first might be called old-line imperialism: the taking over of other countries by force and the incorporation of them within its own domain. Here, the obvious example is the conquest, in 1940, of the Baltic states: Latvia, Estonia, and Lithuania. In this case, Stalin scarcely bothered about theory. Rather, he walked unabashedly in the footsteps of the Tsars. Their conception of the Russian empire had included the territory embraced by these states. His conception of the Soviet empire similarly included this territory. He was strong enough to take what he wanted. Therefore, he took it. Emperors and tyrants back through the centuries made up his "cloud of witnesses."

The brand of terrorism employed in these countries, however, had a *totalitarian,* not a Tsarist, efficiency. Incredible numbers of persons—designated as "anti-Soviet elements" —were transported to forced labor camps in the USSR. The minutely planned manner of their transfer came to light as a result of an uprising in Lithuania on June 23, 1941—after the outbreak of hostilities between the Nazis and the USSR. During this, certain instructions from Moscow to the persons in charge of the mass deportations were seized by the insurgents, and later channeled to the Allied powers. In June 1952, one of these documents was submitted by the United States government to the special United Nations Committee investigating forced labor. It has since been made part of a permanent collection in the Hoover Library at Stanford University.

The document is headed, Top Secret: *Instructions Concerning the Procedure of Deportation of Anti-Soviet Elements from Lithuania, Latvia, and Estonia.* The text begins: "The deportation of anti-Soviet elements from the Baltic republics is a problem of great political importance. . . . It must be borne in mind that operations must be accomplished without noise or panic so as to preclude outbreaks or other excesses by those scheduled for deportation or by those among the local populations known to be hostile to the Soviet regime."

This is followed by a set of minute instructions on matters ranging from how records are to be kept to the proper procedures to adopt if the deportees show resistance. The ethical level—as well as the chill efficiency—of the process is revealed by a section toward the middle of the document: "Since most of the deportees are to be arrested and placed in special prison camps and their families sent to special settlements in remote districts, it is necessary to remove the heads of families along with other members of the family without notifying them of their impending separation. . . .

"The whole family will be conveyed to the loading station on the same cart; only at the station will the head of the family be separated from the family and placed in a special car designated for the heads of families." (2)

As a second variety, the Soviet Union has practiced puppet-government imperialism. By this method, it has "liberated" into subservience to itself the "people's democracies" of Albania, Bulgaria, Roumania, Hungary, Poland, and Czechoslovakia. East Germany, also, of course, has a puppet government; as have the "people's republics" of Outer Mongolia, North Korea, and Vietminh.

No Tsar ever practiced the methods of intrigue, unnoticed penetration, and secret usurpation as skillfully as they were practiced by the Soviet Union, after World War II, in order to reduce the countries of East Europe to the status of satellites. In each instance, moreover—just in case these tactics should not prove sufficient—the Red Army was a visible threat.

Yet in terms of empire-building, not even the manner in which Stalin deprived these countries of their independent status is as important as what has been done to them since. Once having established its *political* control over them, through puppet regimes, the Soviet Union has proceeded with long-range programs of economic exploitation and cultural "Russification."

On the economic front, it has worked to make the satellites increasingly dependent upon itself and to destroy their capacity to operate as normal, balanced economies. To this end, it has employed seven basic methods. It has set up a system of trade treaties under which armaments are sent to the satellites by the USSR and are paid for by goods *at prices favoring the USSR,* so that the countries are never quite able to square their accounts. To make sure that the types of goods it most needs are available, it has skewed the productive systems of all the satellites—and of East Germany —so that no one of them can produce, in any balanced measure, what it needs itself; but each produces in exaggerated measure certain assigned types of goods. Again, it has brought the major industries of the satellites under binational corporations controlled by the USSR. In the fourth place, it has so manipulated loans to the satellites and has so assumed control of their banks that their currencies have been made dependent on the ruble. Fifth, the government in Moscow has appointed managers, advisers, and experts to take charge of the key industries of the satellites. Sixth, it has brought under its control all the agencies in the satellites which supervise the political reliability and efficiency of workers and managers alike. Finally, the Soviet Union "controls the trade of the satellites with the capitalist world and is the main buyer, seller, broker and clearing house of the entire Soviet empire." (3)

On the cultural front, the aim has been to alienate the new generation in each of the satellites from its own heritage and to effect its "Russification." The program has included even the rewriting of history books to be used in the schools, so that the students no longer have a chance to learn about the heroes of their own tradition or the dramatic events of their own people's history. Instead, they learn Communist ideology and a kind of history that plays up the role of the USSR in "liberating" their countries.

The program includes, also, the compulsory learning of Russian as a second language in all schools; the organization of intellectuals into Soviet Friendship Societies to popularize Soviet science and technology; and the blanketing of the satellites with films, plays, books, and music from the Soviet Union.

In connection with this type of empire-building it is significant to recall the orthodox Communist definition of a *nation* as this was worked out by Joseph Stalin. In his *Marxism and the National and Colonial Question,* which he wrote in 1913, Stalin said that a nation was "a historically evolved, stable community of people" with four essential characteristics: a common language, a common territory, a common economic life or "economic cohesion," and a common psychological make-up or "national character," this made manifest in a community of culture. What the Soviet Union has been setting itself to do in the satellite empire has been *to coerce into being* these four characteristics of a nation in a vast territory where they had not "historically evolved."

Khrushchev's determination to keep intact the satellite empire which Stalin built has been underscored again and again. During his tour of Hungary, for example, in April 1958, he scarcely bothered to preserve the fiction that the "liberated" countries enjoy self-determination. He told the Hungarian Communists flatly that they would have to prevent any recurrence of the 1956 uprising and that their own positions depended on their doing so; but he made it clear, likewise, that any "counter-revolutionary" action in any "Socialist country" would be put down by force. At Tatabanya, where a large audience remained sullen and silent, rather than warmly enthusiastic about his speech, he blurted out, "If you don't like my criticism, swallow it anyway and see that it does not leave a bitter taste in your mouth." (4)

In all his demands for Summit conferences, moreover, Khrushchev has stipulated that any agreement acceptable to the Soviet Union must involve the West's recognition of the *status quo*. It must, in brief, involve the free world's acceptance of the fact that 100,000,000 people are going to be kept in a state of vassalage whether they like it or not. It is this demand, we dare not forget, which underlies all the discussion about an agenda for a Summit conference.

The Soviet Union, bent on establishing itself in the eyes of the world, and particularly in the eyes of the backward countries, as a "peace-loving" nation, has had to provide itself with a basis *in Communist theory* for the kind of control it has exercised over the puppet states.

The first part of the rationalization again derives from Stalin's *Marxism and the National and Colonial Question:* "It should be borne in mind that besides the right of nations to self-determination there is also the right of the working class to consolidate its power, and to the latter right the right of self-determination is subordinate. There are occasions when the right of self-determination conflicts with the other, the higher right—the right of a working class that has assumed power to consolidate its power. In such cases—this must be said bluntly—the right to self-determination cannot and must not serve as an obstacle to the exercise by the working class of its right to dictatorship." (5)

To make this Stalinist analysis fit events—as in Hungary, in 1956—and justify intervention in the affairs of presumably "liberated" countries, it has been necessary only for the Soviet Union to interpret every form of resistance, every effort to exercise self-determination, as counter-revolution.

The second part of the rationalization stems from the

Soviet version of how the Communist orbit is politically organized. According to this, there exists a free association of independent republics. Within the association, however, there are two types of states. There is only one socialist state —the USSR; and there are a number of "people's democracies." These are "proletarian dictatorships," but they do not have a *soviet* pattern. Hence, by the yardstick of "scientific socialism," they are on a lower level of development than the Soviet Union. Nothing, therefore, could be more "natural" than for them to be "guided" by the Soviet Union until such time as they achieve their "socialist maturity": a condition which they can readily be kept from achieving. This is one of the neatest formulas ever developed for the rationalizing of empire.

Finland stands alone as an illustration of the Soviet Union's third tactic of imperialism: that of allowing a country to remain "independent"—on good behavior.

It looked for a while as though Poland might be moving toward a similar status. Gestures of independence are still occasionally made by the Poles. When, for example, in April 1958, all the other Soviet-bloc observers at the Seventh Congress of the Yugoslav League of Communists walked out in protest against Tito's "revisionism," the Polish Ambassador, Henryk Grouchulski, stayed in his place—and even applauded the offending speakers. Before a month had passed, however, Poland was officially joining in the denunciation of Tito for threatening the unity of the Communist orbit and thereby weakening the front against imperialism. Thus, there seems little likelihood of Poland's becoming "another Finland."

No one in the free world can give a conclusive reason why Finland has been permitted to maintain its peculiar status. Informed observers, however, suggest that the USSR has not

dared offend world opinion to the extent that an open conquest of Finland would involve; and that, moreover, it does
not think such open conquest to be necessary. It believes
that it can, by penetration, effect an eventual Communist
revolution inside Finland—thus bringing that country into
the orbit "by its own action."

For the time being, in any event, Finland has kept its
sovereignty. Its people enjoy the basic democratic freedoms.
There has been no major purge. The Soviet Union, after
taking western Karelia, has made no further territorial demands. The postwar elections of March 17–18, 1945, were
free elections; and the resulting Parliament was representative. When we consider that Finland was a defeated country
in 1945—having been allied with Germany during the war—
this measure of independence must be counted remarkable.

Why, then, do we bring Finland into the picture of
Soviet empire? There are two reasons. The first is that its
"free" newspapers—and its political figures—are exceedingly
careful not to offend the USSR. Their self-censorship makes
it clear that the country is independent only within limits;
and that its people are free from the terrors of a police state
only so long as they do not make an imprudent use of their
freedom.

The second reason is economic. On September 4, 1944,
Finland signed an armistice with the Soviet Union under
the terms of which it was to pay $300,000,000 in reparations
over an eight-year period: the bulk of this to be paid in
manufactured goods, and chiefly in light machinery of a
type which the Soviet Union needed to fill a gap in its own
heavy-industry program. The Finnish economy, at that time,
was not geared to produce this type of goods. Plants for the
turning out of light engineering products had to be set up
out of all proportion to the country's own long-range needs.

Just as in the satellites, in brief, the basic economy was skewed out of shape to serve Soviet purposes.

This skewing was not the kind that could be set straight as soon as the eight-year reparations period was over. The plants were durably there; and the people's livelihood was at stake in them. Yet neither the home market nor the broad world market could consume their output. Aside from the Soviet bloc—ideologically committed to putting heavy industry first—most countries that could use light machinery could also produce it, and were producing it. Thus, Finland —with its reparations paid off—was still dependent on the Soviet Union as the chief support of its industrial system. Politically sovereign, it comes very close to being an economic satellite.

The fourth imperial policy of the Soviet Union is that of demanding that all Communist-bloc countries, at all times and on all issues, present a united front to the non-Communist world. Here, Yugoslavia has been the chief thorn in its flesh. Khrushchev showed himself, early in his regime, to be determined to re-establish the friendship with Tito which Stalin had dramatically sacrificed in 1948—when Yugoslavia was expelled from the Cominform. Recent events, however, show that the old tensions are still present. The issue of "national Communism," as against "bloc Communism," is still far from resolved.

How far was made evident when Tito and his supporters, at the Seventh Congress of the Yugoslav League of Communists, not only reasserted the right of Yugoslavia to interpret Marxism-Leninism for itself but accused the Soviet Union of "revisionism" and declared the West and the Soviet Union to be equally responsible for the cold war.

When the Soviet observers stalked out, the "procession"

that followed was in its accustomed order—even though the Polish Ambassador did not march in it. Immediately behind the Soviet group came the observers from Red China; then those from the satellites, with the Roumanians last in line. This seems to be the established order of Communist-bloc entrance and exit at all major gatherings; and it is not without significance.

Red China's precedence over the East European countries is a reflection both of Khrushchev's need to preserve the unity of Asian and European Communism and of his awareness that this depends on Mao's being given a sufficient prestige. There is, in fact, no assurance that Mao will permanently accept second place. No one can do more than guess what the future holds for *empire by compelled cohesion;* for cohesion, in the case of Red China, cannot be compelled. It can only be assiduously sought, and preserved as long as possible.

In the fifth place, the Soviet Union has extended its empire by means of ideological outposts: the Communist Parties in non-Communist countries. According to the *Kommunist,* Moscow, October 1957, there are now sixty-two such Parties: eighteen in Europe; twenty in Latin America; ten in southeastern Asia; ten in the Near East, Middle East, and Africa; and one each in Canada, the United States, Australia, and New Zealand.

We have already indicated, with reference to the CPUSA and other Parties of the Western Hemisphere, how these ideological outposts serve the USSR. The important thing, at this point, is simply to emphasize the fact that the hard-core members of these Parties do not belong, intellectually and emotionally, to the countries in which they live. People "belong" to that which they voluntarily serve. On the testimony of their own words and actions, these Parties serve the Soviet Union *by doing whatever it says comes next on the agenda of the world Communist movement*. The Parties are never asked to serve an empire on the make; but in no instance has "what comes next" gone counter to the expansionist ambitions of the Soviet Union.

The sixth tactic for extending the empire has also been ideological rather than territorial. It has been the setting up of front organizations. Lenin called these "transmission belts," because they linked the Party to the masses. They might equally well be called bridges between the Party and the non-Communist world; for countless persons who would never have made the jump across the deep crevasse which divides their own cultural heritage from Communist theory and practice have made a step-by-step passage across by means of one or another front. One of the chief functions of all fronts has, in fact, been to recruit as spokesmen for the Communist line individuals who are too resistant to "monolithic unity" or too preoccupied with their own affairs to be useful Party members but who are enough at odds with their own society to welcome a chance to work for change by means other than those which it provides.

All fronts have thrived best where discontent and idealism have been coupled with political naïveté or with a "high-minded" scorn of practical politics. Thus, they have been more successful in the United States than in Europe; for the types of Europeans who are interested in promoting social change are more likely than are their American counterparts to have worked in *concrete political situations* rather than simply in nonpolitical voluntary groups. In the United States, they have been most successful among the uneducated, on the one hand, and, on the other, among highly educated idea-minded people who have never worked to achieve their social goals through the channels of practical politics.

Most of the international fronts, today, are making a special bid for adherents in Asia, Africa, and Latin America —both because of the importance which the Soviet Union attaches to the winning of these continents, and because they are areas where political inexperience is widespread among both the masses and the intellectuals.

One of the most successful of the international fronts has been the World Peace Council. Formed in 1948 to disseminate the Communist line with regard to "peace-loving" and "war-mongering" nations, it has been more able than most fronts to win the support of non-Communist pacifists, neutralists, internationalists, and Left-wing Socialists—who have tended to take at face value any chance offered them to "work for peace."

In spite of this particular type of success, however, the history of the WPC has been a stormy one. Its original headquarters were in Paris. But in 1951, the French Government expelled it for "fifth-column activities" and it moved to Prague. In 1954, it moved again—this time to Vienna where, under the conditions which then prevailed, the Soviet Union could give it protection. The Austrian Minister of the Interior bitterly protested its move, indicating that it had neither asked nor been given permission to set itself up in Vienna and stating flatly: "A sharp watch will be kept on the World Peace Council, for it has nothing to do with peace." When Austria regained its independence, the WPC was permitted to remain on condition that it obey the laws of the land; but on February 2, 1957, the Ministry of the Interior announced its expulsion on the grounds that it "interfered in the internal affairs of countries with which Austria has good and friendly relations" and that its activities were "directed against the interest of the Austrian State." (6) The World Peace Council thereupon—by invitation—returned to Prague.

The largest and certainly the best organized of the international "fronts" has been the World Federation of Trade Unions (WFTU). This is, we might say, a gigantic monument to frustrated hopes; for it was formed on the initiative of the British Trades Union Congress (T.U.C.) which, at the end of World War II, decided to "believe" that the wartime alliance of the Soviet Union and the West pointed toward a many-sided postwar collaboration between Communists and non-Communists.

By 1948, the futility of this hope was clear; and Arthur Deakin—then its President—stated that the WFTU was rapidly becoming "nothing more than another platform and instrument for the furtherance of Soviet policy." In January 1949, the non-Communist elements withdrew in a body, led by the British T.U.C., the American C.I.O., and the Dutch N.V.V. In a later report to the British Trades Union Congress, Arthur Deakin made a statement of classic simplicity: "We started with an honest intention, but we were not dealing with honest men." In November 1949, the non-Communists organized the International Confederation of Free Trade Unions: probably one of the best-informed bodies in the world with reference both to Communist tactics and the workers' stake in freedom.

To see how far the WFTU falls short of being an honest organization of the world's working people, we need only to observe that when Stalin broke with Tito, the WFTU promptly expelled all the Yugoslav representatives as "traitors"; when Khrushchev went all out to re-establish friendly relations with Tito, the WFTU reversed itself and—unsuccessfully—urged the Yugoslav representatives to return; when the East German strikes took place, in June 1953, the WFTU made no protest against the Soviet Union's intervening to crush them—even though the strikers were among its own members; and in November 1956, it obediently echoed the Soviet line about the "counter-revolutionary" forces which had caused the Hungarian uprising.

Omer Bécu, President of the International Confederation of Free Trade Unions, was saying what millions of workers had come to realize when, in December 1955, he declared, "We regard the WFTU as a Communist espionage apparatus and one of the arms of the Cominform. We regard the WFTU as an enemy of the workers everywhere."

The basic allegiance to the USSR which has marked the World Peace Council and the World Federation of Trade Unions has similarly marked the World Federation of Democratic Youth, the International Union of Students, the International Association of Democratic Lawyers, the Women's International Democratic Federation, and the International Organization of Democratic Journalists. Important as it is, however, for us to know the names of such key groups, and how they operate, it is more important for us to know that front organizations under any name, and regardless of the cause they profess to be serving, are ideological extensions of the Soviet empire.

We have spoken earlier of the fact that the Soviet Union is currently developing a seventh type of imperialism; and because of what it may portend for the free world—and for the United States, in particular—it needs to be studied and understood. It is a specific product of the Khrushchev era of "peaceful competition" and it represents one major aspect of the USSR's effort to take over the world without the risks involved in open warfare. It is, in essence, a new kind of *trade imperialism:* an effort to pry backward countries loose from their trade relations with the Western powers and bind them to itself.

It is nothing new, of course, for the Communists to represent every United States policy as imperialistic. In *Political Affairs* for August 1948, for example, we read, "Widely, in Latin America and elsewhere, the Good Neighbor Policy was mistakenly conceived as an abandonment of imperialism by the United States. . . . But in reality, the Good Neighbor Policy was simply a reformulation of the old imperialism . . . to counter more effectively the growing nationalism and democratic spirit of the Latin American people." (7)

And in similar vein, with reference to our Point Four Program: "The main purpose of the much-vaunted Point Four is to guarantee the economic penetration and the subjugation of the undeveloped colonial areas of the world— Asia and Africa, in particular—by the American monopolies and trusts." (8)

To this steady propaganda line there has now been added a new feature: a portrayal of the recession in the United States as the first stage of a major economic collapse in the Western world. This, the Communists say, will spell stark tragedy for all the countries subject to the "economic imperialism" of the United States—unless they save themselves by transferring their major trade relations to the USSR, "which cannot have a depression or unemployment because the means of production belong to the people."

To encourage the establishment of such trade relations, the Soviet Union is doing on a vast scale what no government truly responsible to its own people could do: it is buying up the surplus materials and goods produced by various countries—particularly in Latin America—without regard to its need of these; is paying whatever price for them is politically strategic, without regard to the world market;

and is then "dumping" them on this world market at prices that suit its own propaganda purposes and that help to create economic crisis.

The Soviet Union, we must note, has every right to establish legitimate trade relations with any country it chooses. But when such relations involve both a constant propaganda barrage against ourselves and other Western powers and the buying up, for reasons of propaganda, of products never fitted into the Soviet economy, we need to recognize that the "peaceful competition" of the Khrushchev era is war with no holds barred. More than this, it is *imperialist* war: a struggle quite as truly calculated *to extend dominion* as if territory were at stake.

Marx and Engels were not imperialists. Their "scientific socialism" had tragic shortcomings as a theory on which to base our human society; but it was no rationalization of empire building. Even Lenin, we might say, was only an unconscious imperialist. Because the Soviet Union remained throughout his lifetime the only country where the "proletarian revolution" had taken place, he could promulgate all the tactics and stratagems for consolidating its power without ever realizing the extent to which he was readying it for a new drive toward empire. Stalin, however—fusing the old Russian dream of world conquest with Marx's theory of the State and Lenin's tactics and stratagems of conspiracy—set the pattern for *totalitarian* empire building. Khrushchev is carrying on from where he left off: repudiating no act of Stalin's, however brutal or cynical, by which the Soviet empire was extended; and developing on his own new ideological and economic measures of empire to fit the nuclear age.

It is against this type of empire that we are now having to pit our powers of understanding and creative initiative.

We might almost say that what we are witnessing on the world stage, now, is a competition between two forms of "internationalism." The old era of sovereign nationalisms is over. What the Communists offer in its place is *Soviet provincialism extended to embrace the planet*. What we and the nations associated with us in freedom must convincingly offer is a *postprovincial internationalism:* one that combines a cosmopolitan respect for the integrity of each nation and culture with a firm sense of realism about the interdependence of all nations and peoples.

SEVENTEEN

NEGOTIATING
WITH OUR EYES OPEN

WHILE Warren Austin was heading our delegation to the United Nations, he was reported as having been taken to task, one day, by a disgruntled critic who complained that all they ever did in the United Nations was to talk; and as having countered with a question: "Would you rather we were shooting each other?"

Most rational persons would regard this question as containing its own answer—and all the more conclusively so if it were rephrased to read, "Would you rather we were bombing each other?" As matters now stand in the sphere of armaments, we can assume that not only all the peoples of earth but all the heads of States—including the USSR—prefer words to bombs.

Thus, we can take it for granted that—barring some trigger incident which unleashes nuclear war—the era ahead will be one in which a vast amount of talk will go on. It will go on inside the United Nations and outside; and it will go on across the line that divides the Communist world from the non-Communist.

A significant portion of this talk will have to do with formal negotiations—at the Summit or at some level below the Summit. It will be talk that explores the feasibility of negotiations; talk that is equivalent to an approach to the council table or to a retreat from it; talk that shapes an agenda; finally, talk that takes place where the heads of State or their representatives sit down to wrestle with specified problems about which some measure of joint agreement has been deemed possible.

The United States will again and again be involved in this complex pattern of words instead of bombs. We, no less than any other people, have a survival stake in the avoidance of war. Also, we hold a position of power that makes us morally accountable to mankind. We cannot, in conscience, refuse to negotiate wherever there is the slightest chance that even the slightest lowering of international tensions might be achieved. Beyond these reasons for our country's involvement, moreover, there is a third. It can be simply stated. *We believe in negotiation.* It makes sense to us as a way of resolving problems.

All this being so, we as citizens owe a peculiar new duty to our government. It is not enough for us to demand that it negotiate whenever the USSR calls for a Summit or pre-Summit conference. It is not enough, certainly, for us to join in the charge that our government is recalcitrant and even war-mongering because it does not hurry into negotiations where the USSR has refused even to allow on the agenda the very problems the resolution of which the West—and equally, of course, the anti-Communist East—counts basic to justice and peace.

Our government, we must hold in mind, owes us a double duty: not only to negotiate wherever there is hope of achieving even small dependable agreements but also *to avoid being trapped into pseudo-agreements that simply magnify danger—because all the good faith is on one side.* We, therefore, owe it to our government to learn enough about the special difficulties and hazards involved in negotiating with the Communists that we will not demand pseudo-agreements.

We cannot learn what we here need to know by engaging our minds solely with foreground events: with what the latest Soviet note has proposed, and what our government has said in reply. Neither can we simply translate our country's long experience in negotiating with non-Communist nations into an understanding of what it means to negotiate with the USSR—or any other Communist nation. Least of all can we impose upon the vastly complex problem a simple faith that something good always happens where people just sit down and talk out their differences.

Within a shared frame of reference, this faith has, many times over, removed both mountains and molehills of confusion and misunderstanding. But how shall those who represent our society—and our Western heritage, and our children's stake in this heritage—talk out their differences with those who have, on ideological ground, declared these to be irreconcilable? What are the best and most honest hopes we can attach to negotiations under these circumstances? What false hopes must we guard against—lest these, disappointed, turn into either a blanket rejection of the whole conference method or into an uninformed denunciation of our own government, or of all the Western governments, for not accomplishing the impossible?

We owe it to those who must decide when and when not to enter into negotiations, and who must bear the brunt of

Communist methods at the conference table, to become realists about the differences that can and cannot be talked out within the frame of "permanent revolution." This means that we must understand both the Communist theory of negotiation and the tactics and stratagems which derive from it.

We cannot possibly get the feel of how Communists negotiate unless we keep in mind the fact that they do not expect peace—or even a significant lowering of tensions— to result from anything that can take place at a conference table.

". . . To Bolsheviks, high tension is the normal state of politics. They do not experience it as something that just cannot go on, but rather as something that necessarily persists. What Westerners call a 'real agreement' seems to Bolsheviks inconceivable. It is often predicted in the West that if particular issues . . . could be settled with the Politburo, an easing of the over-all tension might ensue. For Bolsheviks, this does not follow. There might be less 'noise,' but the basic situation—the presence of two blocs attempting to annihilate each other—would be unchanged." (1)

From the Communist point of view, in brief, the delegates to a conference do not merely represent their nations. Far more deeply, they represent one or the other party to the class struggle; and this is not a struggle which can, in any basic sense, be negotiated. It cannot be negotiated because, according to Marxist-Leninist theory, it cannot eventuate in peace until the capitalist class has been liquidated; and this class "will never voluntarily yield up one iota of its power or privilege." Thus, a conference table—even when it is called a peace table—is simply one more place where war is carried on.

It is clarifying to recall, in this context, a speech which

Lenin made, on December 21, 1920, to the Soviet Congress. He was discussing plans for granting certain "concessions" to capitalists, and was indicating that these meant "the continuation of war in another form, by another means. . . . It would be a great mistake to believe that a peaceful agreement about concessions is a peaceful agreement with capitalists. It is an agreement concerning war." (2)

This, then, is a first fact to pin down in our minds—however reluctant we may be to receive it: when Communists negotiate with non-Communists, they are not seeking to establish peace. They are seeking to maneuver themselves into the best available position for continuing war. We cannot, therefore, require that our own delegates bring home a peaceful settlement of basic differences. Neither, if we are wise, will we want them to delude themselves or the public into believing that this is what they have brought. Both we and they must be satisfied with more modest achievements.

Many of the attitudes and stratagems which mark the Communists' approach to negotiations are baffling in the extreme *so long as we believe that they are seeking peace, or even a significant lowering of tensions.* But they become understandable as soon as we realize that they are seeking only, in Lenin's phrase, "an agreement concerning war."

"Westerners have often commented that there is, in negotiating with the Soviet Union, no common search for a solution to common problems, no discussion in the Western sense of the term: the Soviet delegates elaborate or change their position in strict isolation and then present it in dogmatic fashion. They rarely take account of the views and objections of the other side." (3)

Have the Western negotiators who make this type of report simply failed to create the right atmosphere for discussion?

Have they, somehow, bungled the situation: put the Soviet delegates on the defensive; failed to meet them half way; lacked patience in drawing them out, or in listening to their side of the case? We are easily tempted to jump to some such conclusion. For we know how tragically often such factors play a part in the breakdown of communication between human beings. Also—with our Western orientation—it is easier for us to believe that someone has blundered than to believe that the Soviet delegates have come to the council table, in the first place, *ideologically set against a meeting of minds.* For why, if they were going to be thus set, would they come at all?

Once we have explored our way, however, into the Communist frame of reference, the answer to this question ceases to be obscure: they have come to learn what they can from the enemy and about the enemy; and in the light of this, to get what they can in the way of concessions or favorable agreements, *while warding off the danger implicit in a meeting of minds: the danger of being influenced.*

Here, again, we can go back to Lenin—who was preoccupied throughout his life with the problem of how the Bolshevik Party could enter into expedient relationships with other groups and yet safeguard itself against any obscuring of the sharp line between itself and these others. What he feared most of all was that it might be *influenced* from the outside.

This Leninist fear—which has marked the Party down through the years—is one of the most curious aspects of Communism. Most of us take it for granted that when we enter into a working relationship with others, we will also enter into a kind of give-and-take that involves reciprocal influence. The concept of being thus influenced is not anathema to us. We do not find it incompatible with the maintenance of our own integrity. But in the lexicon of Communism

—and specifically, of Leninism—*to be influenced* means *to be subject to control.* To be influenced by a non-Communist, therefore, is to be controlled, in however slight measure, by the enemy; and this must not happen.

In 1914, Lenin undertook to analyze for the Party the difference between non-Bolshevik and correct Bolshevik behavior in the Duma—which was then made up of parties all across the board. It would be tactically necessary, again and again, he indicated, for the Party to enter into various forms of collaboration and agreement with outsiders. Every Bolshevik, then, to safeguard the ideological purity of the Party, must understand that the word "agreement" has a very different meaning when used by Bolsheviks and non-Bolsheviks. "For non-Party people 'agreement' in the Duma is the *'framing* of a tactical resolution or of a policy.'" It is brought into being after various persons or groups have decided to work together on one or another problem; and it is the joint product of all who enter it. "For Party people, an agreement is an effort to *enlist* others for the purpose of carrying out the Party policy."

No Bolshevik, Lenin made clear, must ever join with a non-Bolshevik in the "free framing" of a policy; for "we have Party decisions on all the important questions of tactics, and we shall never recede from these decisions." By coming to an agreement with others "we mean *enlisting* them on our side, *convincing* them that we are right." (4)

Once we have absorbed this peculiar aspect of Leninist doctrine, we can see why, in negotiating with the Soviet Union, there can be "no common search for a solution to common problems, no discussion in the Western sense of the word." We can see why "the Soviet delegates elaborate or change their position in strict isolation and then present it in dogmatic fashion." For them to enter into a meeting of minds would be for them to fraternize with the enemy in the midst of war—and to risk coming under his influence.

Not only, in brief, are Western delegates unable to bring home from any conference in which Communists are involved any true settlement of differences, but they are unable to reach even limited agreements by any true meeting of minds. This, therefore, is another thing which we cannot demand of them—or criticize them for not doing. Any flexible give-and-take of ideas is definitely out—and not by Western choice.

Another matter about which our delegates have no choice is the constant stalling of procedures. "Even when Western proposals are not really controversial, Soviet delegates are apt to begin with a negative reaction and then to introduce motions for modifications. . . . In top-level contacts one could observe a Soviet disinclination to accept the hour which the Western side would suggest for the next session: the request would be made to meet half an hour earlier or later. To Bolsheviks the complete acceptance of the proposal of an enemy (any non-Communist) tends to signify 'yielding' to that enemy, regardless of how harmless the proposal may appear." (5)

Such action is not, however, simply a safeguard against yielding to the non-Communist enemy. Admiral C. Turner Joy, who was Senior Delegate, United Nations Command, during long months of trying to negotiate a Korean Armistice, reports that it is also a tactic with a function of its own:

"One of the most notable negotiating tactics of the Communists is to delay progress." By such delay, they "hope to exploit to their advantage the characteristic impatience of Western peoples, impatience to complete a task once it has begun. This is a shrewd analysis, particularly as it applies to Americans. We are a people who like to get things *done*."

Hence, the Communists seek "to gain advantage by aggravating our American tendency to impatience through the imposition of endless delays."

Where war is going on during negotiations, as it was in Korea, the Western haste to reach an agreement that will put an end to bloodshed is likewise exploited: ". . . Communist negotiators act upon the premise that if they delay matters long enough, their free-world opponents will recede from previously held positions in order to achieve a measure of progress." (6)

According to Admiral Joy, Western negotiators (and those of the anti-Communist East) have to learn, in the face of this delaying tactic, an infinite patience which their impatient countrymen, back home, are likely to interpret as just not getting anything done. Also—where the stalling gets altogether out of bounds, as it did several times in Korea—they must decisively break off the talks at a point where it is to the Communists' advantage to continue them; and must make a resumption of them contingent upon a demonstrated readiness to get something accomplished. While our Western delegates are practicing these difficult arts, we cannot be demanding that they reach prompt agreements. Patience on our part is in order no less than on theirs.

There is yet another demand—and a crucial one—which we cannot make: we cannot ask our negotiators to guarantee that the Communists will live up to the treaties they sign. During its forty years of existence, the USSR has set a world's record for breaking pacts. This has not been a matter of whimful leadership. Here again the basis of *action* has been *ideology*. No shaper of Communist theory from Marx to the present has ever held that a promise made *across class lines* was to be kept any longer than expediency might dictate. When morality has once been defined as "class morality," promises become tactics; and tactics are subject to change without notice.

We have referred in an earlier chapter to Zinoviev's statement of February 2, 1919: "We are willing to sign an unfavorable peace with the Allies. . . . It would only mean that we should put no trust whatever in the bit of paper we should sign. We should use the breathing space so obtained to gather our strength." If the other party to such a treaty believes that it is being signed in good faith, he is to be rated as a victim of his own naïveté: what Lenin called "petty bourgeois trustfulness."

The Soviet empire rests on broken promises. In 1932, for example, the USSR signed nonaggression pacts with Estonia, Latvia, and Lithuania; and in 1934, these were extended for ten years. Six years later, in 1940, all three countries were invaded and incorporated into the Soviet Union. The satellite empire is a vast monument to the Soviet's disregard of the Yalta agreement. These are not isolated instances. It would not be an exaggeration to say that they could be multiplied hundreds of times over. For the Soviet Union, since 1917, has entered into literally hundreds of agreements, large and small; and has kept almost none of them.

Even the ideological outposts of empire rest on broken promises. Thus, on November 12, 1933, Litvinoff gave a four-point pledge to President Roosevelt—as a condition of the USSR's being officially recognized—guaranteeing that the Soviet Union would refrain from all propaganda and organized activity that had as its aim the overthrow of the United States government or the undermining of our institutions. Five days later, however—with recognition accomplished—he released a statement which said, "The Third International is not mentioned in this document. You must not read into it more than was intended." A month later, the Comintern met in Moscow and adopted resolutions which instructed all Parties—including the CPUSA—that there was no way out of the general crisis of capitalism other than the one demonstrated by the Bolshevik revolution.

In the face of this record, we have no right to ask that our delegates to any Summit or pre-Summit conference negotiate an agreement with the Soviet Union—on disarmament or anything else—so binding, so proof against bad faith, that we can relax and call the problem settled. Neither do we have any right to ask that they sign any treaty so far-reaching in its terms, and so innocent of objective safeguards, that if the Soviet Union—having had a "breathing space" in which to gather its strength—broke the agreement while we were keeping it, the result would be catastrophic for ourselves and the whole free world.

Why, then, negotiate at all? The first answer is implicit in Warren Austin's question: "Would you rather we were shooting each other?" Even if negotiation accomplished nothing more than a postponement of overt warfare, it would be worth while: worth all the patience and the pains it takes. For during this period of postponement unnumbered human beings would still be alive who would otherwise be dead.

This is not the only answer, however. There are reasons to hope and to believe that negotiation can serve positive functions beyond the simple postponing of disaster. It can serve an educative function, on a world scale. The Communists have created out of thin air a platform from which they pronounce their "peace-loving" eagerness to negotiate an end to the cold war. Only by finding out what *specific, limited problems* they are willing to negotiate, and *on what terms,* can their undefined offers be given definition and thus brought within the frame where judgment can operate. So far, they have not been willing even to discuss the status of nations which were brought into the empire, in the first place, by the breaking of treaties. So far, also, they have lost interest in the banning of nuclear weapons whenever such banning has been made conditional upon a program of adequate inspection.

There are, moreover, many kinds of *limited* agreements which might be well worth the effort required to negotiate them—and which would not involve our staking the whole future of the free world on the Soviet Union's good faith: on its readiness to stand by its pledged word even where this had been given *across class lines*. The problem of disarmament, for example, does not have to be taken whole. Special aspects of it might—one after another—be negotiated to the benefit of everyone, Communist and non-Communist alike, and without overwhelming risks.

Here, we can even find some encouragement in Communist theory. While this precludes a genuine meeting of minds and a framing of policies by give-and-take effort, it does not preclude—and even approves—*quid pro quo* agreements. To put the matter differently, it precludes *negotiating* in our traditional Western sense, but not practical *bargaining*.

Lenin, writing in *Pravda*, on April 11, 1922, said, "We must make it a rule not to make political concessions to the international bourgeoisie . . . unless we receive in return more or less equivalent concessions from the international bourgeoisie."

Five years later, Stalin, at the Fifteenth Party Congress, put this rule more succinctly: "Our policy is clear. It is based on the formula: 'If you give us something, we give you something.'"

This formula does not invite to *negotiation;* for where genuine negotiation takes place, the policy arrived at is a new joint creation. It embodies both a respect for what each party has declared indispensable to *separate well-being* and what all parties have agreed on as indispensable to their *common well-being*. The Bolshevik formula invites to *bargaining;* and where true negotiation is ideologically ruled out, bargaining may be ruled in as a useful second best.

In our American branch of the Western tradition, we have had statesmen who have been great creative practitioners of the art of negotiation. Also, however, we have had some very able horse traders. Perhaps these, too, have pointers to give us.

There are two further reasons why we must continue our effort to negotiate—or bargain—with the USSR. The first is that the effort itself is making the free world more conscious than it has been for a long time of the values it is defending —and trying to enact with more and more integrity and consistency. At the NATO conference, for example, in May 1958, fifteen free nations managed, with remarkable success, to *negotiate* their differences in order to agree on a *bargaining* stance with respect to a Summit conference which the USSR was seeking to maneuver on its own terms.

The Communists have always believed that crisis— whether of war or depression—can be exploited to splinter a free country or a combination of free countries, making it ripe for overthrow. But the Communists have never been psychological residents of a free country or a free world. They base their judgment on what takes place where crisis becomes the last straw that makes tyranny intolerable.

If the history of the West teaches anything, it is that free people are most aware of their mutual differences and disagreements, and most at odds with one another, during a time of peace—when a focus on *separate well-being* does not seem too expensive a luxury for them to afford; and that they close ranks under conditions of crisis—when their *common well-being* is clearly at stake.

The Soviet Union's success, since World War II, in dividing to conquer has largely been a product of the West's reluctance to credit the reality of cold war. The West, in short, has been acting as it normally does during peace: giving its internal differences and conflicts free reign. The tedious, repetitive effort to negotiate with the USSR has done more, perhaps, than any other one thing to convince the community of free nations that cold war is not peace. It has, therefore, made for the rediscovery and reaffirmation of common stakes.

The final reason for continuing the effort to negotiate is that every conference earns for the free world a further margin of time: *and time is far kinder to freedom than to totalitarianism.* Totalitarianism, whether Nazi or Communist, depends for its strength upon the *coup d'état,* the sudden attack when an enemy has been put off guard by a mutual nonaggression pact. During its period of intense drive against those who have not yet rallied their forces, totalitarianism always seems stronger than it inherently is. It takes time for the internal weaknesses of a coerced "unity" to make themselves felt.

Within the past year or so, Khrushchev has developed a new line. He has been saying that the Communist world, so long "encircled" by enemies, is now so vast that it is doing the "encircling." The way he has employed this line suggests that he regards it as an effective scare tactic. A united free world, however, can hold in mind that within the vastness of the Communist empire there are the millions of human beings who do not want to be there: who have never wanted to be there. The free world has not established outpost Parties behind the Iron Curtain. Yet it has psychological outposts there, nonetheless: conquered peoples; minds that resist totalitarianism; minds that have been educated to a point where they begin to want stretching space. Time is not kind to "monolithic unity."

In negotiating—or bargaining—with the Communists, however, the free world has to be able to lead from strength. Here, once more, we find a clue in Leninist ideology. To press the enemy to the limit at every point where he shows weakness is basic dogma. To make a strategic retreat in the face of strength is equally basic—as is the avoidance of "adventurism": the taking of chances where success has not been virtually guaranteed by preparatory measures.

By reason of both their ideology and their Party discipline, Communists are less likely than others to go off half-cocked and create a crisis on impulse. No people have ever had less respect for spontaneity and impulse; or greater fear of the consequences that may follow from these. Moreover, their conviction that capitalism is doomed militates against their running risks when strength is not decisively on their side, when the orthodox requirements of a "revolutionary situation" have not been met. Thus, paradoxically, their conviction that we are fated to pass from the stage of history becomes an asset to us. It gives maximum usefulness to the free world's every show of firmness and strength.

In the queer topsy-turvy scheme of things which Communism has created, a show of strength on our part does not bring on a crisis which we might have prevented by a more conciliatory or generous approach. Rather, it is what prevents crisis—and keeps the way as open as it can be kept for constructive bargaining. Every free-world veteran of Summit and pre-Summit conference tables has learned this fact the hard way. We, to whom this veteran delegate must look for understanding as he tries, in the months and years ahead, to fashion some working approximation of peace out of successive limited agreements with the USSR will do well to learn it, also.

EIGHTEEN

DESIGN FOR A COMMITMENT

IT WILL not be at the conference table alone that the free world will be required, in the period that lies ahead, to act on its hard-earned knowledge that cold war is not peace. The rediscovery and reaffirmation of what we hold to be of utmost worth will have to go on all across the board. As Isaiah once heard in the temple the voice of the Lord saying, "Whom shall I send, and who will go for us?" and replied, "Here am I; send me," so each of us is called upon to recognize that the challenge of our time is directed to him as an individual no less than to the organized society and embracing tradition which he calls his own.

"It is often said," Sidney Hook reminds us, "that democracies cannot successfully wage cold wars. They are not geared for it. They are too self-critical. And the factions of normal political life sometimes regard each other with more hostility than the enemy at the gate. All this is true. But a democracy also possesses the virtues of its defects. Once it is informed, its voluntary discipline can accomplish more than columns that are dragooned into goosesteps. It is tougher in crisis than its totalitarian enemies." (1)

It is tougher in crisis—*if it is aware that a crisis exists.* But before our "voluntary discipline" can provide the cause of freedom with the support it needs, we as a people must know the nature of Communism deeply enough to know why it simply will not do as the controlling force of the future and must also know what we take to be the indispensables of a civil order. What are the elements of civilization which must not only be preserved but carried forward if we wish this earth to be a suitable home for the type of creature we take man to be?

Law, certainly, is one such element; for where there is no law, the people perish from the perversions of power. The designation of May 1, 1958, as the first Law Day, U.S.A. (by proclamation of the President) was a dramatically sound choice. For while Khrushchev, in Moscow's Red Square, proclaimed the growing might of Communism to be the world's best safeguard against the "war aims" of Great Britain and the United States, Roscoe Pound, Dean Emeritus of the Harvard Law School, spoke a different language: "The law is the highest inheritance the sovereign people has, for without the law there would be no sovereign people and no inheritance."

Across the continent, other spokesmen—lawyers, judges, teachers of jurisprudence—affirmed this same truth in words of their own and in words borrowed from a tradition centuries old. There were great ghosts abroad that day: Hammurabi, Moses, Justinian, Blackstone, Coke, Marshall, Holmes; and there were great living advocates of law as a living force.

By their common testament, and by that of man's experience, law is not that which coerces human beings who would otherwise be free; it is that which stands between human beings—even the least—and that which would otherwise coerce them, rob them of their freedom, force them to live in terror.

Law, by their common testament, moreover, is no static element in society. It changes as problems change; grows to keep pace with growing insight and conscience. Again and again that day, for example, jurists declared international law to be that which must come next on our human agenda. The essential thing, Roscoe Pound stated, is "a world regime of due process of law."

Significantly, speakers in a score of different places made note—some, almost with surprise—of the free world's resurgent interest in the moral content of law and in natural-law philosophies. The very attitudes, in brief, which fostered British Common Law and the American Constitution are again coming to the fore. Judge Charles E. Wyzanski, of the United States District Court of Massachusetts, gave a reason: "No one trained in the Anglo-American tradition, who paused to consider what 'law' was as administered by Hitler's judges, or who has tried to grasp the essential theories of Soviet jurisprudence, could remain entirely satisfied with a positivist, empirical approach to his profession."

No one, we would believe, whose mind has been shaped by the Anglo-American tradition—be he lawyer or layman—can become familiar with the terrible tawdriness of what passes for law within the Communist orbit and not feel obligated to rededicate himself to the spirit and practice of "liberty under law." Rigged trials, forced confessions, arrests for no specified reasons, the abolition of the writ of *habeas corpus*, the abolition of civil rights, secret police: these are the essence of terror; and these are the demonstrated essence of Communist class law. Also, therefore, they are a basic reason why Communism must not be permitted to extend its empire to embrace—and have at its mercy—yet other human beings.

A second element of civilization, to be cherished and practiced, is respect for the individual. When a person has steeped himself long enough in Communist books, magazines, and pamphlets, he becomes conscious of a startling fact. Nowhere in all the interminable verbiage that purports to deal with human situations has he encountered the *individual.*

Instead, on page after page, he has encountered the *masses,* the *proletariat,* the *bourgeoisie, imperialist warmongers, agents of Wall Street, hirelings of capitalism,* *bourgeois reformists, revisionists, renegades, witch-hunters, stool-pigeons;* and always and everywhere, the *revolutionary vanguard,* the *Party.* Where the single Party member is spoken of, he is rendered psychologically aseptic by having his individuality removed: he becomes a *comrade* or a *cadre.* These strange figures—larger than life and empty of life— make up the cast of characters in the Communist drama of class struggle, overthrow, the dictatorship of the proletariat, and the coming of the classless society.

It is no accident that the human being in all his vital, stubborn identity is absent from Communist writings. He has no place in these because he has no place in either the ideology or the program of Communism. The ideology is interested in man only as a member of a class; and so far as the program is concerned, the only elements worth reckoning with are those which can be manipulated *en masse* or, if revolutionary ends so require, liquidated *en masse:* these, and the leaders who will do the manipulating and liquidating.

To the extent that an individual remains *himself,* he is

animated by personal interests and hopes; given to doubts and rectifying laughter; capable of being touched by the mystery of life; unpredictably compassionate; unpredictable, too, in holding to his own opinion; given to intense absorptions, but incorrigibly given, also, to going off on tangents and taking time out; warmed by affection for a beloved few and by a general good will toward a random lot of fellow human beings.

The very qualities which make him thus an individual render him unfit for Party purposes. He is too likely to go off half-cocked; to look skeptical at the wrong time; to become bored with reiterated abstractions; to have qualms about methods; to hold to an opinion even after the official line has been reversed; to resist the pressures of Party discipline; and, not least, to like and dislike people without permission from the Central Committee. He is, therefore, "unreliable." He has either to be "developed" or else left as part of the "mass" that will, when the Party fulfills its "historic mission," be dealt with according to "proletarian justice."

According to Communist dogma, the forces and relationships of society become significant only as they are "politicalized": that is to say, interpreted—and manipulated—in the light of the class struggle. All aspects of the human being that are not amenable to being "politicalized" are "bourgeois." As over against this grim erasure of the unique, we ourselves believe that the *individual,* as the vessel of life, has unalienable rights because he has unalienable worth. Government derives its just powers from his consent and from that of his fellow individuals; and society derives its richness of texture from variety and uniqueness as well as from the deep communality of tradition and shared experience.

One curious intellectual cult in our own midst insistently portrays the American people as "conformist." This view has, in fact, become so orthodox in certain circles that the person who sees the mass as made up of all kinds and varieties is looked upon with some disapproval: he is nonconformist, is not putting the social scene in order by imposing upon it the proper classifications. Variousness in human society, however, is a product not only of *what people are* but also of how they are regarded. Nothing makes two men in grey flannel suits look so much alike as looking at the suits instead of the men.

This, curiously enough, is one lesson that we learn as we study the terrifying conformism of Marxist-Leninist writings. Pushed to its extreme limit, the tendency to classify creates the image of man as a member of a class and nothing more; and it reduces all the criss-crossing interests and influences of life to the rigid, lifeless dimension of the class struggle.

There is a certain readiness, then, which each of us owes to our cultural heritage and to man's future. It is that of seeing what is *individual* in one another—not merely what can be classified. Only as we thus experience individuality as real, can we devote ourselves to safeguarding its rights and giving it room to thrive.

Precisely as the individual is "downgraded" in Communist theory and practice, so likewise are the emotions we have counted basic to sound human relationships: love, friendliness, compassion, neighborliness, tenderness. These add up to a far healthier dynamic for life than hatred can ever be. But to read Communist writings is to find oneself in an atmosphere of dedicated, dictated hatred for all who do not wear the ideological straitjacket.

Bella V. Dodd, who joined the Party while she was a teacher in New York City, and who worked for years in its service, has since reported that she did not really qualify as a "full-fledged Communist" until she had made the Party's hates her hates. "In the long ago," she writes, "I had been unable to hate anyone; I suffered desperately when anyone was mistreated. . . . Now, little by little, I had acquired a whole mass of people to hate: the groups and individuals who fought the Party. How it came about I cannot tell. All I know as I look back at that time is that my mind had responded to Marxist conditioning. For it is a fact, true and terrible, that the Party establishes such authority over its members that it can swing their emotions now for and now against the same person or issue. It claims such sovereignty even over conscience as to dictate when it shall hate." (2)

Other ex-Communists have made similar reports. The instilling of hatred is a prescribed part of each comrade's indoctrination, they tell us, because it is a requisite part of the Party's elaborate machinery of defense and aggression.

Of defense. The Party member is deliberately isolated from warm association with non-Communists and taught to regard them with hostility and contempt because only thus can the Party protect itself against both "penetration" by "bourgeois ideas" and the danger that a comrade may, fraternizing with outsiders, reveal secret tactics or name underground functionaries. Thus, also, it reduces the risk that he may "deviate" or defect. We have, by now, the word of a multitude of different ex-Communists to the effect that the dreadful isolation they saw before them, in the world "outside," made them postpone their break with the Party long after disillusionment had set in.

Of aggression. The Party member is deliberately turned into an emotional alien within the larger non-Communist society which he inhabits; for only thus can he be brought to desire its overthrow. The tactics of alienation are brought to bear upon all comrades and are, by means of propaganda and united fronts, extended beyond the Party to sympathizers and collaborators. They are applied in their most extreme form, however, where the Soviet Union, through its foreign network, is engaged in selecting and training espionage agents.

The best "textbook," perhaps, for the study of these tactics in precise, documented detail is the *Report* of the Canadian Royal Commission on espionage. "In virtually all cases," this *Report* states—referring to an espionage network uncovered after World War II—"the agents were recruited from among 'cells' or study groups of secret members or adherents of the Communist Party (Labour-Progressive Party)."

The members of these cells had been carefully selected in the first place; and the alienating process which had then been set in motion was a double one: schooling in Marxist-Leninist doctrine and schooling in secrecy. The program was designed to accustom the adherents "to an atmosphere and an ethic of conspiracy. The general effect . . . over a period of time of *secret* meetings, *secret* acquaintances, and *secret* objectives, plans and policies, can easily be imagined. The technique seems calculated to develop the psychology of a double life and double standard. . . .

"The curriculum includes the study of political and philosophic works, . . . selected to develop in the students an essentially critical attitude toward Western democratic society. . . .

"Linked with these studies at all stages, moreover, goes an organized indoctrination calculated to create in the mind of the study-group member an essentially uncritical acceptance at its face value of the propaganda of a foreign state. . . .

"Thus it seems to happen that through these study-groups some adherents, who begin by feeling that Canadian society is not democratic or not equalitarian enough for their taste, are gradually led to transfer a part or most of their loyalties to another country, apparently without reference to whether that other country is in actual fact more or less democratic or equalitarian than Canada." (3)

Instilled hatred serves a second aggressive function, also. Only the person who himself hates is likely to become a willing and skillful fomenter of hatred—able to stir up, "develop," and exploit animosities wherever the Party, for tactical reasons, wants them to exist. In 1920, we may recall from an earlier chapter, Lenin stated that wherever mutual animosities and rivalries exist between non-Communist groups and nations, the Party's "practical task . . . is to take advantage of this hostility and to incite one against the other." (4) The Communists have been following this tactic ever since: setting nation against nation, employee against employer, race against race. It takes experienced haters, with no qualms, to apply a method of this sort.

To turn from the hate-saturated writings of the Communists to books that affirm the abiding principle of good will is like a spiritual homecoming. We can feel how sharp the contrast is if we put side by side the statement quoted from Lenin and a statement made by a top American psychiatrist, Karl Menninger. The latter, long experienced in working with people who have been disastrously at odds with themselves and others, declares the chief "practical problem" of any psychiatrist to be that of finding out how to "encourage love and diminish hate." (5)

Menninger speaks as a physician of the mind; but also he speaks for our tenacious conviction that it is better to build a life or a society on good will than on hatred. In going against this conviction—as they do at every turn, and as their ideology compels them to do—the Communists offer our individual human nature and our cumulative human experience an affront we cannot ignore.

Most of us are so aware of how far we fall short of loving our enemies—or even of handling our friendships with the creative imagination they deserve—that we lose sight of the multitudinous ways in which we practice good will and take it for granted. A study of Communism shocks us into realizing what it would be like to be *forbidden* to love our enemies and to be obligated to define as enemies—regardless of their individual deserts—all who are outside the ideological pale.

We might almost say that what we are basically defending in our struggle against Communism is our unalienable right to like people and wish them well—and to grow in our understanding of them—*without asking permission from a political authority;* our right to feel affection and compassion *as spontaneous emotions.*

His refusal to give up this unalienable right was what made Arthur Koestler break with the Communist Party; and his story points up what is at stake in the crisis of our time. Arrested for his Communist activities during the Spanish War, Koestler spent four months in prison—expecting from day to day to face a fascist firing squad. When he was finally released, through the intervention of the British Government, he discovered that his own outlook had subtly changed without his realizing it. In prison, he had learned to feel a type of pity not allowed to Communists: a pity that extended to suffering individuals *regardless of their ideology or their class.*

He had learned, he tells us, "that man is a reality, mankind an abstraction; . . . that ethics is not a function of social utility, and charity not a petty bourgeois sentiment but the gravitational force which keeps civilization in its orbit." Any such view "was incompatible with the Communist faith which I held." (6) So far as he was concerned, therefore, the Communist faith had to go—as we can believe it will go from the world when the emotional impoverishment which it prescribes for its adherents is finally understood.

The moral impoverishment which it prescribes is equally destructive. Perhaps the most tragic and heartbreaking evidence of what happens to people when they are not allowed to bring their own moral sense to bear upon the human scene is to be found in the "confessions" of Soviet writers who have publicly condemned themselves for "errors" offensive to the Party. Here, one example can stand for many. It was not under Stalin, but under Khrushchev, in October 1957, that Margarita Aliger—one of the Soviet Union's most gifted authors—was "persuaded" to say, openly and humbly, at a meeting of writers and Party functionaries in Moscow:

"I committed a number of gross mistakes in my public work. . . . It is my peculiarity at times to substitute morally-ethical categories for political categories. . . . Obviously I must now be much more exacting with myself, liberate myself from a certain speculativeness. . . . All the work of a Soviet writer is political work, and to accomplish it honorably is possible only when one follows firmly the party line and party discipline." (7)

Where it has been made a "peculiarity" to apply moral judgments to the human scene, and where "speculativeness" is equivalent to "error," the individual is denied the right to become a psychological, and not merely a physical, vertebrate.

Where "morally-ethical categories" are ruled out, what is ruled in is the doctrine of the *expedient*, the politically "necessary": as Arthur Koestler has put it, the "necessary lie, the necessary slander; the necessary intimidation of the masses to preserve them from shortsighted errors; the necessary liquidation of oppositional groups and hostile classes." (8)

If expediency is accounted a sufficient basis for policy-making, obedience is a sufficient virtue in those to whom the policy is handed down. So long as they adhere to the line, they need have no qualms: they can feel right about themselves—and superior to all non-Communists. But *overt* obedience on their part is not enough. *Inner* obedience is also demanded. All comrades must *feel* the "correctness" of whatever the Party ordains.

When we study the history and workings of the CPUSA, we make a significant discovery in this connection: that *inner* obedience of the type required is not always easy to deliver. "Speculativeness" and the moral sense, it would appear, have a stubborn way of coming back even after they have been ruled out. In any case, whenever Party members have had to do an abrupt about-face, in order to adjust to a sharp reversal in Soviet policy, they have made haste not only to change their programs and propaganda but also *to fortify themselves against doubts and misgivings.* To this end, they have plunged into both an intensified study of Marxism-Leninism and a veritable orgy of "Communist self-criticism." It is as if they have felt the need to exorcise some residue of "bourgeois morality" within themselves, lest this move them to "revisionism" or defection.

By thus combining dogma and self-criticism, Party members seem able to perform a peculiar "miracle." They convince themselves that they were at fault for having been caught off guard by the abrupt change in policy. Had they not been guilty of "errors of interpretation," they would have seen that "socialist realism" demanded the precise policy which the Soviet Union has "correctly" instituted.

Thus, for the Communists, *self-discipline* means a determined effort to get the inner self lined up with dictates that come from the outside. It does not mean the integrating of the self around a firm and flexible core of values. Emphatically, it does not mean the individual's readying of himself to make his own decisions and to assume responsibility for them. Communist self-discipline is the most efficient mass tactic ever devised for the voluntary renouncement of the right to grow up. We must make no mistake about this: *the triumph of Communism on a world scale would mean the fixating of mankind at a level far short of moral maturity.*

It would mean, also, the fixating of mankind at a level far short of intellectual maturity. The right to grow is inseparable from the right to learn.

More shocking than the Soviet Union's launching of its first two sputniks was the widespread tendency in this country to interpret their launching as proof that the Communists were far ahead of us in *education.* It need not mean a belittling of their accomplishments nor a glossing over of our own shortcomings to say that this is not true. Their accomplishments have been in fields that make people amenable to indoctrination and in those that make them able to render specialized service to the monolithic State. Our shortcomings are those of a far more complex and daring venture: the education of a whole people for the enactment of democratic freedom. The Soviet effort and our own are simply not comparable. They do not belong within the same frame of intention.

The Soviet Union has achieved literacy on a remarkable scale. We must recall, however, that Lenin instituted the vast literacy program for political, not educational, reasons. His stated purpose was to make it possible to indoctrinate, through the classroom, a people who could not otherwise be brought to understand and accept the "dictatorship of the proletariat." The very textbooks used for the teaching of literacy taught Communist dogma, also. From that time to the present, the capacity to read has been tethered to an iron control—and Iron Curtain control—over what is available for reading.

During the past few years, the Soviet Union has forged ahead in the teaching of foreign languages—a field in which we have notoriously lagged. But again the purpose has been strictly ideological and strategic. As part of its policy of "peaceful co-existence"—that is, of taking over the world without nuclear war—the USSR has been stepping up the training of persons who can carry the Party line convincingly into all countries.

We cannot, for example, dissociate the intensified study of Spanish and Portuguese from the intensified propaganda effort to alienate Latin America from the United States and strengthen its ties with the Soviet Union. In behalf of this effort, Radio Moscow broadcasts to Latin America, chiefly in Spanish, programs that total a hundred hours a week. Thus, on April 30, 1958, shortly before Vice-President Nixon's visit to eight South American countries, Radio Moscow broadcast in both Spanish and Portuguese a detailed announcement of his tour and labeled it as "an attempt to save U.S. prestige in Latin America." The broadcast then continued: "In Peru, Chile, Colombia, Venezuela and several other countries there is a powerful upsurge of the strike movement, and this has an open anti-imperialist character." Every Communist leader in Latin America—and particularly in the specified countries—could translate these words into a command: "Make the most of this occasion to stir up trouble." While it would be folly for us to ascribe the unrest and hostility in Latin America wholly to such propaganda, it would also be folly for us to underestimate the extent to which it is, by calculated intent, making our problems harder to solve.

The Soviet Union, in short, has learned that the study of foreign languages is an exceedingly useful weapon in the cold war: a useful weapon for extending the domain of Communist provincialism. However inadequately we have taught such languages, we have at least assigned a larger purpose to the learning of them. We have sought to educate minds out of provincialism into some measure of cosmopolitanism.

Now, the Soviet Union is raising a generation schooled in mathematics, technology, and science. But this does not mean that it is educating a generation to seek truth wherever it may find it. The role of the Soviet scientist as a servant of the State—not a free seeker of truth in the world community of science—was conclusively spelled out, as we have noted earlier, in the September 1957 issue of *Kommunist,* in an article by A. Topchiev, called "Building of Communism and Science."

"Our scientists," wrote Topchiev, "cannot and should not stand on the sidelines of the ideological struggle between communism and capitalism." He then went on to reproach —and to set straight—those who took too literally and too broadly Khrushchev's slogan about "peaceful co-existence": "Some scientific workers attempt automatically to extend to the field of ideology the slogan of peaceful co-existence of countries with different social-economic systems. The time has come, so they say, when we can permit ourselves such co-existence of the two ideologies. This is a profoundly mistaken conclusion. . . . Now more than ever, vagueness, neutrality, indifference to politics, which V. I. Lenin constantly opposed, should not be tolerated among us." (9)

We in this country have good reason to be concerned about the quality and future of our educational system. We need to raise the literacy level; to do a better job of teaching foreign languages; to foster the accuracies of mathematics and science. We profoundly need, also, to communicate to young people that drama of freedom which has been received from the past and which must be projected into the future.

But we certainly cannot let the Soviet Union be our guide

in this. Neither can we let it be our chief stimulus. Our stimulus must be found in our own purposes: our own concept of man in society. For we do not want either the child in the classroom or the scientist in the laboratory to think of himself as, above all, an obedient servant of the State. We want the skills of learning to enhance the freedom of learning; and the freedom of learning to enhance the mind's responsible freedom as it copes with the problems and possibilities of a world in which answers not only resolve questions but open up ever new questions to be resolved.

Here, then, are certain matters that are at stake in the cold war that is not peace: the principle of liberty under law; respect for the integrity and uniqueness of the individual; the right to enact friendliness and compassion as broadly and spontaneously as our own stage of emotional growth makes possible; the right to apply moral judgments, not merely political judgments, and to assume moral responsibility for our own actions; and the right to learn what we need to know in order to make our enactment of freedom a living proof that freedom is the proper condition for our human selves.

These stakes are not psychological museum pieces. The rights which we affirm for ourselves and others are designed for use in the open market places of man's society. We have, therefore, a stake in certain *methods* as well as in basic *principles*.

In the first place, we have a stake in the very method of "reformism" which all Communists from Marx down have despised and deprecated. To them, "reformism" has meant doing just enough to ward off the necessity of doing what should be done. They have seen it thus because they have conclusively "known" what should be done. Believing themselves possessed of a total answer to social ills, they have rejected the thesis that this ideological answer can co-exist with any other except on a temporary and tactical basis. Also, being under no moral compulsion to respect the rights or the lives of persons outside one favored class, they have been able to want total revolution in behalf of their total answer.

For ourselves, in contrast, "reformism" has meant going as far *in action* as we have, to date, gone *in insight*. Claiming no total answer, we have claimed instead the right to keep the future open and to discover answers on a broad front without our search for these being restricted by arbitrary power. "Reformism" has meant growing in our awareness of what needs to be done next by doing what we see to do, and then moving beyond this. If reform has the gradualness of evolution, not the swiftness of revolution, it has also, we believe, the soundness of organic growth.

We have a stake, likewise, in a second method which the Communists have condemned: *parliamentarism*. This, as we are here using the term, is not a political concept only. More basically, it has to do with the right of human beings to have their point of view represented wherever their basic welfare is at issue; and it expresses our common faith that social problems are best worked out, in the long run, by the pooling of insight and experience across lines of difference —not by totalitarian edict that tolerates no dissent.

Further, we have a stake in what we have called *federalism*. Again, we would say, this must be regarded as far more than a political concept. It has to do with the existence— and the peaceful co-existence—of many different experiment centers within society. We noted in Chapter One, for example, that the State of Oregon introduced the initiative and referendum; that Wisconsin passed the first direct-primary law; and that Maryland enacted the first state workmen's compensation law. What these facts testify to— as do thousands of others in our history—is our belief that many different organizations, localities, and states need to be constantly at the business of trying out solutions to social, political, educational, and economic problems: learning what works and what does not work; learning, then, from one another; and thus moving toward an acceptable conclusion about what the common welfare requires.

Reform, the *parliamentary process, federal structure:* Communism cannot tolerate any one of these three, and a free society needs all of them. *It needs them because they provide for getting things done while keeping the future open.* For this reason, we can dare to believe that the world needs them also. When we say this, we do not mean that our particular type of social and political organization should be transplanted to lands where it is not indigenous. On the contrary, we mean that the world must have the right to tackle its problems, as we have tackled ours, by methods that keep the future open. It must not be coerced into a rigid *either-or* choice as a preface to its being coerced into one rigid pattern with no choice at all.

The Communists continue to declare, in Lenin's words, that "*the only choice is:* either bourgeois or socialist ideology. There is no middle course . . ." They continue to declare that "humanity has not created a 'third' ideology . . ." We must learn to say to the peoples of the earth, with their many different cultures, that they *need not choose* between the Soviet brand of Communism and our particular brand of capitalism; nor between the "monolithic state" represented by the USSR and our particular type of democratic state. We must learn to say to them that the mind of man is more socially ingenious than the Communists give it credit for being; that the planet is large enough for many experiment centers, many trial-and-error learnings, many points of view that deserve to be represented.

To say this to them does not express indifference to their

urgent needs. It does not mean leaving them to shift for themselves as they strive to satisfy these needs. It means only that we help them to realize that the open way of life has proved more fruitful of human well-being than has any closed way. It has been our experience—and we have every right to say so—that where minds are permitted to move freely, ingenuity has its best chance to give to the raw materials of earth those forms which eventuate in a high standard of living.

The Communists are telling the peoples of the backward countries that their quickest and surest course to a high standard of living is through the "dictatorship of the proletariat." But so far the Soviet Union has chiefly demonstrated two things. The first is that a "monolithic state," by wholly subordinating the individual to its own purposes, and wholly subordinating the present to the future, *can* coerce heavy industry into being. The second is that when a country is "liberated" by Communism, it is forthwith subordinated, both politically and economically, to the Soviet Union.

No matter what the Communists may say, it is on the books of history that our Western way of life—growing and changing through the years, and yet remaining its intrinsic self—has come closer than any other way thus far to delivering both political freedom and a high standard of living. It is not chauvinism for us to underscore this fact. Not to underscore it would be morally irresponsible. We must not let Communist verbiage obscure tangible evidence; for the restless, searching peoples of earth have a human right to *both* food and freedom—not simply one or the other.

As we bring this book to a close, we recall two statements that may well serve us as a conclusion. The first was made by a body of American scientists; the second by an American editor.

"Man is breaking with the past," said the scientists; "its limitations, and its safeguards. The prize is greater than ever before—and so are the risks. The question is not 'Do we like this?' The question is 'What role do the people of the United States wish to play in the drama of the future?' " (10)

It seemed almost as if in direct reply to this question that editor Norman Cousins spoke. He was talking to an American forum about nuclear weapons and the acute crisis in our foreign policy created by these weapons. "The question is not what policy we should devise that seems to make sense for America alone but rather what policy makes sense in human terms." (11)

These two statements, we believe, pose the issue as we now must see it: *We Americans not only have a role to play but have one that is as wide as mankind.* The scientists, obviously, in saying that man is "breaking with the past," were not calling for any total repudiation of the cumulative experience of man nor of the principles of responsibility and relationship that have been distilled from this experience. They were not, in short, advocating the type of break with the past which Communism seeks to enact in the name of Marx's theory of the State: that theory which contends that the only way to better the human lot is to replace one owning class by another; and that when this replacement has been made, all the codes and institutions of society must be changed to support the regime inaugurated by the new power class—the new "dictatorship."

What the scientists were talking about is made explicit in their reference to *limitations* and *safeguards*. They were saying that man is breaking out of old *confines* and is taking a larger social and physical universe for his province. As we face the hazards and the promise of the future, we will need all that mankind has ever learned about the factors that release life for new growth.

What we are seeking to preserve and carry forward—from liberty under law to multiple experiment centers—is of great worth, not simply because it has served us well in the past, but because it can be stretched to serve the peoples of earth. The emphasis of the two statements we have quoted is on *inclusiveness*. The age ahead is to be one of a new compelling morality: an age in which the powerful can survive only if they care enough about what happens to "the least of these" to enact mercy, justice, and humility.

Inclusiveness appears to be what history is calling for today—and it is that in terms of which all the powers of earth stand condemned. We ourselves stand condemned to the extent that we have, on so many fronts, stopped tragically short of enacting what we believe. But the Communists stand more irrevocably condemned, because their basic doctrine divides man from man. "Monolithic unity"—brought into being by coercion, and based on a theory of irreconcilable antagonism—is a sorry substitute for an inclusive unity of free peoples who, with the future open, can seek still further unities and freedoms.

BIBLIOGRAPHY

BOOKS FROM COMMUNIST SOURCES

Adoratsky, V. *Dialectical Materialism*. International Publishers, New York, 1934.

Allen, James S. *World Monopoly and Peace*. International Publishers, New York, 1946.

Aptheker, Herbert. *A Documentary History of the Negro People in the United States*. Citadel Press, New York, 1951.

Cornforth, Maurice. *Science and Idealism*. International Publishers, New York, 1947.

Dennis, Eugene. *Letters from Prison*. International Publishers, New York, 1956.

Dimitroff, Georgi. *The United Front*. International Publishers, New York, 1938.

Foster, William Z. *Toward Soviet America*. Coward-McCann, New York, 1932.

————— *The Twilight of World Capitalism*. International Publishers, New York, 1949.

————— *Outline Political History of the Americas*. International Publishers, New York, 1951.

————— *History of the Communist Party of the United States*. International Publishers, New York, 1952.

————— *The Negro People in American History*. International Publishers, New York, 1954.

———— *History of the Three Internationals.* International Publishers, New York, 1955.

———— *Outline History of the World Trade Union Movement.* International Publishers, New York, 1956.

Guest, David. *A Textbook of Dialectical Materialism.* International Publishers, New York, 1939.

Lenin, V. I. *Selected Works.* International Publishers, New York, 1943.

Losovsky, A. *Marx and the Trade Unions.* International Publishers, New York, 1935.

Mao Tse-tung. *Selected Works* (Four Volumes, Based on Chinese Edition, Peking, 1951). International Publishers, New York, 1954.

Marx, Karl. *Selected Works in Two Volumes.* Prepared by the Marx-Lenin Institute, Moscow. Ed. V. Adoratsky. International Publishers, New York.

Marx, Karl and Engels, Friedrich. *Selected Correspondence—1846–1895.* International Publishers, New York, 1942.

———— *The Russian Menace to Europe. A Collection of Articles, Speeches, Letters and News Dispatches.* Selected and Edited by Paul W. Blackstock and Bert F. Hoselitz. The Free Press, Glencoe, Illinois, 1952. (NOTE: We have included this book in the list of Communist sources because it is compiled from the works of Marx and Engels. The Editors, however, Blackstock and Hoselitz, are non-Communists; and they have made up this volume from works of Marx and Engels not normally included in Communist editions. Had we been listing the book in terms of its *Introduction,* instead of in terms of its major content, it would have been put under *Non-Communist Sources.*)

Reed, John, *Ten Days that Shook the World,* pp. 271–274. Boni and Liveright, New York, 1919.

Selsam, Howard. *Handbook of Philosophy.* International Publishers, New York, 1949.

———— *Philosophy in Revolution.* International Publishers, 1957.

Stalin, J. V. *Works.* Foreign Languages Publishing House, Moscow, 1949, 1952, 1953, 1954.

———— *Foundations of Leninism.* International Publishers, New York, 1932.

———— *Problems of Leninism.* International Publishers, New York, 1934.

J. V. *Stalin.* (A Commemoration volume by the Central Committee, Communist Party of the Soviet Union). Workers Library Publishers, New York, 1940.

Trotsky, Leon. *Stalin.* Hollis and Carter, London, 1947.

BOOKS FROM NON-COMMUNIST SOURCES

Acton, Harry B. *The Illusion of the Epoch: Marxism-Leninism as a Philosophical Creed.* British Book Center, New York, 1955.

Alexander, Robert J. *Communism in Latin America.* Rutgers University Press, 1958.

Almond, Gabriel A. *The Appeals of Communism.* Princeton University Press, 1954.

Aron, Raymond. *The Century of Total War.* Doubleday, New York, 1954.

Baldwin, Roger N., Editor. *A New Slavery: The Communist Betrayal of Human Rights.* Oceana Publishers, New York, 1953.

Bauer, Raymond A. *The New Man in Soviet Psychology.* Harvard University Press, 1952.

Belov, Fedor. *The History of a Soviet Collective Farm.* Praeger, New York, 1955.

Borkenau, Franz. *European Communism.* Harper, New York, 1953.

Berman, H. J. and Kerner, Miroslav, Editors. *Documents on Soviet Law and Administration.* Harvard University Press, 1955.

Brzezinski, Z. *Permanent Purge.* Harvard University Press, 1956.

Budenz, Louis. *The Techniques of Communism.* Regnery, Chicago, 1954.

Counts, George S. *The Challenge of Soviet Education.* McGraw-Hill, New York, 1957.

———— and Lodge, Nucia. *The Country of the Blind: The Soviet System of Mind Control.* Houghton Mifflin, Boston, 1949.

Crankshaw, Edward. *Russia without Stalin.* Viking, New York, 1956.

Crossman, Richard, Editor. *The God That Failed.* Harper, New York, 1949.

Dallin, David J. *The New Soviet Empire.* Yale University Press, 1951.

———— *Soviet Espionage.* Yale University Press, 1955.

———— and Nicolaevsky, Boris I. *Forced Labor in Soviet Russia.* Yale University Press, 1947.

Djilas, Milovan. *The New Class.* Praeger, New York, 1957.

Dodd, Bella V. *School of Darkness.* Kenedy, New York, 1954.

Ebon, Martin. *World Communism Today.* McGraw-Hill, New York, 1948.

Einaudi, Mario. *Communism in Western Europe.* Cornell University Press, 1953.

Ernst, Morris L. and Loth, David. *Report on the American Communist.* Holt, New York, 1952.

Fainsod, Merle. *How Russia Is Ruled.* Harvard University Press, 1954.

Fischer, George. *Russian Liberalism.* Harvard University Press, 1958.

Friedrich, Carl J. and Brzezinski, Z. *Totalitarian Dictatorship and Autocracy.* Harvard University Press, 1956.

Gliksman, Jerzy G., Editor. *International Commission against Forced Labor Camps.* Beacon, Boston, 1953.

Gurian, W. *Bolshevism: Theory and Practice.* Macmillan, New York, 1932.

Herling, Albert Konrad. *The Soviet Slave Empire.* Funk, New York, 1951.

Hicks, Granville. *Where We Came Out.* Viking, New York, 1954.

Hodgkinson, Harry. *The Language of Communism.* Pitman, New York, 1955.

Hook, Sidney. *Heresy, Yes—Conspiracy, No.* John Day, New York, 1953.

Hoover, J. Edgar. *Masters of Deceit.* Holt, New York, 1958.

Hunt, R. N. Carew. *The Theory and Practice of Communism.* Macmillan, New York, 1957.

Huxley, Julian. *Soviet Genetics and World Science.* Chatto and Windus, London, 1949.

Joy, Admiral Charles Turner. *How Communists Negotiate.* Macmillan, New York, 1955.

Kampelman, Max M. *The Communist Party vs. the C.I.O.* Praeger, New York, 1957.

Kelsen, Hans. *Political Theory of Bolshevism.* University of California Press, 1948.

Kintner, William R. *The Front Is Everywhere.* University of Oklahoma Press, 1954.

Kirkpatrick, E. M. *Target the World: Communist Propaganda Activities in 1955.* Macmillan, New York, 1956.

Kulsky, W. W. *The Soviet Regime.* Syracuse University Press, 1954.

Leites, Nathan. *A Study of Bolshevism.* Free Press, Glencoe, Illinois, 1953.

———— *The Operational Code of the Politburo.* McGraw-Hill, New York, 1951.

Lyons, Eugene. *Assignment in Utopia.* Harcourt, New York, 1937.

———— *The Red Decade.* Bobbs-Merrill, Indianapolis, 1941.

MacEoin, Gary. *The Communist War on Religion.* Devin-Adair, New York, 1951.

Malaparte, Curzio. *Coup d'État: The Technique of Revolution.* Dutton, New York, 1932.

Markham, Ruben H. *Communists Crush Churches in Eastern Europe.* Meador, 1950.

Meerloo, Joost A. M. *The Rape of the Mind.* World, Cleveland, 1956.

Meyer, Alfred G. *Marxism: the Unity of Theory and Practice.* Harvard University Press, 1954.

Milosz, Czeslaw. *The Captive Mind.* Knopf, New York, 1953.

Mitrany, David. *Marx and the Peasants.* University of North Carolina Press, 1951.

Nagy, Imre. *On Communism.* Praeger, New York, 1957.

Nolan, William A. *Communism vs. the Negro.* Regnery, Chicago, 1951.

Nyardi, Nicholas. *My Ringside Seat in Moscow.* T. Y. Crowell, New York, 1952.

Oneal, James and Werner, G. A. *American Communism.* Dutton, New York, 1947.

Philbrick, Herbert A. *I Led Three Lives.* Grosset, New York, 1952.

Pilat, Oliver. *The Atom Spies.* Putnam, New York, 1952.

Popper, Karl R. *Open Society and Its Enemies.* Princeton University Press, 1950.

Record Wilson. *The Negro and the Communist Party.* University of North Carolina Press, 1951.

Rossi, A. *A Communist Party in Action.* Yale University Press, 1949.

Schub, David. *Lenin, a Biography.* Doubleday, New York, 1948.

Schwartz, Solomon M. *The Jews in the Soviet Union.* Syracuse University Press, 1951.

———— *Labor in the Soviet Union.* Praeger, 1952.

Selznick, Philip. *The Organizational Weapon.* McGraw-Hill, New York, 1952.

Seton-Watson, Hugh. *The East European Revolution.* Praeger, New York, 1951.

———— *From Lenin to Malenkov: The History of World Communism.* Praeger, New York, 1953.

Shuster, George N. *Religion Behind the Iron Curtain.* McGraw-Hill, New York, 1952.

Steinberg, Julien, Editor. *The Verdict of Three Decades:* From the Literature of Revolt Against Communism. Duell, New York, 1950.

Stowe, Leland. *Conquest by Terror.* Random House, New York, 1951.

Walker, Richard L. *China under Communism: The First Five Years.* Yale University Press, 1955.

Walsh, Edmund A. *Total Empire.* Bruce, Milwaukee, 1951.

Wolfe, Bertram D. *Three Who Made a Revolution.* Dial, New York, 1948.

———— *Six Keys to the Soviet System.* Beacon, Boston, 1956.

DOCUMENTS FROM PUBLIC SOURCES

The Communist Conspiracy: Strategy and Tactics of World Communism. Prepared and released by the Committee on Un-

American Activities, U. S. House of Representatives. U. S. Government Printing Office, Washington, D.C., 1956.

Congressional Investigations of Communism and Subversive Activities: Summary-Index, 1918–1956, United States Senate and House of Representatives. Compiled by Senate Committee on Government Operations. U. S. Government Printing Office, Washington, D.C., 1956.

Forced Labor in the Soviet Union. U. S. Information Service, Washington, D.C.

The Great Pretense: A Symposium on Anti-Stalinism and the 20th Congress of the Soviet Communist Party. Issued by the Committee on Un-American Activities, U. S. House of Representatives. U. S. Government Printing Office, Washington, D.C., 1956.

Handbook for Americans: The Communist Party in the U.S.A., What It Is, How It Works. Issued by the Senate Internal Security Committee. U. S. Government Printing Office, Washington, D.C., 1956.

Report of the Commission on Government Security. U. S. Government Printing Office, Washington, D.C., 1957.

Report of the Royal Commission on Espionage, Commonwealth of Australia. Printed for the Government of the Commonwealth of Australia by A. H. Pettifer, Government Printer for New South Wales. Sydney, Australia, 1955.

Report of the Royal Commission, Canada. Edmund Cloutier, Printer to the King's Most Excellent Majesty. Ottawa, Canada, 1946.

Report of the ad hoc *Committee on Forced Labour,* International Labour Office, United Nations. Geneva, Switzerland, 1953.

Report of the Special Committee on the Problem of Hungary, General Assembly, United Nations. Official Records: Eleventh Session. Supplement No. 18 (A/3529). New York, 1957.

Soviet Atomic Espionage. Joint Committee on Atomic Energy. U. S. Government Printing Office, Washington, D.C., 1951.

Soviet Political Agreements and Results. Staff Study, Senate Internal Security Committee. U. S. Government Printing Office, Washington, D.C., 1956.

Soviet Total War. Prepared and Released by the Committee on Un-American Activities, U. S. House of Representatives. U. S. Government Printing Office, Washington, D.C., 1956.

Speech of Nikita Khrushchev Before a Closed Session of the XXth Congress of the Communist Party of the Soviet Union, February 25, 1956. Senate Internal Security Committee. U. S. Government Printing Office, Washington, D.C., 1957.

United States Court of Appeals, For the Second Circuit. Brief for the United States. United States of America vs. Eugene Dennis, also known as Francis X. Waldron, Jr., John B. Williamson, Jacob Stachel, Robert G. Thompson, Benjamin J. Davis, Jr., Henry Wriston, John Gates, also known as Israel Regenstreif, Irving Potash, Gilbert Green, Carl Winter and Gus Hall, also known as Arno Hust Halberg. 6164—Brief—June 10, 1950— Record Press, 214 William Street, New York.

United States Court of Appeals, For the Second Circuit, No. 242 —Oct. Term, 1949. (Argued June 21, 22 and 23, 1950 Decided August 1, 1950) Docket No. 21538. United States of America vs. Eugene Dennis et al. Judgment handed down by Learned Hand, Circuit Judge. Record Press, 214 William Street, New York.

United States Supreme Court. No. 336. October Term, 1950. Dennis et al vs. The United States of America. Judgment handed down by Mr. Chief Justice Vinson.

PERIODICALS—COMMUNIST

Mainstream, 832 Broadway, New York 3.

Political Affairs, 832 Broadway, New York 3.

The Worker, 35 East 12 St., New York 3.

PERIODICALS—NON-COMMUNIST *

ACEN News. A monthly review of the Assembly of Captive European Nations, 29 W. 57th St., New York 19.

East Europe. A monthly review of East European Affairs, 2 Park Ave., New York 17.

Problems of Communism (bimonthly). United States Information Agency, 1728 L St., N.W., Washington, D.C.

The New Leader (weekly). 7 East 15 St., New York 3.

United Nations Review (monthly). Columbia University Press, 2960 Broadway, New York 27.

PAMPHLETS

Anti-Stalin Campaign and International Communism: A Selection of Documents. Edited by the Russian Institute, Columbia University. Columbia University Press, New York, 1956.

Brief on Communism: Marxism-Leninism. American Bar Association. 1155 E. 60th Street, Chicago 37, Illinois.

Crimes of the Stalin Era: Special Report to the 20th Congress of the Communist Party of the Soviet Union, by Nikita S. Khrushchev. Annotated for this edition by Boris I. Nicolaevsky, Formerly of the Marx-Engels Institute, Moscow. *The New Leader,* 7 East 15 Street, New York 3.

Hungarian Situation and the Rule of Law. International Commission of Jurists, The Hague, 1957.

Let a Hundred Flowers Bloom: The Complete Text of "On the Correct Handling of Contradictions Among the People," by Mao Tse-tung. With notes and an Introduction by G. F. Hudson, Director of Far Eastern Studies, St. Anthony's College,

* Many other magazines carry informative articles about Communism. We have limited our list to the few that have a specialized relation to this problem.

Oxford. *The New Leader,* 7 East 15 Street, New York 3. September 9, 1957.

Meaning of Hungary, Raymond Aron. *The New Leader,* 7 East 15 Street, New York City. March 24, 1958.

Primer on Communism. Prepared by Anti-Defamation League of B'nai B'rith, 515 Madison Avenue, New York 22, 1951, 1955.

Revolt in Hungary: A Documentary Chronology of Events, Based Exclusively on Internal Broadcasts by Central and Provincial Radios, Oct. 23, 1956–November 4, 1956. Free Europe Committee, 2 Park Avenue, New York 17.

Slave Labor in the Soviet World. Free Trade Union Committee, A.F. of L., Box 65, Radio City Station, New York 19. 1950.

Soviet Crimes and Khrushchev's Confessions: A factual report with a chronology of 72 citations in the 38-year criminal record. Based on a study prepared by Chester S. Williams. Freedom House, 20 W. 40 Street, New York 18.

Survey of Recent Developments in Nine Captive Countries: February 1956–February 1957. Published by the Assembly of Captive European Nations, 29 West 57 Street, New York 19.

Survey of Recent Developments in Nine Captive Countries: February 1957–October 1957. Published by the Assembly of Captive European Nations, 29 West 57 Street, New York 19.

The Greater Danger: The Post-Stalin Pattern for Communist World Conquest. A.F. of L.–C.I.O., 815 16th Street, N.W., Washington, D.C.

Under the Soviet Heel: Destruction of Jewish Life in Eastern Europe. Peter Meyer. The American Jewish Committee, 386 Fourth Avenue, New York 16.

RESEARCH CENTERS

GENERAL

Mid-European Studies, 4 West 57 Street, New York 19.

Rand Corporation, 1625 I Street, N.W., Washington, D.C.

The Institute for the Study of the USSR, Munich, 26, Schliessfach 8, Germany.

CENTERS ATTACHED TO UNIVERSITIES

Center of International Studies, Princeton University, Princeton, New Jersey.

Center for International Studies, Massachusetts Institute of Technology, Cambridge, Massachusetts.

Center of Slavonic Studies, University of Montreal, Montreal, P.Q., Canada.

Department of Slavic Studies, Indiana University, Bloomington, Indiana.

East Asian Institute, Columbia University, New York 27.

Hoover Institute and Library, Stanford University, Stanford, California.

Institute of Contemporary Russian Studies, Fordham University, New York 58, N.Y.

Program on East Central Europe, Columbia University, New York 27.

Russian Institute, Columbia University, New York 27.

Russian Research Center, Harvard University, Cambridge, Massachusetts.

School of Advanced International Studies, Johns Hopkins University, Baltimore, Maryland.

Slavic Institute, University of California, Berkeley, California.

NOTES TO THE TEXT

Chapter One—FROM ST. PETERSBURG TO BUDAPEST

(1) V. I. Lenin, "The Revolution of 1905," *The Handbook of Marxism,* p. 620. New York: International Publishers, 1935.

(2) *Op. cit.,* pp. 614–615.

(3) *Op. cit.,* p. 612.

(4) United Nations, *Report of the Special Committee on the Problem of Hungary,* p. 9. Official Records, General Assembly, Eleventh Session, Supplement No. 18 (A/3529). New York, 1957.

(5) *Op. cit.,* p. 6.

(6) *Ibid.*

Chapter Two—THE THEORY BEHIND THE SYSTEM

(1) J. Peters, *The Communist Party: a Manual on Organization,* pp. 26–27. New York: Workers Library Publishers, 1929.

(2) *Report of the Special Committee on the Problem of Hungary,* p. 13. General Assembly of the U.N., Supplement No. 18 (A/3529), 1957.

(3) J. V. Stalin, *Works,* Vol. XII, pp. 380–381. Moscow: Foreign Languages Publishing House, 1955.

(4) William Z. Foster, *The Twilight of World Capitalism,* pp. 101–102. New York: International Publishers, 1949.

(5) M. Kammari and F. Konstantinoff, "Science and Superstructure," *Political Affairs,* February, 1953. Translated and condensed from *The Bolshevik,* Moscow, February, 1952.

Chapter Three—THE MAN BEHIND THE THEORY

(1) Karl Marx and Friedrich Engels, *Selected Correspondence, 1846–1895,* p. 55. New York: International Publishers, 1934. Heinzen, a doctor by profession, was editor of several German-American newspapers and an advocate of democracy.

(2) *Op. cit.,* p. 22.

(3) Karl Marx, *The Civil War in France,* p. 319. New York: International Publishers, 1940.

(4) Marx and Engels, *Selected Correspondence, 1846–1895,* pp. 161–162.

(5) Istvan Vizinczei, "A Young Writer's Story," *East Europe,* February, 1958, p. 7.

(6) From *The People, Yes* by Carl Sandburg, copyright, 1936, by Harcourt Brace and Company, Inc.

Chapter Four—THE ROOTS OF CONSPIRACY

(1) V. I. Lenin, *Selected Works,* Vol. II, p. 53. New York: International Publishers, 1943.

(2) *Op. cit.,* Vol. II, p. 64.

(3) *Op. cit.,* Vol. II, p. 68.

(4) A. Topchiev, "Building of Communism and Science," *Kommunist* (Moscow), September, 1957.

(5) Lenin, *Selected Works,* Vol. IX, p. 475.

(6) V. I. Lenin, *Lenin on Organization,* p. 99. Chicago: Daily Worker Publishing Company, 1926.

(7) Lenin, *Selected Works,* Vol. II, pp. 139–140.

(8) *Op. cit.,* Vol. II, p. 33.

(9) William Z. Foster, *The Worker,* July 8, 1945.

(10) Lenin, *Selected Works,* Vol. II, p. 105.

(11) *Op. cit.,* Vol. II, p. 100.

(12) V. I. Lenin, "Letter to a Comrade on Our Organizational Tasks," *Works* (Moscow), 3rd Edition, Vol. V, p. 184.

(13) V. I. Lenin, *Selected Works,* Vol. II, p. 140.

(14) *Op. cit.,* Vol. II, p. 89.

(15) *Op. cit.,* Vol. II, p. 105.

(16) *Op. cit.,* Vol. IX, p. 4.

(17) *Op. cit.,* Vol. II, p. 53.

(18) *Op. cit.,* Vol. II, p. 19.

(19) *Op. cit.,* Vol. II, pp. 21–22.

(20) *Op. cit.,* Vol. V, p. 146.

(21) *Op. cit.,* Vol. X, p. 172.

(22) *Op. cit.,* Vol. X, p. 95.

Chapter Five—THE REACTIONARY REVOLUTION

(1) Lenin, *Selected Works,* Vol. X, p. 287.

(2) *Op. cit.,* Vol. VI, p. 475.

(3) Lenin, *Selected Works,* Vol. VI, p. 71.

(4) *Op. cit.,* Vol. IX, p. 137.

(5) Joseph Stalin, *Problems of Leninism,* p. 133. Moscow: Foreign Languages Publishing House, 1947.

(6) Hugh Seton-Watson, "1917–1957: An Historical Perspective," *Problems of Communism,* November–December, 1957, pp. 1–2. United States Information Agency, Washington, D.C.

(7) *Op. cit.,* pp. 2–3.

(8) Lenin, *Selected Works,* Vol. X, p. 65.

(9) Julien Steinberg (Ed.), *The Verdict of Three Decades,* Introduction, p. 9. New York, Duell, Sloan and Pearce, 1950.

(10) Lenin, *Selected Works,* Vol. X, p. 67.

(11) *Op. cit.,* Vol. X, pp. 68–69.

(12) Karl Kautsky, "The New Theory," in Steinberg (Ed.), *The Verdict of Three Decades.*

(13) Lenin, *Selected Works,* Vol. VI, pp. 216–217.

(14) *Op. cit.,* Vol. VI, p. 468.

(15) John Reed, *Ten Days That Shook the World,* pp. 271–274. Boni and Liveright, New York, 1919.

(16) Lenin, *Selected Works,* Vol. VI, p. 477.

(17) *The New Leader,* February 10, 1958, p. 35.

Chapter Six—THE REVOLUTION BECOMES PERMANENT

(1) Karl Marx, *Selected Works,* Vol. II, p. 161. New York: International Publishers.

(2) *Op. cit.,* Vol. II, pp. 163–164.

(3) *Op. cit.,* Vol. II, p. 168.

(4) Lenin, *Selected Works,* Vol. X, p. 199.

(5) *Op. cit.,* Vol. IX, p. 298.

(6) M. Olgin, *Why Communism?* pp. 59–60. New York: Workers Library Publishers, 1933.

(7) Lenin, *Selected Works,* Vol. VIII, p. 33.

(8) *Op. cit.*, Vol. X, pp. 18–19.

(9) *Op. cit.*, Vol. VIII, pp. 148–149.

(10) *Op. cit.*, Vol. X, pp. 100–101.

(11) *Op. cit.*, Vol. X, p. 113.

(12) *Op. cit.*, Vol. VIII, pp. 179–180.

(13) *Op. cit.*, Vol. VIII, p. 284.

(14) N. S. Khrushchev, "Report to the XX Congress, CPSU," *Political Affairs*, March, 1956, p. 59.

(15) Admiral C. Turner Joy, *How Communists Negotiate*, pp. 167–168. New York: The Macmillan Company, 1955.

(16) *Propaganda i Agitatsiya*, No. 18, Leningrad, 1945, p. 3.

(17) Lenin, *Selected Works*, Vol. VIII, p. 33.

(18) Marx, *Selected Works*, Vol. II, pp. 163–164.

(19) *Report on the Bolshevik Movement in Russia*, sent by Secretary of State Robert Lansing to the Senate Committee on Foreign Relations, 1920, p. 20. Document 172, 66th Congress, 2nd Session. Washington, D.C.: U. S. Government Printing Office, 1920.

Chapter Seven—LENIN'S PARTY

(1) Marx, *Selected Works*, Vol. II, p. 162.

(2) Lenin, *Selected Works*, Vol. X, p. 214.

(3) *Op. cit.*, Vol. VIII, p. 26.

(4) *Op. cit.*, Vol. IX, p. 112.

(5) *Op. cit.*, Vol. VI, p. 473.

(6) *Op. cit.*, Vol. II, pp. 154–156.

(7) *Op. cit.*, Vol. II, p. 69.

(8) *Op. cit.*, Vol. II, p. 136.

(9) *Op. cit.*, Vol. II, p. 226.

(10) *Op. cit.*, Vol. II, p. 217.

(11) *Op. cit.*, Vol. X, p. 97.

(12) *Op. cit.*, Vol. IX, p. 254.

(13) *Op. cit.*, Vol. VII, pp. 123, 254.

(14) *Op. cit.*, Vol. VI, pp. 276–277.

(15) *Op. cit.*, Vol. VI, p. 479.

(16) *Op. cit.*, Vol. VIII, p. 93.

(17) *Op. cit.*, Vol. VIII, p. 34.

(18) *Op. cit.*, Vol. VII, p. 369n.

(19) Alexander Berkman, "The Kronstadt Rebellion," in Steinberg (Ed.), *The Verdict of Three Decades,* p. 97.

(20) *Op. cit.*, p. 108.

(21) *Op. cit.*, p. 90.

Chapter Eight—LENIN'S PROBLEMS BECOME KHRUSHCHEV'S

(1) Alexander Berkman, "The Kronstadt Rebellion," in Steinberg (Ed.), *The Verdict of Three Decades,* p. 97.

(2) Peter Meyer, "The Soviet Union: a New Class Society," in Steinberg (Ed.), *The Verdict of Three Decades,* p. 495. Meyer's article originally appeared in *Politics,* March and April, 1944.

(3) Milovan Djilas, *The New Class,* p. 69. New York: Praeger, 1957.

(4) Theodore Lit, "The Proletariat vs. the Dictatorship," *Problems of Communism,* November–December, 1953. United States Information Agency, Washington, D.C.

(5) United Press dispatch, August 12, 1957.

(6) Guyla Illyes, *Tyranny. Irodalmi Ujsag,* November 2, 1956. For the complete poem and other writings of this creative interval, see *East Europe,* Free Europe Committee, 2 Park Avenue, New York City, August 1957.

(7) For a survey of the new humanist writings of the Communist orbit, see Thomas P. Whitney, "Humanist Specter in Eastern Europe," *The New Leader,* October 7, 1957, pp. 16–20.

(8) Stalin, *Works,* Vol. I, pp. 22–23.

(9) *ACEN News,* April–May, 1957, p. 62. Issued by the Assembly of Captive European Nations, 29 West 57th Street, New York 19, N.Y.

(10) *Kommunist* (Moscow), No. 10, August, 1956.

(11) *Washington Post and Times Herald,* November 3, 1957.

Chapter Nine—KHRUSHCHEV'S PARTY

(1) All quotations from Khrushchev's speech are taken from the version released by the U. S. Department of State in 1956, and republished for the use of the Committee of the Judiciary as Senate Document 84293, 85th Congress, First Session. U. S. Government Printing Office, Washington, D.C., 1957.

(2) Lenin, *Selected Works,* Vol. II, p. 17.

(3) Foreign Broadcast Information Service, Daily Report, August 29, 1957. Supplement No. 12, Khrushchev's Speeches, May–July, 1957.

(4) USIA, Office of Research and Intelligence Report, *Eastern European Reactions to Top Leadership Changes in the USSR,* July 17, 1957.

Chapter Ten—MOSCOW DIRECTIVES AND THE COMMUNIST PARTY U.S.A.

(1) William Z. Foster, "Draper's 'Roots of American Communism,'" *Political Affairs,* May, 1957, pp. 34–35.

(2) Lenin, *Selected Works,* Vol. X, p. 31.

(3) *Op. cit.,* Vol. X, pp. 45–46.

(4) *Op. cit.,* Vol. X, pp. 202–204.

(5) *Theses and Statutes of the Third (Communist) International,* p. 1. Moscow; Publishing Office of the Communist International.

(6) *Program of the Communist International,* p. 64. New York: Workers Library Publishers, 1936.

(7) "Andrei Zhdanov, 'On the International Situation,'" *Political Affairs,* December, 1947.

(8) William Z. Foster, "World Democracy's Struggle Against American Imperialism," *Political Affairs,* March, 1948, p. 201.

(9) John Gates, "The Failure of Communism in America," *The Progressive,* March, 1958, p. 39.

(10) *Ibid.*

Chapter Eleven—TACTICS AND STRATAGEMS: THE UNITED FRONT

(1) P. 21.

(2) John Gates, "Time for a Change," *Political Affairs,* November, 1956, p. 46.

(3) *Ibid.*

(4) *Investigation of Communist Propaganda, Hearings, House of Representatives,* Part I, p. 384. Washington, D.C.: U. S. Government Printing Office, 1930.

(5) S. Tsirul, *The Practice of Bolshevik Self-Criticism,* p. 17. New York: Central Committee, CPUSA, 1932.

(6) Georgi Dimitrov, *The United Front,* p. 30. New York: International Publishers, 1938.

(7) Earl Browder, *Teheran and America,* p. 21. New York: Workers Library Publishers, 1944.

(8) William Z. Foster, *History of the Communist Party of the United States,* p. 437. New York: International Publishers, 1953.

(9) Lenin, *Selected Works*, Vol. III, pp. 377–378.

(10) William Z. Foster, "The War Danger in the Present World Situation," *Political Affairs*, May, 1951, p. 35.

(11) Alex Bittelman, "Where Is the 'Monthly Review' Going?" *Political Affairs*, May, 1951, p. 35.

(12) Hyman Lumer, "The Truth About Hungary," *Political Affairs*, July, 1957, pp. 21–22, 30.

(13) Martin Fisher, "Urgent Tasks for Strengthening the Party," *Political Affairs*, November, 1951, pp. 31–32.

(14) John Williamson, "Trade-Union Tasks in the Struggle for Peace, Jobs, and Negro Rights," *Political Affairs*, November, 1950, p. 53.

(15) Richard Walker, "The Issues Behind the Truman-Shvernick Exchange," *Political Affairs*, September, 1951, p. 44.

Chapter Twelve—THE AMERICAN PEOPLE AS A TARGET

(1) Eugene Dennis, "Peace—the Supreme and Over-Riding Issue," *Political Affairs*, April, 1951, p. 7.

(2) Claude Lightfoot, "Leadership Quality and the Draft-Program Perspectives," *Political Affairs*, June, 1954, p. 38.

(3) Carl Ross, "The Youth in the Fight for Peace, Against Militarization," *Political Affairs*, February, 1951, p. 178.

(4) Gus Hall, "The Present Situation and the Tasks of Our Party," *Political Affairs*, October, 1951, p. 11.

(5) Editorial, *The Worker*, May 11, 1952.

(6) William Weinstone, "The Fight to Repeal the Legislative Blueprint for Fascism," *Political Affairs*, October, 1950, p. 35.

(7) V. J. Jerome, "Restore American-Soviet Cooperation for Peace," *Political Affairs*, November, 1947.

(8) *The Daily Worker*, May 30, 1952.

(9) *The Daily Worker*, January 14, 1957.

(10) *The Daily Worker*, March 24, 1957.

Chapter Thirteen—TARGET GROUPS AND THE PARTY LINE

(1) William Z. Foster, "The Party Crisis and the Way Out," *Political Affairs*, December, 1957, p. 52.

(2) Max M. Kampelman, *The Communist Party vs. the C.I.O.*, with an Introduction by Hubert H. Humphrey, p. 4. New York: Praeger, 1957.

(3) *Op. cit.*, Hubert H. Humphrey, Introduction, pp. vii–viii.

(4) J. Edgar Hoover, *Masters of Deceit*, p. 246. New York: Henry Holt, 1958.

(5) Lenin, *Selected Works*, Vol. XI, p. 68.

Chapter Fourteen—THE PARADOX OF LEGALITY

(1) *The Communist*, Vol. XIX (July, 1940), p. 611.

(2) *The Communist*, Vol. XX (August, 1941), p. 682.

(3) *Theory and Practice of the Communist Party*, prepared by the Education Department of the CPUSA, pp. 21–22.

(4) Earl Browder, *Communism in the United States*, p. 309. New York: International Publishers, 1935.

(5) *Farmers' Call to Action*, p. 4. National Committee for Action, Washington, D.C., 1933.

(6) Lenin, *Collected Works*, Vol. XVIII, p. 375.

(7) William Z. Foster, *Toward Soviet America*, p. 273. New York: Coward-McCann, 1932.

(8) *The Communist*, Vol. I (October, 1921), p. 6.

(9) *The Communist*, Vol. I (July, 1922), p. 2.

(10) National Committee, CPUSA, "Restore Democratic Rights!" *Political Affairs*, October, 1953, p. 3.

(11) National Committee, CPUSA, "Answer the Attack on the Communist Party and the Labor Movement," *Political Affairs*, September, 1954, p. 5.

(12) *The New York Times*, May 13, 1958, p. 13.

Chapter Fifteen—THIS SIDE OF THE PLANET

(1) Alex Bittelman, Introduction to *Communism in the United States*, Earl Browder, p. xxi. New York: International Publishers, 1935.

(2) William Z. Foster, "Communication Concerning Edward Kardelj's Article," *Mainstream*, February, 1957, p. 54.

(3) A. B. Magil, "Mexico: Gathering Storm," *Political Affairs*, August, 1953, p. 23.

(4) Tim Buck, *Canada: The Communist View*. Toronto: Progress Publishers, 1948.

Chapter Sixteen—THE SHADOW OF EMPIRE

(1) See Marx and Engels, *The Russian Menace to Europe, a Collection of Articles, Speeches, Letters and News Dispatches*, Selected and Edited, with an Introduction, by Paul W. Blackstock and Bert F. Hoselitz. Glencoe, Illinois: The Free Press, 1952.

(2) For the complete text of this document, see *Problems of Communism,* No. 3, pp. 40–43. Washington, D.C., Documentary Studies Section, International Information Agency.

(3) *Primer on Communism,* p. 58. The Anti-Defamation League of B'nai B'rith, 515 Madison Avenue, New York 22, New York, 1955.

(4) Editorial, "Swagger Through Hungary," *Washington Post and Times Herald,* April 11, 1958.

(5) P. 68. New York: International Publishers, 1934.

(6) *The Observer,* February 3, 1957.

(7) William Z. Foster, "Specific Features of American Imperialist Expansion," *Political Affairs,* August, 1948, p. 676.

(8) Benjamin J. Davis, "On the Colonial Liberation Movements," *Political Affairs,* December, 1950, p. 43.

Chapter Seventeen—NEGOTIATING WITH OUR EYES OPEN

(1) Nathan Leites, *A Study of Bolshevism,* p. 59. Glencoe, Illinois: The Free Press, 1953.

(2) Lenin, *Works* (Moscow), 3rd Edition, Vol. XXVI, pp. 6, 21.

(3) Leites, *A Study of Bolshevism,* p. 61.

(4) Lenin, *Selected Works,* Vol. IV, p. 201.

(5) Leites, *A Study of Bolshevism,* p. 55.

(6) Admiral C. Turner Joy, *How Communists Negotiate,* pp. 39–40. New York, Macmillan, 1955.

Chapter Eighteen—DESIGN FOR A COMMITMENT

(1) Sidney Hook, "A Foreign Policy for Survival," *The New Leader,* April 7, 1958, p. 12.

(2) Bella V. Dodd, *School of Darkness,* p. 57. New York: P. J. Kenedy and Sons, 1957.

(3) *Report of the Royal Commission,* pp. 69, 71, 73. Ottawa: Edmund Cloutier, 1946.

(4) Lenin, *Selected Works,* Vol. VIII, p. 284.

(5) Karl Menninger, *Love Against Hate,* p. 5. New York: Harcourt, Brace and Company, 1942.

(6) Arthur Koestler, in *The God That Failed* (Richard Crossman, Ed.), p. 68. New York: Harper and Brothers, 1949.

(7) *Literaturnaia Gazeta* (Moscow), October 8, 1957.

(8) Arthur Koestler, in *The God That Failed,* p. 60.

(9) *Kommunist* (Moscow), September, 1957.

(10) Statement by the 1958 Parliament of Science, held in Washington, D.C., under the auspices of the American Association for the Advancement of Science. *Science*, April 19, 1958, p. 852.

(11) *The New Leader*, April 21, 1958, p. 12.

INDEX

absolutism, 21

Address to the Communist League,
Marx, 84, 171

Albania, 72, 96, 263

Albanian Workers' Party, 146

Aliger, Margarita, 303

America, *see* separate national entries

American liberalism, *see* Liberalism

American Committee for Spanish Freedom, 178

American Federation of Labor, 201, 203

American League for Peace and Democracy, 180

American Legion, 214

American Peace Mobilization, 180

American Veterans Committee, 214

American Veterans of World War II, 214

American Youth for Democracy, 178, 207

"anti-imperialist" front, in Western Hemisphere, 247

April Theses, Lenin, 77

Argentina, Communist Party in, 242, 249

armed forces, Communist propaganda directed at, 65–66, 206–207, 220–223

atomic weapons control, 190

Austin, Warren, 278, 288

Austria, World Peace Council issue, 272—273

Bauer, Bruno, 47–48

Bécu, Omer, 274

Bentley, Eric, 220

Beria, Lavrenty, 142

Bittelman, Alex, 244

Bloody Sunday, 15–17, 19

Bolivia, Communist Party in, 249

Bolsheviks, 19, 206, 283–285
as core of conspiracy, 59, 62
Lenin's shaping of, 108–110
in revolution of 1917, 74–81

Brazil, Communist Party in, 243, 249–250

British Common Law, 295

Brooks, John Graham, 24

Browder, Earl, 61, 63, 98–99, 178, 225

"Browderism," 236

Buck, Tim, 252

Budapest, uprising of 1956, 19–22, 144

Fonseca, Ricardo, 242
foreign-language teaching, in Soviet Union, 306–307
foreign policy, American, CPUSA and, 196–199
For a Lasting Peace, For a People's Democracy, 157, 160, 190, 241, 244, 253
Fortune, 97
Forward, 47
Foster, William Z., 40, 99, 152, 155, 159, 176, 198, 201, 213, 225, 244
  on Latin America, 254
  on legal system, 228
Foundations of Leninism, Stalin, 175
France, Communist Party in, 98, 236
Front organizations:
  intellectuals in, 210
  Soviet empire-building through, 271–274
Fundamentals of Marxism, 227

Gapon, George, 16, 17, 20
Gates, John, 61, 63, 174
  on Moscow direction, 161, 162
General Literary Gazette, 47
Georgia, Ingram affair, 205
German-French Yearbook, Ruge and Marx, eds., 46
Germany, 96
  revolution in, 84–86
  see also East Germany
Gomez, Eugenio, 243
Gompers, Samuel, 24
Good Neighbor Policy, 275
Gorky, Maxim, 81–83
Gosplan, 140–141
Gottwald, Klement, 230
Greece, 197
Grotewohl, Otto, 122
Grouchulski, Henryk, 267
Grün, 49
Guatemala, Communist Party in, 249
Guides to Speakers, 193
Gunter, George, 24

Harding, W. G., 26
hatred, essential to Communist theory, 298–303
Hegel, G. W. F., 32, 33
Heinzen, 49
Herr Vogt, Marx, 257, 258
Hints on How to Organize Open-Air Meetings, 192
Hitler, A., 99, 156, 222, 223, 295
  Soviet pact, 179
Holy Family (The): Bruno Bauer and his Associates, Marx, 48
Homestead strike (1892), 22
Hook, Sidney, 293
Hoover, Herbert, 226
Hoover, J. Edgar, 204, 218, 219
Hoover Library, Stanford University, 262
House Un-American Activities Committee, 204
humanism, Communist attack on, 129
humanitarianism, 29–31, 45
Humphrey, Hubert H., 202, 219
Hungary, 96, 128, 263, 265
  Cominform meeting in, 159
  Communist Party in, 146
  Soviet interpretation of uprising, 184–185
  student unrest, 130
  United Nations committee on, 38, 184
  uprising of 1956, 19–22, 38, 123, 184–185

ideology:
  Marxist, 29–41
  as social force, 21
imperialism, *see* empire-building, Soviet
India, Communist Party in, 236
individual, worth of, 296–298
industrial unions, 201
infiltration, Communist, in trade unions, 202–203
Information Bureau of the Communist and Workers' Parties, *see* Cominform
Inge, Dean, 211